EDUCATIONAL INTERVENTIONS AND SERVICES FOR CHILDREN WITH EXCEPTIONALITIES

Second Edition

EDUCATIONAL INTERVENTIONS AND SERVICES FOR CHILDREN WITH EXCEPTIONALITIES

Strategies and Perspectives

By

GEORGE R. TAYLOR, PH.D.

*Coppin State College
and
Core Faculty
The Union Institute*

Charles C Thomas
PUBLISHER • LT D.
SPRINGFIELD • ILLINOIS • U.S.A.

Published and Distributed Throughout the World by

CHARLES C THOMAS • PUBLISHER, LTD.
2600 South First Street
Springfield, Illinois 62704

©2001 by CHARLES C THOMAS • PUBLISHER, LTD.

ISBN 0-398-07112-8 (cloth)
ISBN 0-398-07113-6 (paper)

Library of Congress Catalog Card Number: 00-057735

With THOMAS BOOKS *careful attention is given to all details of manufacturing
and design. It is the Publisher's desire to present books that are satisfactory as to their
physical qualities and artistic possibilities and appropriate for their particular use.*
THOMAS BOOKS *will be true to those laws of quality that assure a good name
and good will.*

Printed in the United States of America
SM-R-3

Library of Congress Cataloging-in-Publication Data

Taylor, George R.
   Educational interventions and services for children with exceptionalities :
strategies and perspectives / by George R. Taylor.-- 2nd ed.
      p.   cm.
   Rev. ed. of: Educational strategies and services for exceptional children /
[edited] by George R. Taylor and Stanley E. Jackson. c1976.
   Includes bibliographical references and index.
   ISBN 0-398-07112-8 (cloth) -- ISBN 0-398-07113-6 (pbk.)
   1. Special education--United States. I. Educational strategies and services
for exceptional children. II. Title.

LC3981 .E38 2000
371.9'0973--dc21   00-057735

CONTRIBUTORS

Helen Brantley, M.Ed., Ph.D. is Professor of Special Education at South Carolina State University, where she has held several administrative positions. She has been actively involved with the education of individuals with disabilities and has made significant contributions to special education through publication, participation, and conducting local and national workshops and conferences.

Frances Harrington, M.Ed., Ph.D. is teacher of individuals with disabilities at the Showtown Middle School, Lillington, North Carolina. She has had extensive teaching experiences on the college level and has been active in local and national organizations that serve individuals with disabilities. She has added to the body of research through several publications, curriculum development, program evaluation, and is participating in and conducting local and national conferences and workshops.

Loretta MacKenney, M.Ed. is Adjunct Professor of Special Education at Coppin State College, where she has instructed undergraduate students in strategies for working with children with disabilities in grades K-3 in Baltimore County Public Schools for several years. She has made contributions to the field of special education through publications.

Thaddaus L. Phillips Ph.D. is Associate Professor in the Department of Special Education at Coppin State College. In addition to his teaching responsibilities, he is Assistant to the Chair of Special Education. His research interests are in the areas of learning disabilities, inclusion and assessment. He has contributed to the professional literature in the field of special education.

Richard Rembold, Ed.D. currently serves as an Adjunct Faculty member in the Department of Special Education and as Assistant Vice President for Academic Affairs at Coppin State College. His past experiences with individuals with disabilities include teaching in Baltimore City Public Schools and other local colleges, and he was Coordinator of Alcoholism Services at Sinai Hospital in Baltimore, Maryland. He is active in community and professional organizations, and has made significant contributions to the field of special education through publications.

George R. Taylor, Ph.D. is Professor and Chairperson of the Department of Special Education at Coppin State College in Baltimore, Maryland and Core Faculty, The Union Institute. He has published six textbooks and over 20 articles related to special education, and has conducted numerous workshops at the local, state, and national levels.

PREFACE

The Second Edition of *Educational Interventions and Services for Children with Exceptionalities* will provide educators and community agencies serving children with exceptionalities strategies and perspectives for serving them. The text has been updated to include the most recent federal legislation, incidences of exceptionality, behavioral styles, behavioral management, technology, trends, intervention, research, assessments, IEP development, and curriculum development. Specific examples are given for each area addressed. A special chapter has been written on the role and importance of parental involvement. Current events and research relating to various exceptionalities have been highlighted throughout the text. Each chapter ends with a summary or concluding remarks.

G.R.T.

ACKNOWLEDGMENTS

This text was developed to address critical issues for providing quality services to children with exceptionalities. A significant amount of services for children with exceptionalities have been mandated by federal and state legislation. Methods and procedures employed have been developed over years of professional involvement in the field of special education.

This awesome task could not have been completed without the assistance of others. A deep sense of gratitude is extended to the graduate students at Coppin State College, The Maryland State Department of Education, The Baltimore City Public Schools, and the faculty of the Department of Special Education at Coppin State College. A sense of gratitude is extended to Dr. Thomas Terrell for proofing the manuscript and Mrs. Emma Crosby for typing the manuscript.

CONTENTS

EDUCATIONAL INTERVENTIONS AND SERVICES FOR CHILDREN WITH EXCEPTIONALITIES

Chapter 1

INCIDENCE OF EXCEPTIONALITY

George R. Taylor and Frances Harrington

INTRODUCTION

DURING THE PAST TWO DECADES, tremendous progress has been made in the field of special education. One of the major outgrowths of this thrust has been directed toward making special education a part, rather than a separate entity, of regular education.

Traditionally, special education programs were not initiated in response to the needs of exceptional individuals, but rather as expedient measures to resist a perceived threat to the existing goals for normal children. The anticipated purpose of such classes was to develop within the pupil basic attitudes, habits, and skills which would enable the student's satisfactory adjustment to life in an increasingly complex society. Basic to the achievement of this goal was the inability of the pupils to use these attitudes, habits, and skills in securing and holding a job. Much controversy exists because many specialists agree that special education has not provided exceptional individuals with a viable education.

Today, many organizational structures are being developed to maintain exceptional individuals in the mainstream of education. These structures do not appear to eliminate categorical labels that have plagued special education since its inception. Another type of classification system is needed which will focus on educational variables rather than etiology. This chapter is designed to review incidence and provide an overview of the classification system in use by some school districts.

HISTORICAL OVERVIEW

Prior to the early part of the nineteenth century, exceptional individuals were at the mercy of the societies in which they lived. Notions regarding handicapping conditions were closely linked with spirits and mysticism. Since there was no universal understanding of individual differences, some exceptional individuals were avoided, or placed in institutions and ignored. Inhuman treatment was rather pronounced for many of the mentally and physically handicapped. The gifted individual was usually exploited as his abilities were used to promote selfish interests within his society. Research concerning the exceptional individual was practically unheard of prior to the eighteenth century.

The early history of the United States was closely linked with a strong religious philosophy. The consensus generally held was that imperfect individuals were bedeviled. Consequently, exceptional individuals were considered to be outside the realm of religion. Since religion played a dominant role in the politics of the United States during this time frame, realistic planning and treatment for the exceptional individual was severely hampered.

During the early nineteenth century, improved attitudes toward exceptional individuals were expounded by such leaders as Horace Mann, Samuel Gridley Howe, Dorothea Dix, and Reverend Gallaudet. Horace Mann and Samuel Gridley Howe spoke out on behalf of the retarded; Dorothea Dix pleaded for the socially maladjusted; and Revered Gallaudet was instrumental in promoting programs for the deaf. These leaders gave impetus to the movement establishing residential schools for the exceptional. It was proven that appropriate teaching procedures could be successful in helping exceptional individuals become useful citizens. Societal pressure, including numerous protests from the parents of exceptional children, led to the change from residential schools to day schools.

Classification of exceptional children was accelerated by Godard. He brought the Binet-Simmon Intelligence Test to this country in 1914, and it was standardized for American children by Lewis Terman in 1916. This opened the era of mental testing in the United States. Mental testing revealed that distinct differences existed between individuals. Practices and attitudes began to change from concepts of custody, care, and treatment to creating programs of education and rehabilitation for exceptional individuals. The influence of World Wars I and II had far-reaching effects on the education of exceptional individuals. Many individuals who had gone into the services with no handicaps frequently returned with a disability; thus, public attention was focused more and more on disabilities. Combined, these factors caused public agencies, especially the schools, to give increasing attention to individuals who had exceptional differences.

PRESENT DAY TRENDS

The role of public schools in this country parallels the social and historical movements reflected in our culture. Education was viewed as such an important function that it was reserved as a right of the individual states. Since a democracy accepts the responsibility for the education of all youth, the constitution of each state provides for a system designed to provide educational opportunities for all children. Children who deviated in mental, physical, social, or emotional traits to such a degree that they could not reach their optimum growth in regular classes were not covered in most state constitutions until the beginning of the nineteenth century. Today, most states provide educational opportunities for all exceptional individuals.

Interest in special education has greatly increased because of the events of recent years. The influence of parent movement groups shows their deep concern for the future welfare of exceptional individuals. A significant factor is the social change in attitude toward the exceptional individual which was instilled into the minds of the general public by parents. Changes in attitude with regard to the education of the exceptional have led to their inclusion in the public school system. Advances in scientific fields have enabled many exceptional individuals to enter the mainstream of education. A case in point is the development of electronic devices which promoted the practicability of maintaining the hard-of-hearing in the schools. Another advance is the launching of the Russian *Sputnik* which, by spurring technology, renewed interest in education of the gifted.

As a result of these developments, many reforms in educational philosophy and administration have ben instituted. Various trends have emerged that appear to be leading to significant changes in the education of the exceptional. President John F. Kennedy was the first president to introduce a national plan to combat mental retardation. Since then, federal, local, and state governments are financially supporting programs for exceptional individuals through several agencies. Therefore, special education is being presented with a new thrust which stresses continuity and appropriateness of educational programs and also emphasizes effectiveness in delivering services to exceptional individuals (Taylor, 1999).

Advancements have been made in knowledge, program development, remedial techniques, behavior modification, evaluation, and a variety of individualized techniques unparalleled in the history of special education. These various techniques will be dealt with in subsequent chapters. Significant advances have also been made during the past decade toward the economic and social integration of exceptional individuals into society, rectifying some of the ills resulting from segregating exceptional individuals. Unfortunately, modifications in instructional strategies are still based upon psychological or medical models as well as conventional classification systems. Chapter 5 highlights the major trends in special education.

CONVENTIONAL DEFINITIONS AND CLASSIFICATIONS OF EXCEPTIONAL CHILDREN

The conventional term "exceptional children" denotes many different degrees of disability. According to numerous authorities, the term is difficult to define because exceptionality represents a variety of medical and psychological categories. The consensus, therefore, is that a general definition for an exceptional child is one who deviates mentally, physically, socially, or emotionally so markedly from what is considered normal growth and development that the child can not receive maximum benefit from a regular school program unless modifications are made in the instructional program, or special instruction and ancillary services are provided to enable the child to achieve at a level commensurate with the child's respective abilities (Blackhurst & Berdine, 1993; Gallagher & Ansastasiow, 1993; Handman & Drew, 1993; Haring & McCormick, 1990; Heyward & Orlansky, 1992; Kaplan, 1996; Taylor, 1998).

These authors generally agreed that many operational definitions of exceptionality are statistical and quantitative in nature. The mentally retarded can be defined as the intellectually lowest 2 or 3 percent of the population as indicated by intelligence tests; whereas, the intellectually gifted can be defined in terms of test scores at the upper 1 or 2 percent of the general population. The hard-of-hearing and the deaf can be identified in terms of hearing loss as measured in decibels by a standard audiometer. Blindness is typically defined legally as a visual acuity of 20/200 or less in the better eye after maximum correction, or as a possession of a visual field limited to 20 degrees or less. There are no conventional quantitative indices of most other types of deviant individuals, such as the orthopedically handicapped, the socially maladjusted, the emotionally disturbed, the epileptic, and the individual with speech defects. In most of these conditions, the diagnostic judgment of trained specialists replaces quantitative measurement. All of the above definitions appear to operate from medical or psychological terminology which has little relevancy for educational intervention.

Exceptional individuals are generally grouped on the basis of their major deviation or handicap, and may be classified as follows: (1) the physically handicapped, (2) the mentally handicapped, (3) the intellectually gifted, (4) the emotionally unstable, (5) those with special health impairments, (6) the blind and hard-of-seeing, (7) the deaf and hard-of-hearing, (8) those with speech defects, (9) the socially maladjusted, and (10) the multiple handicapped. Chapter 3 gives specific information on the various types of exceptionalities.

Various authorities have advanced different categories for areas of exceptionality in the following areas: (1) communication disorders, (2) mental deviations, including the gifted and the mentally retarded, (3) sensory handicaps, including individuals with auditory and visual handicaps, (4) neurologic, orthopedic, and other health impairments, and (5) behavior disorders, including the socially maladjusted and the emotionally disturbed (Ysseldyke, Alozzine, & Thurlow, 1992; Meyen, 1990; Norris & Haring, 1994; Kaplan, 1996). Similarly, Cruickshank (1963) divided the areas of deviations into the following categories: (1) the intellectually exceptional individual, including the gifted and the mentally retarded, and (2) the physically handicapped, including visual and auditory handicaps, speech handicaps, orthopedic and neurological impairments.

INCIDENCE OF EXCEPTIONAL CHILDREN

It is estimated that exceptional children constitute approximately seven to 12 percent of the general population. Part of the difficulty in determining the number of exceptional children is due to various definitions used by different disciplines in identifying the exceptional individual, and the lack of consensus concerning the classification and selection criteria. States differ in their classification systems, and to compound the problem, local school districts in various states also differ.

The number of children identified as retarded reflects certain political connotations. In the United States, the number of retarded individuals is generally accepted as approximately three percent of the total population. In some countries, such as the Soviet Union, there is a generally accepted figure of one percent. The difference in the Soviet figures reflects two basic concepts: firstly, that mental retardation is a condition caused by heredity or some central nervous system condition (approximately 1%); secondly, that the two percent additionally identified in the United States, according to Soviet authorities, were the direct result of social inadequacies reflecting the evils of capitalism and exploitation. There is a growing number of scientists, in the United States, who are beginning to recognize that there are large numbers of individuals who function as though they are retarded due to factors in society. Factors such as social class, race, inappropriate use of tests, inadequate environments, attitude, health, diet, and quality of education modify performance as measured by intelligence tests. How many of these factors were the result of capitalism and exploitation, as suggested by the Russians, is difficult to assess. However, there is no question that changes in social policies and attitudes may alter the number of children classified as retarded.

A different way of looking at incidence is to identify the severity of the handicap. This is especially true when the need arises to provide school programs and services. The severely to profoundly handicapped, the totally deaf, the multiple handicapped, the blind, the severely retarded, and the psychotic are such a comparatively small number (less than 1% of the population), and are usually identified long before they come to school. Most children with severe handicaps are currently served outside of the regular public school and require the efforts of many public and private programs in health, education, and welfare.

U.S. Office of Education statistics appear to provide the best data on the number of exceptional children in schools. The Office of Education has provided estimates since 1922. In 1964, Congress created the Bureau of Education for the Handicapped within the Office of Education. In order to provide more reliable data from the states, federal regulation in 1967 required all state departments of education to submit reports on the number of exceptional children the schools were serving. The office is presently housed in the U.S. Department of Education and is called the Office of Special Education Programs (OSEP). This office is presently engaged in providing updated, precise data for future use. The data in Table 1 are based on estimated 1994-1996 population statistics as reported by the Office of Special Education Programs.

TABLE 1

Number of Students Served Under IDEA, Part B by Age Group:
School Years 1994-95 Through 1995-96

Age Group	1994-95	Percent of Total	1995-96	Percent of Total	Change Number	Percent
3-5	522,710	9.63	548,441	9.76	25,731	4.9
6-11	2,515,487	46.32	2,581,061	45.93	65,574	2.6
12-17	2,153,448	39.66	2,237,124	39.81	83,676	3.9
18-21	238,578	4.39	252,473	4.49	13,895	5.8
6-17	4,668,935	85.98	4,818,185	85.75	149,250	3.2
6-21	4,907,513	90.37	5,070,658	90.24	163,145	3.3
3-21	5,430,223	100.00	5,619,099	100.00	188,876	3.5

Source: U.S. Department of Education, Office of Special Education Programs. Data Analysis Systems (DANS).

AGE GROUPS OF STUDENTS SERVED UNDER IDEA, PART B

The largest age group of students (2,581,061 or 45.9 percent) with disabilities served in 1995-96 under IDEA, Part B were ages 6 through 11. Students with disabilities ages 12 through 17 were the next largest age group served; 2, 237, 124 (39.8 percent) students received services in this age group (see Table 1). The remaining age groups, ages 3 through 5 (548,441 children) and ages 18 through 21 (252,473 students) made up less than 15 percent of the students served. The largest increase in the percent of students serve occurred in the 18 through 21 (5.8 percent) and 3 through 5 (4.9 percent) age groups.

Child count data by age group for all children served under IDEA, Part B only exist from 1987-88 forward. The largest percentage increase between 1987-88 and 1995-96 occurred in the 3 through 5 age group, which increased by 63.3 percent (212, 670). This was followed by the 12 through 17 (25.8 percent or 459,511) and 6 through 11 (21.9 or 463,535) age groups. The 18 through 21 age group only increased by 12.2 percent over the same period. There was a concomitant increase in the percentage of children served under IDEA, Part B in the resident population. These increases occurred in all age groups.

DISABILITIES OF STUDENTS SERVED

OSEP collects information on the primary disability condition of children ages 6 through 21 served under IDEA. As in the past, the largest disability categories continue to be specific learning disabilities (2,597,231 or 51.2 percent), speech or language impairments (1,025,941 or 20.2 percent), mental retardation (585,308 or 11.5 percent), and serious emotional disturbance (438,217 or 8.6 percent) (refer to Table 2).

The largest relative increases from 1994-95 to 1995-96 occurred in the traumatic brain injury (30.1 percent), autism (27.2 percent), and other health impairments (24.5 percent) categories (see Table 2). Most states attributed the increases in the two newest categories, traumatic brain injury and autism, to the reclassification of students at the time of triennial reevaluations. The increase in the other health impairments category was generally attributed to increased service to students with attention deficit/hyperactivity disorder.

By way of review, classification and estimations of exceptional individuals have been based upon the total population within given age ranges. Educational institutions should be dedicated to providing the best opportunities possible for assisting exceptional individuals in reaching their optimum growth. In order to achieve this, the focus of special education must be radically shifted from a categorical model to one which stresses serving the needs of individuals.

OSEP provides information on preschoolers to school districts. This information is important in aiding school districts to appropriately plan for these children. Data are provided on the local and national levels. The reader is referred to the Nineteenth Annual Report to Congress for information relevant to his or her state.

TABLE 2

Change in the Number of Students Age 6-12 Served Under IDEA,
Part B From 1994-95 to 1995-96 by Disability

Disability Category	1994-95	Percent of Total	1995-96	Percent of Total	Change Based on Number Served	
					Number	Percent[a]
Specific Learning Disability	2,510,224	51.2	2,597,231	51.2	87,007	3.5
Speech or Language Impairments	1,020,331	20.8	1,025,941	20.2	5,610	0.5
Mental Retardation	570,518	11.6	585,308	11.5	14,790	2.6
Serious Emotional Disturbance	428,049	8.7	438,217	8.6	10,168	2.4
Multiple Disabilities	89,620	1.8	94,156	1.9	4,536	5.1
Hearing Impairments	65,204	1.3	68,070	1.3	2,866	4.4
Orthopedic Impairments	60,467	1.2	63,200	1.2	2,733	4.5
Other Health Impairments	107,133	2.2	133,419	2.6	26,286	24.5
Visual Impairments	24,713	0.5	25,484	0.5	771	3.1
Autism	22,664	0.5	28,827	0.6	6,163	27.2
Deaf-blindness	1,331	0.0[b]	1,362	0.0[c]	31	2.3
Traumatic Brain Injury	7,259	0.1	9,443	0.2	2,184	30.1
All Disabilities	4,907,513	100.00	5,070,658	100.0	163.145	3.3

a. The percent of change is calculated in the following manner: The number served in 1994-95 is subtracted from the number served in 1995-96. The result is then divided by the total number served in 1994-95.

b. This percent is rounded to the nearest tenth. The actual percent is .027.

c. This percent is rounded to the nearest tenth. The actual percent is .026.

Source: U.S. Department of Education, Office of Special Education Program, Data Analysis System (DANS).

EDUCATIONAL PLACEMENTS OF
PRESCHOOLERS WITH DISABILITIES

OSEP collects data on preschoolers with disabilities who are served in each of eight different placements: regular class, resource room, separate class, separate school (public and private), residential facility (public and private), and homebound/hospital. Because these placement categories may not reflect all of the placement categories specific to preschoolers, OSEP provides optional instructions to States and Outlying Areas about reporting counts of preschoolers in each of the placement categories. Table 2 includes a definition of each placement category as it applies to preschoolers with disabilities.

As shown in Figure 1, just over 50 percent of children ages 3-5 with disabilities were served in regular class placements on December 1, 1995. This is a 2 percent increase over the percentage served on December 1, 1994. The second most frequently used setting was separate class placement, fol-

FIGURE 1

Number and Percentage of Children Ages 3 - 5 Served in Different
Educational Placements on December 1, 1995

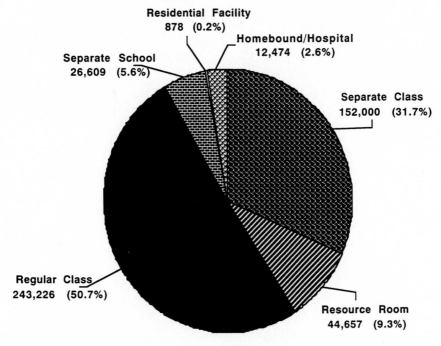

Source: U.S. Department of Education, Office of Special Education Programs, Data
    Analysis System (DANS).

lowed by resource room. The percentage of children served in these two settings remained fairly stable from December 1, 1994, to December 1, 1995.
The use of separate facilities, both public and private, has declined (from
8.92 percent), while the use of residential facilities has remained stable (0.3
percent to 0.2 percent) and the use of home/hospital placements rose slightly (1.9 percent to 2.6 percent).

The number of children served each year continues to increase, although
the funds appropriated have remained almost level over the past 2 years.
States continue to use the full continuum of placement options. However,
there has been an increase in the number of children served in regular class
placements, and the use of separate facilities has declined.

Creative ways of administering services are being developed. As shown
in the examples in this module, State and local agencies are increasing the
level of collaboration among agencies. This, in turn, is making access of services easier for families.

TOTAL NUMBER OF CHILDREN AND YOUTH SERVED

A total of 5,619,099 children and youth with disabilities ages 3 through
21 were served under IDEA, Part B during the 1995-96 school year (see
Table 3), an increase of 188,876 (or 3.5 percent) from the previous year. The
increase in the number of students with disabilities served resulted in an
increase in the percentage of children with disabilities enrolled in school.
The percentage of children ages 6 through 17 with disabilities enrolled in
school increased from 10.4 percent in 1994-95 to 10.6 percent in 1995-96.
There was also an increase in the percentage of children in the resident population served in special education. The percentage of children with disabilities ages 3 through 21 in the resident population increased from 7.7 percent in 1994-95 to 7.9 percent in 1995-96.

Total school enrollment decreased from 45,090,301 in 1976-77 to
38,925,000 in 1984-85. Since 1985-86, enrollments have steadily increased.
The 1995-96 enrollment count of 45,363,691 represents a net increase of
6,438,691 (16.5 percent) in enrollment since the 1984-85 school year.

The resident population ages 6 through 17 decreased from
46,337,802 in 1976-77 to 41,436,000 in 1985-86, and then gradually increased
to 45,109,401 in 1995-96. There has been a net decrease of 1,228,401 (2.7
percent) in the number of students ages 6 through 17 since 1976-77. There
was also a decrease in the 18 through 21 age group, from 17,014,687 in 1976-
77 to 14,032,177 in 1995-96 (-2,982,511 or -176.5 percent). The 3 to 5 age
group increased during this period, from 9,429,510 to 12,060,235.

TABLE 3

Students Served Under IDEA, Part B: Number and Percentage
Change, School Years 1976-77 Through 1995-96

School Year	Change in Total Number Served From Previous Year (%)	Total Served	Percentage of 0-21 Population
1976-77	—	3,708,601	4.52
1977-78	1.9	3,777,300	4.65
1978-79	3.8	3,919,073	4.87
1979-80	3.0	4,036,219	4.98
1980-81	3.5	4,177,689	5.15
1981-82	1.3	4,233,282	5.20
1982-83	1.5	4,298,327	5.40
1983-84	1.0	4,341,399	5.50
1984-85	0.5	4,363,031	5.50
1985-86	0.2	4,370,248	5.56
1986-87	1.2	4,421,601	5.64
1987-88	1.4	4,485,702	5.73
1988-89	1.8	4,568,063	5.82
1989-90	2.4	4,675,619	5.93
1990-91	2.8	4,807,441	6.07
1991-92	3.7	4,986,039	6.20
1992-93	3.4	5,155,853	6.38
1993-94	4.0	5,363,766	6.60
1994-95	1.2	5,430,233	6.63
1995-96	3.5	5,619,099	6.79

SUMMARY

There has been a steady increase in the number of students served under IDEA, Part B. It is important to note that two different underlying demographic factors existed during this period. During the first 10 years of the program, the growth in the IDEA, Part B count occurred while population and enrollment counts were decreasing. Early growth in the special education count occurred as IDEA was more fully implemented, and services were expanded to more fully serve the eligible population.

During the second 10 years of the program, growth in the special education counts coincided with increases in enrollment and population. However, the percentage of students enrolled in special education has increased at a slightly higher rate than has the total school age population. The percentage of children receiving special education ages 6 through 17 enrolled in schools increased from 9.6 percent in 1987-88 to 10.6 percent in 1995-96. The percentage of children ages 3 through 21 receiving special education in the resident population increased from 6.6 percent in 1987-88 to 7.9 percent in 1995-96.

There are several explanations for the growth in the special education population over this period. There was a natural growth in the numbers in the early years of the program as States fully implemented IDEA. The ability to identify children with disabilities may have also improved as a result of new developments in the assessment of children and in medical tests. The program has also expanded the age range of students served. These data are essential for school districts to plan appropriately for exceptional children, as well as meeting the federal mandates concerning educating these children.

REFERENCES

Blackhurst, A. E., & Berdine, W. H. (1993). *An introduction to special education* (3rd ed.). Lexington: Harper Collins College Publishers.

Cruickshank, W. A. (1963). *Psychology of exceptional children and youth.* New Jersey: Prentice Hall.

Gallagher, K., & Ansastasiow, N. (1993). *Educating exceptional children.* Boston: Houghton Mifflin.

Handman, M. L., Drew, C. J., Egan, M. W., & Wolf, B. (1993). *Human exceptionality: Society, school, and family.* Needham Heights, MA: Allyn & Bacon.

Haring, N., & McCormick, L. (1990). *Exceptional children and youth* (5th ed.). Columbus: Merrill.

Heyward, W., & Orlansky, D. (1992). *Exceptional children* (4th ed.). New York: Merrill.

Kaplan, P. (1996). *Pathways for exceptional children.* Minneapolis: West Publishing Company.

Meyen, E. (1990). *Exceptional children in today's schools.* Denver: Love.

Norris, G., Haring, L., & Haring, T. (1994). *Exceptional children and youth* (6th ed.). New York: MacMillan.

Taylor, G. R. (1998). *Curriculum strategies for teaching social skills to the disabled.* Springfield, IL: Charles C Thomas.

Taylor, G. R. (1999). *Curriculum models and strategies for educating individual with disabilities in inclusive classrooms.* Springfield, IL: Charles C Thomas.

Ysseldyke, J., & Alozzine, B. (1990). *Introduction to special education.* Boston: Houghton Mifflin.

Chapter 2

FEDERAL LAWS AFFECTING
EXCEPTIONAL INDIVIDUALS

RICHARD REMBOLD AND GEORGE R. TAYLOR

INTRODUCTION

IN THE NINETEENTH ANNUAL REPORT to Congress (1997) concerning exceptional individuals, it was found that:

1. there are more than eight million children with disabilities in the United States today;
2. the special educational needs of such children are not being fully met;
3. more than half of the children with disabilities in the United States do not receive appropriate educational services which would enable them to have full equality of opportunity;
4. one million children with disabilities in the United States are excluded entirely from the public school system and will not go through the educational process with their peers;
5. there are many children with disabilities throughout the United States participating in regular school programs whose disabilities prevent them from having a successful educational experience because their disabilities are undetected;
6. because of the lack of adequate services within the public school system, families are often forced to find services outside the public school system, often at great distance from their residence and at their own expense;
7. developments in the training of teachers and in diagnostic and instructional procedures and methods have advanced to the point that, given appropriate funding, state and local educational agencies will provide effective special education and related services to meet the needs of children with disabilities;
8. state and local educational agencies have a responsibility to provide education for all children with disabilities, but present financial

resources are inadequate to meet the special education needs of children with disabilities; and

9. it is in the national interest that the Federal Government assist state and local efforts to provide programs to meet the educational needs of children with disabilities to secure equal protection of the law.

Educating children with special needs provides both challenges and opportunities. Today, American schools are meeting the special education service needs of 5.373 million children from birth to age 21–a figure that is expected to increase (Seventeenth Annual Report to Congress, 1995).

THE EXCEPTIONAL AND THE EVOLUTION
OF SPECIAL EDUCATION

Current mandates to provide equal access and an appropriate education to the disabled are primarily the result of Federal congressional actions, often taken in response to litigation, as well as the encouragement and persistence of parents, professionals, and advocacy groups. Prior to the 1970s, efforts to meet the needs of the disabled within the public schools varied widely in form and intent. The landmark decision in *Brown v. Board of Education* (1954) established the right of all children to an equal educational opportunity. The sentiment of the following language, contained in the Supreme Court's opinion, is common to litigation and legislation of the past four decades seeking equal educational access and opportunity for the disabled:

> Today, education is perhaps the most important function of state and local governments. Compulsory school attendance laws and the great expenditures for education . . . demonstrate our recognition of the importance of education to our democratic society. It is required in the performance of our most basic public responsibilities, even service in the armed forces. It is the very foundation of good citizenship. Today, it is a principal instrument in awakening the child to cultural values, in preparing him/her for later professional training, and in helping him/her to adjust normally to his environment. In these days, it is doubtful that any child may reasonably be expected to succeed in life if he/she is denied the opportunity of an education. Such an opportunity, where the state has undertaken to provide it, is a right which must be made available to all on equal terms.

Although Congress (through the adoption of the Education of Handicapped Act of 1970) attempted to overcome the historical inadequacy of educational services to the disabled, it was two court cases decided during 1971-72 that helped establish the right of access of the disabled to a free appropriate public education and outlined the protection that such students could be afforded.

IMPACT OF COURT DECREES

In *Pennsylvania Association for Retarded Children v. Commonwealth* (1997), the court was asked to examine policies that permitted Pennsylvania to deny access and a free appropriate educational to mentally retarded children.

The consent decree, approved by the district court, enjoined the state from denying education to mentally retarded children and required that retarded children be provided a free, public program of education and training appropriate to the child's capacity, within the context of the general education policy that, among the alternative programs of education and training required by statute to be available, placement in a regular public school class is preferable to placement in a special public school class [i.e., a class for "handicapped" children] and placement in a special public school class is preferable to placement in any other type of program of education and training.

The consent decree further required that retarded children be provided procedural due process and periodic reevaluation. *Mills v. Board of Education of the District of Columbia* (1972), also approved by consent decree, greatly expanded the *PARC* decision to include all disabled children and incorporated an extensive plan created by the District of Columbia Board of Education to provide: (1) a free appropriate education, (2) an Individualized Education Plan, and (3) due process procedures. The language of the final order provided significant guidance for litigants in cases in other states as well as for the development of appropriate state and federal legislative responses to provide equal educational access and opportunity for the disabled.

IMPACT OF FEDERAL LEGISLATION

Federal legislation was introduced following the *PARC* and *Mills* decisions to eliminate discrimination against the disabled. Section 504 of the Vocational Rehabilitation Act of 1973 (PL 93-112), considered the first major legislation protecting the civil rights of disabled persons, provides that:

> No otherwise qualified handicapped individual in the United States...shall, solely be reason of his handicap, be excluded from participation in, be denied the benefits of, or be subjected to discrimination under any program or activity receiving Federal financial assistance.

A principal concern of Section 504 is discrimination in employment and the provision of health, welfare, and other social services. However, it does recognize the educational needs of disabled children and requires five issues be considered in meeting those needs: (1) location and notification; (2) free appropriate public education; (3) educational setting; (4) evaluation and placement; and (5) procedural safeguards. Failure to comply with these requirements could result in the withdrawal of Federal funding.

In 1975, Congress amended the Education of the Handicapped Act (EHA) with the Education for All Handicapped Children Act (EAHCA) (PL 94-142). The new law was intended to make certain that disabled children receive equal educational access, and provided extensive rules and regulations to guide state and local school actions in providing an appropriate education. The basic educational rights of the EAHCA [see 20 U.S.C. §1401 (16-91)] has been described by Turnbull (1993) in six primary principles as:

1. Zero reject—every disabled child (regardless of the severity of his/her disability) must be provided a free, appropriate, publicly supported education—no child may be excluded.
2. Non-discriminary assessment—each child must be provided a multifactored evaluation (free of race, cultural, or native language bias) to determine the presence of a disability and guide special education program development.
3. Appropriate education—an individualized education program (IEP) is to be developed and implemented to meet the child's unique needs and to ensure a meaningful educational experience.
4. Least restrictive environment (LRE)—each disabled child is to be educated with non-disabled peers to the maximum extent practicable—favoring inclusion as a means of supporting the child's right to normalization.
5. Due process—procedures to protect the rights of disabled children and their parents must be provided—safeguarding the right to protest program planning and placement decisions or records confidentiality issues by providing an impartial hearing and appeals process to resolve disputes.
6. Parent participation—parents have the right to participate in planning their child's educational program—mutual benefits can be realized through collaboration in program development.

The EHA was amended in 1990. Though the basic provisions established in PL 94-142 were retained, several modifications were made as follows:

1. Public Law 101-476 changed the title to the Individual with Disabilities Education Act—better known today by its acronym IDEA. The same title change was made applicable to all laws making reference to the original Education of the Handicapped Act as well replacing the term *handicap* with *disability* (e.g., "handicapped children" became "children with disabilities"). Such modifications also made the language consistent with the American with Disabilities Act (PL 101-336) enacted earlier in the year.
2. Autism and Traumatic Brain Injury were added to the list of distinct disabilities.

3. Monies were made available to establish centers to organize, synthesize, and disseminate current knowledge relating to children with attention deficit disorder.
4. Students' IEPs are to include transition services as may be required by individual need. Transition services are defined as a coordinated set of activities for a student, designed within an outcome-oriented process, which promotes movement from school to postschool activities.
5. Included the support services of "assistive technology devise" and "assistive technology service" as they appeared in the Technology-Related Assistance for Individuals with Disabilities Act of 1988.
6. Added rehabilitation counseling to the definition of related services.

It is essential that teachers working with disabled children, whether in fully included or self-contained classrooms, have a basic understanding of the key provisions of current law. Three such provisions–least restrictive environment, individualized education program, and appropriate education–can have a significant impact on the curriculum strategies that may be employed in the teaching of social skills to the disabled.

The Individuals with Disabilities Education Act requires:

> . . . to the maximum extent appropriate, children with disabilities, including children in public or private institutions or other care facilities, are educated with children who are not disabled and that special classes, separate schooling, or other removal of children with disabilities from the regular educational environment occurs only when the nature or severity of the disability is such that education in regular classes with the use of supplementary aids and services cannot be achieved satisfactorily.

Unfortunately, neither the statutory law nor the following language of the regulations clearly prescribes how school districts are to determine what the least restrictive environment is:

a. Each public agency shall ensure that a continuum of alternative placements is available to meet the needs of children with disabilities for special education and related services.
b. The continuum required under paragraph (a) of this section must:
1. Include the alternative placements listed in the definition of special education under §300.17 (instruction in regular classes, special classes, special schools, home instruction, and instruction in hospitals and institutions); and
2. Make provision for supplementary services (such as resource room or itinerant instruction) to be provided in conjunction with regular class placement. (Sixteenth Annual Report to Congress, 1995)

As greater efforts are made to provide instruction to disabled children in inclusive settings, the possibility exists to misinterpret or misapply the concept of "maximum extent possible." The United States Court of Appeals

(Sixth Circuit) in *Ronker v. Walter* identified three exceptions to inclusive placement that may be helpful to remember. Such placements may be precluded if there exists: (1) no benefit to the child, (2) greater benefits in segregated settings even after the feasibility standard is applied, and (3) the potential for disruption to a non-segregated setting (*Ronker v. Walker,* 1983). These are important considerations when creating the child's individualized education program.

An essential element of free appropriate education is the development of an individualized education program. The IDEA defines individualized education program as

> . . . a written statement for each child with a disability developed in any meeting by a representative of the local educational agency or an intermediate educational unit who shall be qualified to provide, or supervise the provision of, specially designed instruction to meet the unique needs of children with disabilities, the teacher, the parents or guardian of such child, and whenever appropriate, such child, which statement shall include—
> a. a statement of the present levels of educational performance of such child,
> b. a statement of annual goals, including short-term instructional objectives,
> c. a statement of the specific educational services to be provided to such child, and the extent to which such child will be able to participate in regular educational programs,
> d. a statement of the needed transition services for students beginning no later than age 16 and annually thereafter (and, when determined appropriate for the individual, beginning at age 14 or younger), including, when appropriate, a statement of the interagency responsibilities or linkages (or both) before the student leaves the school settings,
> e. the projected date for initiation and anticipated duration of such services, and
> f. appropriate objective criteria and evaluation procedures and schedules for determining, on at least an annual basis, whether instructional objectives are being achieved (Individuals with Disabilities Education Act, 1972).

For younger children, ages birth through two years of age, PL 99-457 (The Education of the Handicapped Amendments of 1986) provided that the multidisciplinary team develop an individualized family service plan (IFSP). The development of an individualized education program (or IFSP) and the provision of that program utilizing the continuum of services associated with the least restrictive environment are fundamental to providing an appropriate education.

As defined in the Individual's with Disabilities Education Act (PL 101-476):

The term "free appropriate public education" means special education and

related services that:
  a. have been provided at public expense, under public supervision and direction, and without charge,
  b. meet the standards of the State educational agency,
  c. include an appropriate preschool, elementary, or secondary school education in the State involved, and
  d. are provided in conformity with the individualized education program under section 1414 (a) (5) of this title.

Differences of interpretation of the language of the statutory law were common. The Supreme Court, in *Board of Education of Hendrick Hudson Central School District v. Rowley* attempted to minimize confusion by establishing a standard to determine compliance. The Court indicated that a child's education program would be appropriate if it met the following criteria. First, has the state complied with the procedures set forth in the Act? And second, is the individualized education program developed through the Act's procedures reasonably calculated to enable the child to receive educational benefits. Further, the Courts did not agree that an appropriate education was one that assisted a child in reaching his/her maximum potential; rather, "the intent of the Act was more to open the door of public education to children with disabilities on appropriate terms than to guarantee any particular level of education once inside." Special education programs were to provide "a basic floor of educational opportunity."

An examination of the case law following Rowley seems to indicate that judges are unwilling to overturn the decisions of education professionals as to what constitutes an appropriate education as long as the procedures, services, and rights afforded by the Act are provided. However, the courts appear to be moving away from such procedural evaluations to substantive evaluations of proposed education programs as the movement toward full inclusion continues. One substantive issue impacting curriculum decisions or strategies employed could be the need to respond to the Act's "related services" requirement (Seventeenth Annual Report to Congress, 1997).

Title 34 §300.16 describes related services.

  a. As used in this part, the term "related services" means transportation and such developmental, corrective, and other support services as are required to assist a child with a disability to benefit from special education, and includes speech pathology, and audiology, psychological services, physical and occupational therapy, recreation, including therapeutic recreation, early identification and assessment of disabilities in children, counseling services, including rehabilitation counseling, and medical services for diagnostic or evaluation purposes. The term also includes school health services, social work services in the schools, and parent counseling and training.

Subsequent sections of the regulation, taken collectively demonstrate a recognition of the importance of having diverse services available to support the development of appropriate social skills.

> *"Counseling services"* means services provided by qualified social workers, psychologists, guidance counselors, or other qualified personnel.
>
> *"Parent counseling and training"* means assisting parents in understanding the special needs of their child and providing parents with information about child development.
>
> *"Psychological services"* means
> (i)   Administering psychological and other assessment procedures;
> (ii)   Interpreting assessment results;
> (iii) Obtaining, integrating, and interpreting information about child behavior and conditions relating to learning.
> (iv)   Consulting with other staff members in planning school programs to meet the special needs of children as indicated by psychological tests, interviews, and behavioral evaluations; and
> (v)   Planning and managing a program of services, including psychological counseling for children and parents.
>
> *"Social work services in schools"* include -
> (i)   Preparing a social or developmental history on a child with a disability;
> (ii)   Group and individual counseling with child and family;
> (iii) Working with those problems in a child's living situation (home, school, and community) that affect the child's adjustment in school; and
> (iv)   Mobilizing school and community resources to enable the child to learn as effectively as possible in his or her education program.

Underwood and Mead (1985) suggested three questions that must be considered to determine whether a child will be eligible for related services:

> Is the service necessary for the student to gain access to or remain in the special program?
>
> Is the service necessary to resolve other needs for the student before educational efforts will be successful? Is the service necessary for the student to make meaningful progress on the identified goals?

The EHA was amended in 1997 and is scheduled to be implemented July 1, 1998. Though the basic provisions established in IDEA 1990 were retained, several modifications were made as follows:

1. Participation of children and youth with disabilities in state and district-wide assessment (testing) programs;
2. Development and review of the Individualized Education Program (IEP), including increased emphasis upon participation of children and youth with disabilities in the general education classroom and the general curriculum, with appropriate aids and services;
3. Parent participation in eligibility and placement decisions;

4. The way in which re-evaluations are conducted;
5. The addiction of transition planning;
6. Voluntary mediation as a mean of resolving parent-school controversies.
7. Discipline and behavior issues of children and youth with disabilities (Underwood & Mead, 1985; IDEA Reauthorization Special Report, 1997).

The lengthy comprehensive and extension of IDEA does not provide enough space in this chapter to cover all of the changes. The reader may obtain a copy of the New Law by contacting the following sources:

1. Your Senator or Representative and refer to S.717/H.R.5).
2. Office of Special Education and Rehabilitative Services (OSERS) (http://www.ed.gov/offices/OSERS/IDEA.
3. Education Administration On-Line (http://www./rp/com/ed).
4. Internet web sites (refer to Appendix A).

The authorization of IDEA (PL 105-17) has several areas of change that influence the manner in which educators, psychologists, and researchers conduct their professional responsibilities within the context of the classroom. One change promoted in PL 105-17 involves changes in the IEP process. These changes make the IEP document and process a better tool for instruction, accountability/assessment, and involvement of parents. Another change involves promoting discipline procedures that provide safety for all. In particular, this change is challenging in that discipline procedures must be developed and implemented to meet the needs of children and at the same time, not giving up on any student. A third change includes exploring inclusive classrooms and collaborative general/special education teaching. Efforts in this area have been underway for several years now. Interestingly, little attention is given to the fact that the reauthorization of IDEA insures a continuum of services model that meets the needs and strengths of all children and provides collaboration between early intervention and preschool programs. Underscoring this change is the need for looking at early screening, early preventative measures/interventions for all students who may be at-risk for academic, discipline, physical and mental health issues (the new IDEA Reauthorization Law, 1998).

Although the above changes are only a few of the changes that must be addressed through the new IDEA Reauthorization, they may be interpreted as examples of invitations to engage in research. One such invitation is extended to researchers who are interested in exploring the large number of issues related to children who may be at-risk for failure in school due to their: (1) diverse ethnic backgrounds, (2) environmental/home situations, (3) physical, academic, and emotional disabilities, and (4) social/emotional situations. The following examples are a few invitations that might be considered as future research endeavors. Researchers may find that these endeavors actually affect the future educational success of children from diverse backgrounds and who have disabilities.

An Invitation to Explore the IEP/Assessment Process

Development research questions in the area of the IEP and assessment process may begin with researchers asking questions concerning the involvement of parents—especially of parents who are of different cultures and who do not speak Standard English. Some questions may include how professionals involve parents so that they are respected, their needs are met, and their participation is valuable as well as valued.

The assessment process will continue to ask research questions concerning the appropriateness of tests as well as whether an overrepresentation of students from diverse backgrounds are receiving special education services. Additionally, greater expectations are being placed on students to improve their test scores. Questions concerning whether testing procedures accommodate students with disabilities must be addressed. This question is expanded when the variables of ethnicity, culture, and language are factored into a research agenda.

An Invitation to Explore Discipline Procedures

This issue of discipline in the schools is of great interest to professionals dealing with the new IDEA regulations. Some invitations for research in this area may include the following; Are discipline measures effective in inclusive classrooms? Is the use of expulsion avoided because of alternative disciplinary actions being exercised? Are the number of student dropouts decreasing due to the changes in the school disciplinary policies?

An Invitation to Explore Services that Meet the Needs and Strengths of All Children

Because the new IDEA emphasizes the importance of meeting the needs of all children, researchers must ask questions that encourage the development of effective teaching procedures for all children in a variety of settings. Determining whether these interventions work for children in certain settings is a primary concern. Currently, researchers are finding that the majority of students from different ethnic backgrounds and who have disabilities can benefit from specific instruction in an inclusive classroom. With this success, it is important to ask why some children did not succeed and what is being done to eliminate failure for these students.

An Invitation to Explore Early Detection and Preventive Interventions for All Young Children

Today, a great number of children are failing in school at an early age. Because IDEA has specific provisions for early childhood programs, researchers might want to investigate whether early detection measures and universal intervention programs reduce the number of children receiving special education services. A question that extends this vein of inquiry might include the identification of those children who do not respond to universal interventions, why they do not respond, and what target interventions are needed to promote success at an early age.

SUMMARY

Congressional investigations clearly have shown that the needs of exceptional individuals were not met in this country. These investigations were chiefly prompted by demands from parents, professional groups, court cases, and advocacy groups for disabled individuals. The results of these investigations were the reenactment of several federal laws being passed to provide equal educational opportunities for all disabled individuals in inclusive settings as much as possible. The federal laws are summarized below.

Public Law 94-142

The systematic identification of disabled individuals is required of states receiving federal aid under Public Law 94-142. States are mandated to develop procedures resulting in the identification of all children who may be disabled, regardless of type or severity of disabling conditions, as well as making a determination of special education needs in terms of children currently being served or children not currently being served.

The law made available a free and appropriate public education to all school-aged students with disabilities. It directed that students with disabilities must be educated in the least restrictive environment, and mandated that an individualized education program (IEP) be developed for all disabled students using non-discriminatory evaluation techniques. Additionally, a due process provision was outlined which was designed to protect the rights of the family and the child. Finally, the law stated that no student may be excluded from public education because of a disability, and that each state must take action to locate children who may be entitled to special education services.

The emphasis on PL 94-142 and subsequent revisions are the requirements that parental consent be obtained for any decision made in the IEP process. Also that parents always be informed of any steps taken in the IEP process, whether they concern pre-referral, referral, evaluation, service, treatment, progress, annual review, and modifications of the IEP. Parental consent is the voluntary agreement of the parent or guardian after being apprised of all information in a comprehensible form. Parent awareness and approval are essential.

Public Law 99-457

Public Law 94-142 was amended in 1986 to EHA PL 99-457. This act extended the authority of PL 94-142 in the following ways:
1. Provided a free and appropriate education to preschool children.
2. Disability categories were not required to be reported by the states.
3. The law provided for the development of cost-effective methods of service delivery in early childhood.
4. A grant program was developed to provide financial incentive for states to establish programs for infants and toddlers who were developmentally delayed.

Public Law 99-457 (Part H Infants and Toddlers Program) is designed, in part, to assist states in setting up early intervention programs for children from birth through age two who need special services. Early intervention services include the following: physical, mental, social, emotional, language and speech, and self-help skills. The total family is involved, the focus for service is on the total family (Bailey, Buysse, Edmondson, & Smith, 1992). Special education services may be provided to children from birth through age two who have special needs, such as a physical disability, partial or total loss of sight, severe emotional problems, hearing or speech impairment, mental handicap, or learning disabilities. The key is early intervention, which should be designed to treat, prevent, and reduce environmental factors associated with disabling conditions and the impediment of social growth and development.

The PL 99-457 piece of legislation was greatly needed due to the public dissatisfaction with earlier legislation created for the disabled. There was also a need for early care and education not just for the disabled child, but also for the normal child. Two factors also contributed to educators searching for early child care services: (1) the increase in the number of mothers who were working outside the home, and (2) the realization that many of these children were disadvantaged. Many disabled individuals are not developmentally ready for school. Early intervention can reduce or eliminate many of the conditions attributed to development delays. Public Law 99-457 places the family in the center of the early intervention process. The major thrust of the law is to develop meaningful parent-professional partnerships to support the development of infants and toddlers (Summers, 1990). Hanson (1992) wrote that the issues of which families and professionals focus in providing services for infants and toddlers are closely related to the families' beliefs, values, and childbearing practices. Consequently, when working with families from diverse backgrounds, professionals should be cultural sensitive. This is particularly true when developing the IEP. Family preferences should be respected and included when legally possible. Objectives and outcomes should be written in terms familiar to the family.

Public Law 101-476

In 1990, the Congress of the United States amended the Education of the Handicapped Act and renamed it the Individuals with Disabilities Act (IDEA) PL 101-476.

1. The term "handicapped" was removed and the term "disabled" was substituted.
2. Autism and traumatic brain injury were added to the list of disabling conditions.
3. The definition of special education was broadened to include instruction in all settings where disabled individuals are educated, including workplaces and training centers.
4. Related services were expanded to include rehabilitation counseling and social work services.
5. The IEP was modified to include a transition planning statement for students by age 16 or younger.
6. Assessing, identifying, and placing disabled individuals require the use of non-discriminatory and multidisciplinary assessment in constructing the IEP.
7. Parental involvement in the total process was mandated. Procedural safeguards (due process) were reinforced to protect the child and family.
8. The rights of all children to learn in the least restrictive environment with non-disabled peers was affirmed.

In 1997, Congress amended IDEA to expand the following components: (1) participation of children in assessment and the IEP process, (2) parental participation in placement decisions, (3) required transition planning, (4) voluntary mediation, and discipline and behavior issues of children.

Public Law 105-17 chiefly addressed changes in the IEP process and LRE requirement. Changes were proposed in instruction, accountability, assessment, and parental involvement. Other proposed changes included exploring discipline procedures in the schools, services that meet the needs of all children, and early detection and preventative interventions for all young children. During the 1998 school year, many of the proposed changes never happened because the regulations were not released in time. After months of debates, the regulations on (IDEA) 1997 were released.

These federal laws have had widespread implications for educating disabled individuals in this country. These laws have revolutionized education for disabled individuals. The acts have made it possible for millions of disabled individuals to receive a free and appropriate education in the public schools. Recent impact of federal legislation has extended special education to include all instruction in all settings, including the workplace, rehabilitation centers, and shelter workshops (Special Education Law Update, 1999).

These laws were specific in many areas. One of the areas included was that exceptional individuals must be educated in the least restrictive environment. For many exceptional individuals this meant that many of them would be educated with their normal peers. Research findings have shown that many exceptional individuals do not display appropriate skills (Gresham, 1993; Hanson, 1990; Odom, 1988; Peck, 1983; Sasso, 1990). With this mandate, exceptional individuals must be instructed in several areas. Many experiences may be integrated into the regular curriculum. Early intervention is necessary in order to reduce the amount of isolation and rejection experienced by many exceptional individuals in regular classes.

Because educators may find themselves unable to respond in the affirmative to these queries, access to the services described above may be severely limited or entirely prohibited. Therefore, having access to innovative and successful curriculum strategies in the development of communication, mathematics, science, social, effective and psychomotor and character skills to the exception is highly endorsed.

REFERENCES

Bailey, D. B., Buysse, V., Edmondson, R., & Smithe, T. M. (1992). Creating family center services in early intervention: Perception of professionals in four states. *Exceptional Children, 58,* 298-309.

Brown v. Topeka, Kansas, Board of Education. (1954). 347- U.S. 483.

Congress passed IDEA. (1997). IDEA Reauthorization Special Report [Special Supplement to The Special Educator]. Horsham, PA: LRP.

Gresham, F. M. (1993). Social skills and learning disabilities as a type III error: Rejoinder to Conte and Andrews. *Journal of Learning Disabilities, 26* (3), 154-158.

Hanson, M. J. (1990). Ethnic, cultural, and language diversity in intervention settings. In E. W. Lynch, & M. J. Hanson (Eds.), *Developing cross-cultural competence: A guide for working with young children and their families.* Baltimore: Paul H. Brookes.

Individuals with Disabilities Education Act. (1972). U.S. Office of Education. Washington, D.C.: U.S. Government Printing Office.

Mills v. Board of Education (1972) District of Columbia, Washington, D.C.

Nineteenth Annual Report to Congress. (1997). U.S. Department of Education. Washington, D.C.: U.S. Government Printing Office.

Odom, S., & McEvoy, M. (1988). Integration of young children with handicapped and non-handicapped children: Mainstreamed versus integrated special education. In S. Odom & M. Karnes (Eds.), *Early intervention for infants and children with handicaps: An empirical base* (pp. 241-267). Baltimore, MD: Paul H. Brookes.

Peck, C.A., & Cooke, T. P. (1983). Benefits of mainstreaming at the early childhood level: How much can we expect? *Analysis and Intervention in Developmental Disabilities, 3,* 1-22.

Pennsylvania Association for Retarded Citizens v. Commonwealth of Pennsylvania. (1971). 334 F. Supplement. 1257 (E.D. Pa. 1971).

Rowley v. Board of Education of Hendrick Hudson School District. (1982). 458 US. 176.

Ronker v. Walter, 700 F21058, 1063 (6th Cir.) 1983.

Sasso, G. M., Melloy, K. J., & Kavale, K. A. (1990). Generalization, maintenance, and behavioral in variation associated with social skills training through structured learning. *Behavioral Disorders, 16* (1), 9-22.

Sixteenth Annual Report to Congress. (1995). U.S. Department of Education. Washington, D.C.: U.S. Government Printing Office

Special Education Law Update. (1999). *A report of Court decisions, legislation, regulations, and law review articles affecting special education for students with disabilities, 8* (17).

Summers, J. A., Dell, O. C., Turnbull, A. P., Benson, H. A., Santeili, E., Campbell, M., & Siegel-Clausey, E. (1990). Examining the individualized family service plan process: What are family and practitioner preferences? *Topics in Early Childhood Special Education, 10,* 78-99.

The New IDEA Reauthorization Law. (1998). U.S. Department of Education. Washington, D.C.: U. S. Government Printing Office.

Turnbull, H. R. (1993). *Free appropriate public education: The law and children with disabilities* (4th ed.). Reston: Love Publishing Company.

Underwood, J., & Mead, J. (1985). *Legal aspects of special education and pupil services.* Needham Heights: Allyn and Bacon.

U.S. Department of Education. (1995). *Sixteenth Annual Report to Congress on the Implementation of the Individuals with Disabilities Act.* Washington, D.C.: U. S. Government Printing Office.

U.S. Department of Education. (1997). *Individuals with Disabilities Education Act Amendment.* Washington, D.C.: U. S. Government Printing Office.

U.S. Department of Education. (1997). *Seventeenth Annual Report to Congress on The Implementation of the Individuals with Disabilities Education Act.* Washington, D.C.: U.S. Government Printing Office.

Chapter 3

ISSUES IN EDUCATING CHILDREN
WITH EXCEPTIONALITIES

GEORGE R. TAYLOR, FRANCES HARRINGTON AND THADDAUS PHILLIPS

OVERVIEW

THE HISTORY OF EDUCATION AS IT RELATES to children with exceptionalities had a poor beginning. For many years, just getting an education was no
easy matter for children with exceptionalities. Before 1800, most people with
exceptionalities were not recognized unless their disabilities were severe.
Those that were recognized were mostly people with mental retardation.
They were considered to be inhuman and possessed by demons or evil spirits. They were also thought of as fools or jesters, and there was an increase
in infanticide. According to Blackhurst and Berdine (1993) when
Christianity was introduced into the church, it changed some of the negative
thinking toward individuals with exceptionalities.

Gallagher and Ansastasiow (1993) noted that there were some advancements for the exceptional during the eighteen hundreds in that although
physically and mentally handicapped children received some attention in
the nineteenth-century primarily through the establishment of philanthropic
and state institutions for the blind and deaf and for the mentally subnormal,
most exceptional youth did not receive public attention (Hardman, Drew,
and Egan, (1996). It was during this time period, 1789, that Victor and Wild
Boy were found roaming wild in the forest by Jean Marc Gaspard Itar. Itar,
also known as the father of special education, did not believe as the others
that the child was an incurable idiot. He launched a program to civilize and
educate Victor and some improvement was made. This was also known as
the era of institutions. Institutions, or human warehouses, kept the "unde-
sirables from interacting with the mainstream." According to Haring,
McCormick, and Haring (1990), most of the programs evolved into custodial approaches that provided no meaningful treatment or education to their
participants. There was no care to promote or enhance the quality of life for

the exceptional; they just existed.

In the early 1900s, ungraded classes were developed in larger public schools to deal with the mildly retarded students who appeared normal but could not succeed in the graded school system that had been established. During the nineteen hundreds, Alexander Graham Bell was instrumental in deinstitutionalization. He suggested to educators to form public schools to provide classes for individuals with deaf, sight, and mental retardation disabilities. He urged special education be provided so that these individuals could attend schools instead of being sent to institutions. Hardman, Drew, and Egan (1996) asserted that individuals with special needs ought to function in as normal an environment allowable, thereby eliminating institutionalized behaviors.

The 1900-1970s were recognized as the years for public schools special classes. Blackhurst and Berdine (1993) and Gallagher and Ansastasiow (1993) proclaimed that individuals with mental retardation were the first group to establish special classes along with the visually and hearing impaired. Many students with physical, hearing, and visual impairment were integrated with more success than those with mental retardation (Hardman, Drew, & Egan, 1996). The severely handicapped were viewed as something less than human creatures, to be treated as decently as limited charity would allow, not as persons with rights.

The first law to provide funding for training teachers in mental retardation, National Defense Education Act PL 85-926, was passed in 1958. Since that time there have been no less than a dozen new laws and amendments to prior laws. Those laws were the foreground to the most important law on this subject. In 1975, the Education for All Handicapped Children Act (PL 94-142) was passed. It is considered as the capstone for the movement. It was amended in 1990 and renamed the Individuals with Disabilities Education Act (IDEA). The primary benchmark of the law was its stipulation that all children must be provided with a free, appropriate education that includes due process and delivery of education in the least restrictive environment. The IDEA defines special education as specially designed instruction, at no cost to parents or guardians, to meet the unique needs of a child with a disability (Kaplan; 1996).

These laws ensured due process and equal access to education for all disabled children in the least restricted environment. Additionally, the laws were considered as a victory for parents with disabled children who believed that institutions were not the best placement for their children (refer to Chapter 2 for a detailed analysis of federal laws).

Classifying and Defining Exceptionalities

Several classification systems are used in schools in the United States today. Different terms are used in different states to specify the handicapped conditions that entitle a student to special education services. The most frequently used terms and criteria are those required for reporting under the regulations of the Individuals with Disabilities Education Act (IDEA). The definitions used in regulations for IDEA (34 CFR 300.7) are listed below.

AUTISM

Autistic students are those who demonstrate developmental disability significantly affecting verbal and non-verbal communication and social interactions generally evident before age three, that adversely affects a child's educational performance. Other characteristics often associated with autism are engagemental change or change in daily routines, and unusual responses to sensory experiences. The term (autism) does not apply if a child's educational performance is adversely affected primarily because the child has a serious emotional disturbance. Students with suspected autism are usually evaluated by speech and language specialists and psychologists. When the student has limited intellectual ability, it is often very difficult to distinguish autism from severe forms of mental retardation.

MENTAL RETARDATION

Mentally retarded pupils are those who demonstrate significant subaverage intellectual functioning that exists concurrently with deficits in adaptive behavior, and manifests during the developmental period which adversely affects a child's educational performance. Students who are eventually labeled "mentally retarded" are often referred because of generalized slowness. They lag behind their age mates in most areas of academic achievement, social and emotional development, language ability, and perhaps physical development. This slowness must be demonstrated on an individually administered test of intelligence that is appropriate for the student being assessed. Thus, the test must be appropriate not only for the age of the student but also for the pupil's acculturation and physical and sensory abilities. However, a test of intelligence is not enough. The pupil must also demonstrate slowness in adaptive behavior. An assessment for mental retardation should always contain an assessment of achievement, intelligence, and adaptive behavior.

LEARNING DISABILITY

Learning disabled pupils are those who demonstrate a disorder in one or more of the basic psychological processes involved in understanding or in using language, spoken or written, that may manifest itself in the imperfect ability to listen, think, read, write, spell, or do mathematical calculations. The term *learning disabilities* includes such conditions as perceptual handicaps, brain injury, minimal brain dysfunction, dyslexia, and developmental aphasia. The term does not apply to children who have learning problems that are primarily the result of visual, hearing, or environmental, cultural, or economic disadvantage. Students who are eventually labeled "learning disabled" are often referred because of inconsistent performance; they are likely to have pronounced patterns of academic and cognitive strengths and weaknesses. For example, learning to read, no matter what her teacher tries; Joyce may be reading at grade level, be a good speller, have highly developed language skills, but not able to master addition and subtraction facts.

The criteria for eligibility of services for the learning disabled vary considerably from state to state. Generally, a pupil must demonstrate normal (or at least non-retarded) general intellectual development on an individually administered test of intelligence. The student must also demonstrate, on an individually administered test of achievement, some areas that are within the normal range, while demonstrating significantly delayed development in other areas of achievement, and demonstrate (correct) hearing and vision within normal limits. Eligible pupils would not have significant emotional problems or cultural disadvantage. Finally, the basic process disorder that causes the learning disability may or may not have to be tested, depending on the particular state's education code. If it is assessed, measures of visual and auditory perception, as well as measures of linguistic and psycholinguistic abilities, could be administered.

EMOTIONALLY DISTURBED

Emotionally disturbed pupils exhibit one or more of the following characteristics over a long period of time and to a marked degree that adversely affects educational performance: (a) an inability to learn which cannot be explained by intellectual, sensory, or health factors; (b) an inability to build or maintain satisfactory interpersonal relationships with peers and teachers; (c) inappropriate types of behavior or feelings under normal circumstances; (d) a general pervasive mood of unhappiness or depression; or (e) a tendency to develop physical symptoms or fears associated with personal or school problems. Students who are eventually labeled "emotionally disturbed" are often referred for problems in interpersonal relations (for example, fighting or extreme non-compliance) or unusual behavior (for example, unexplained non-compliance) or unusual behavior (for example, unexplained episodes of crying or extreme mood swings). Requirements for establishing a pupil's eligibility for, or special education services for the emotionally disturbed, vary markedly among the states. Some or all of the following sources of information may be used in determining eligibility: observational data, behavioral rating scales, psychological evaluations, and examination by a board-certified psychiatrist or psychologist.

TRAUMATIC BRAIN INJURY

Students with traumatic brain injury have an acquired injury to the brain caused by an external physical force, resulting in total or partial functional disability or psychology impairment, or both, that adversely affects a child's educational performance. The term applies to open or closed head injuries resulting in impairments in one or more areas, such as cognition; language; memory; attention; reasoning; abstract thinking; judgment; problem-solving; sensory, perceptual and motor abilities; psychosocial behavior; physical functions; information processing; and speech. The term does not apply to brain injuries that are congenital or degenerative, or brain injuries induced by birth trauma. Students with traumatic brain injury have normal development until they sustain a severe head injury. As a result of the injury, they are disabled. Most head injuries are the result of an accident (frequently automobile accidents) but may also occur as a result of physical abuse or intentional harm (for example, being shot). Traumatic brain injury will be diagnosed by a physician, who is usually a specialist (a neurologist), and educators identify the school-based deficits.

SPEECH OR LANGUAGE IMPAIRMENT

A student with a speech or language impairment has a communication disorder such as stuttering, impaired articulation, a language impairment, or a voice impairment that adversely affects a child's educational performance. Many children will experience some developmental problems in their speech and language. For example, children frequently have difficulty with the "r" sound and say "wabbit" instead of "rabbit." Similarly, many children will use incorrect grammar, especially with internal plurals; for example, children may say, "My dog has four foots." Such difficulties are so common as to be considered a part of normal speech development. However, when such speech and language errors continue to occur beyond the age when most children have developed correct speech or language, there is cause for concern. School personnel identify the educational disability, while speech and language specialists use a variety of assessment procedures (norm-referenced tests, systematic observation, and criterion-referenced tests) to identify the speech and language disability.

VISUAL IMPAIRMENT

A student with a visual impairment has an impairment in vision that, even with correction, adversely affects child's educational development. Visual impairment includes both partial sight and blindness. Students with severe visual impairments are usually identified before entering school, although some partially sighted students may not be identified until school age, when visual demands increase. Assessments of previously undiagnosed visually impaired students may indicate gross-and fine-motor problems or variable visual performance (that is, performance that varies with the size of print, amount of light, and fatigue, for example). Visual acuity and visual field are usually assessed by an ophthalmologist. A specialist assesses functional vision through systematic observation of a student's responses to various types of paper, print sizes, lighting conditions, and so forth.

DEAFNESS AND HEARING IMPAIRMENT

Deafness is an impairment in hearing that is so severe that the child is impaired in processing linguistic information through hearing, with or without amplification, (and) that adversely affects the child's educational performance. A student with a hearing impairment has an impairment in hearing, whether permanent or fluctuating, that adversely affects a child's educational performance but this is not included under the definition of deafness. Even severe hearing impairments may be difficult to identify in the first years of life, and students with milder hearing impairments may not be identified until school age. Referrals for undiagnosed hearing-impaired students may indicate both expressive and receptive language problems, variable hearing performance, problems in attending to aural tasks, and perhaps problems in peer relationships. Diagnosis of hearing impairment is usually made by audiologists, who identify the auditory disability, in conjunction with school personnel, who identify the educational disability.

ORTHOPEDIC IMPAIRMENTS

An orthopedic impairment adversely affects a child's education performance. The terms include impairments caused by congenital anomaly (e.g., clubfoot, absence of some member, etc.), and impairments caused by disease (e.g., poliomyelitis, bone tuberculosis, etc.), and impairments from other causes (e.g., cerebral palsy, amputations, and fractures or burns that cause contractors). Pupils with physical disabilities are generally identified prior to entering school. However, accidents and disease may impair a previously normal student. Medical diagnosis establishes the presence of the condition. The severity of the condition may be established in part by medical opinion and in part by systematic observation of the particular student.

OTHER HEALTH IMPAIRMENTS

Other health impairments are conditions that limit strength, vitality or alertness, (or) chronic or acute health problems such as a heart condition, tuberculosis, rheumatic fever, nephritis, asthma, sickle cell anemia, hemophilia, epilepsy, lead poisoning, leukemia, or diabetes that adversely affect a child's educational performance. Diagnosis of health impairments is usually made by physicians, who identify the health problems, and school personnel, who identify the educational disability.

THE PROCESS OF DETERMINING EXCEPTIONALITY

In practice deciding whether a student is exceptional can be complex. MDT evaluations frequently (and correctly) go beyond the information required by the entitlement criteria. MDTs collect information to rule out other possible disabling conditions. Sometimes the condition that initiates the referral is not the disabling condition. Those who are responsible for classification of pupils must adopt a point of view that is, in part, disconfirmatory, a point of view that looks to disprove the working hypothesis. Assessors must collect information that would allow them to reject the classification if a pupil proves either to be not disabled or suffers from a different disability (Ysseldyke & Alozzine, 1990).

An analysis of definitions, criteria, and diagnostic procedures in the classification of exceptional individuals must be predicted upon an understanding of the interrelationships among the various disabling conditions. Others avoid categorical definitions when describing exceptional individuals. The classification system used by the various states are designed to facilitate identification, evaluation, placement, and programming for disabled individuals.

Most states provide a written description of characteristics based upon the IDEA for each categorical type for whom they provide an education. Most states have added two additional categories not found in PL 94-142; they are: (1) multiple disabled, and (2) homebound and hospitalized.

SPECIFIC CHARACTERISTICS OF CHILDREN WITH EXCEPTIONALITIES

There is general agreement among professionals that exceptional children and youth exhibit behavior that cause problems in school (Ysseldyke, Algozzine, & Thurlow, 1992; Milich, McAnnich, & Harris, 1992; Polloway, Patton, Epstein, Cullinan, & Luebke; 1986). These behaviors may interfere with employment opportunities (Agran, Salzberg, & Stowitschek, 1987; Baron, Trickette, Schmid, & Leone, 1993; Sullivan, Vitello, & Foster, 1988; Zetlin & Hosseini, 1989). Additionally, that may serve as the primary factor in dropping out of school (Butler-Nalin & Padilla, 1989; Nelson, 1988).

Behavioral characteristics of pupils who have mild learning and behavior problems indicate that many of these pupils talk out, do not pay attention, do not follow the rules, get angry easily, start fights, use obscene language and sarcasm, interfere with the work of others, and frequently engage in temper tantrums and out-of-seat behavior (Farmer & Farmer, 1986; Roberts & Zubrick, 1992). In 1991, Forness and Kavale reported that the classmates of children with learning and behavior problems expressed that they actively dislike them. Because social acceptance is closely related to self-esteem (Henley, Roberts, & Algozzine, 1993), the peer rejection experienced by pupils with mild learning and behavior problems contributes to a low self-esteem. In addition, academic success and attending behavior are related to acceptance by peers, whereas, disruptive and aggressive behaviors are related to rejection by peers (Roberts & Zubrick, 1992).

Generally, children are expected to regulate and manage their own behavior in school (Farmer & Farmer, 1989). The socially competent individual generates social interactions; that is, the socially competent individual initiates or participates in a reciprocal social exchange which is mandated through natural reinforces (Nelson, 1988). Further, social competence ratings are lower for children with mild handicaps when compared to regular education pupils (Merrell, Merz, Johnson, & Ring, 1992). The absence of offers to share, smiling, making eye contact when speaking, asking for help, saying thank you, or following directions could potentially nullify a social interaction (Nelson, 1988).

Deficits in appropriate age-level social skills may be a contributing factor in the exceptional's inability to get along with peers. Social immaturity is often observed in antisocial behavior and failure to recognize responsibility and the rights of others.

A confounding variable that must be considered in examining peer relationships of the exceptional is the influence of labels. Milich, McAnnich, and Harris (1992) reviewed studies that disorder can lead to peer stigmatization which results in disturbed or disrupted peer relationships. These authors concluded that expectancy effects do occur among children and the effects occur in response to even minimal stigmatizing information; the stigmatizing information affects not only how the perceive feels about the exceptional child, but also how the exceptional child feels about the ensuing interaction. Finally, the authors pointed out that negative behavior of the exceptional may have immediate and long-term consequences for peer relations.

According to the International Study of the Center for Health, Education and Social System Research (Butler-Nalin & Padilla, 1989), the graduation rates of youths with disabilities (56-59%) are considerably lower than non-disabled youths (70-74%). Independent variables, namely the youths' behavior, experience, and the degree of social integration are examined as particular behaviors and experiences that influence the chance of pupils dropping out directly. These variables were examined on the basis of whether or not students had one or more of the following incidents: (1) being fired from a job, (2) leaving school because of suspension or expulsion, and (3) being arrested or incarcerated. Social integration was measured by whether the parent reported that the youth belonged to a school or community group in the past year. The results pointed out two measures of youth behavior as related to many exceptional individuals. They exhibit negative behaviors and seldom belong. Negative behavior is consistently related to dropping out of school. Belonging to a group is also significantly related to dropout and graduation.

Finally, in 1976, Sirvis and Carpignanoi analyzed the status of the disabled populations as having unique social status parallel to what occurs with minority groups including the disadvantages of discrimination and prejudice which accompanies that status. Fourteen years later, in 1990, the Americans with Disabilities Act (ADA 101-336) was passed with an intent to end discrimination against public services, public accommodations, transportation, and telecommunications. ADA required four years for employers and businesses to make reasonable modification (Blackhurst & Berdine, 1993). Although the jury is out regarding the effects of ADA, we expect research to report productive changes in the lives of the disabled members of our society.

While the introductory portion of this chapter focused on the history, classification, and general behavioral-social characteristics of students who have mild and severe learning and behavior problems, the next section will provide an overview of specific behavioral-social and academic characteristics of specific categories for exceptional children and youth. Behavior disorders, learning disabled, mental retardation, communication disorders, visual impairment, orthopedic, health impairments, and learning disabilities will be discussed in general terms, for specific information, the reader is referred to any basic book on exceptionality.

Please note that within each exceptional category, conditions may exist in mild, moderate, and severe forms. The mild to moderate levels are those pupils who have more contact with regular education programs. Pupils who have severe disabling conditions are most often educated in more restrictive settings with less interaction with the regular education program. All exceptional children should be educated with their normal peers to the extent that their disabilities will permit in the regular classroom.

For each exceptional group mentioned, there are several types and degrees of disabilities and each type will require a different type of assessment and intervention strategy.

BEHAVIORAL DISORDERS

Children with behavior disorders are more likely than any other category of exceptional youth to drop out of school. Dropout rates are reported at 55% with nearly half of the dropout rate, 26.8%, due to behavior problems (Butler-Nalin & Padilla, 1989). The behaviors observed interfere with the establishing and maintaining positive relations with others (Zargota, Vaughn, & McIntosh, 1991). Problems in adapting to the school environment, relating socially, and responsibly to teachers and authority figures are evident.

In addition, behavior disordered students are skilled at eliciting emotional responses of others (Henley, Ramsey, & Algozzine, 1993). These behaviors affect the social climate of the classroom and are of particular concern to the teacher because they require the teacher to take time to arbitrate disputes and encourage appropriate social interaction. Defiance, aggression, and non-compliance toward authority figures are likely to alarm the teachers and other school officials (Carr & Pungo, 1993; Blackhurst & Berdine, 1993).

Behavior disordered children and youth are also characterized by distractibility and impulsivity (Carr & Pungo, 1993). Frequently, there are difficulties in listening, asking for teacher assistance, bringing materials to class, following directions, and completing assignments. Many behavior disordered students are unable to ignore distractions and often cannot deal with anger and frustration. Introducing oneself, beginning and ending a conversation, sharing social problems, solving problems, and apologizing are generally difficult social skills for behavior disordered students to master (Hardman, Drew, Egan, & Wolf, 1993).

Some children with behavior problems avoid peer and social relationships (Glassberg, 1994; Henley, Ramsey, & Algozzine, 1993). They withdraw and isolate themselves. Others have engaged in social behaviors that are unacceptable to their peers and are, thereby, rejected by their peers (Kirkcaldy & Mooshage, 1993). Older behavior disordered students are described as destructive and intractable (Glassberg, 1994).

Zargota, Vaughn, and McIntosh (1991) reviewed 27 studies that examined social skills interventions for behavior disordered youth. These studies validate the behaviors discussed previously. The independent variables in the research included: nine studies which used interpersonal problem solving, smiling, conversation skills; following instructions, and joining a group were targeted in ten; one study addressed coping with anger, two included one or more of social cognition, coping with conflicts, and forming friendships; three addressed peer interactions; one examined moral development, choice, perspective taking and consequences; and finally, a study addressed self-control and coping behaviors.

It becomes obvious from the prior discussion that behavior disordered children will most likely experience academic deficits as an indirect result of their behaviors. According to Heyward and Orlansky (1992), many more behavioral disordered children than normal score in the slow learner or mildly retarded range on IQ tests. These authors define a score of about 90-95 as the average score for behavior disordered children and youth. Kaufman (1989) concurs but uses a range of 80-100. He also cites the average IQ score for children who are severely disturbed to range around 50.

DEAF AND HARD-OF-HEARING

The social-emotional development of children with hearing impairments follows the same basic pattern found among their peers (Meyen, 1990). Young deaf children are like hearing children in many ways—few differences exist. In language development, the deaf and the hearing children coo, gurgle, and babble. However, within eight to 12 months of age, vocalizations cease for deaf children and they withdraw and become silent. Children who are hard-of-hearing continue to vocalize (Moore, 1987). During the next few years of the child's life, parents become concerned and realize that something is wrong. The child, thus, becomes confused and frustrated (Bigge & O'Donnell, 1976). The beginning of school may involve the deaf and hard-of-hearing in mutual play interests that are not impeded by communication differences (Meyen, 1990). However, the social interactions of the deaf and hard-of-hearing child may, because of social immaturity, result in impulsivity (Haring & McCormick, 1990; Greenberg & Kusche, 1989). In addition, deaf children may be less capable of interpreting emotional states and situations due to limited opportunities for social interaction (Cole, 1987). Although the graduation rates of deaf and hard-of-hearing children–school-age youth that approach the rate of the non-disabled (Butler-Nalin & Padilla, 1989), their environment of deaf or hearing parents, severity of the loss (severity of the hearing loss is positively correlated with social adjustment), and the family climate (Hardman, Drew, Egan & Wolf, 1993; Greenberg & Kusche, 1989).

Greenberg and Kusche's (1989) review of current research regarding the development of deaf children and adolescents summarized that on verbal tests of intelligence deaf children scored lower than hearing peers. On measures of non-verbal intelligence the deaf scored within the normal range. Caution however, is suggested in interpreting these findings because the tests that were used to test the deaf pupils were standardized on hearing children and because the language background of deaf students is different from that of hearing peers (Geers, 1985).

Tests of academic achievement show deficits among deaf children, in part, because achievement is based upon language (Greenberg & Kusche, 1989; Haring & McCormick, 1990).

Intellectual development for individuals with hearing impairments is more a function of language than cognitive ability. Difficulties in performance appear to be closely associated with speaking, reading, and writing the English language (Hardman, Drew, Egan & Wolf, 1993). Children who are hard-of-hearing experience difficulty in reading achievement, thereby, suggesting that any hearing loss appears to be detrimental with regard to reading achievement (Higgins, 1980). Moore's (1987) interpretation is that deafness imposes no limitations on the cognitive abilities of individuals.

MENTAL RETARDATION

According to the American Association of Mental Deficiency, mental retardation refers to subaverage general intellectual functioning . . . which interpreted, means that a retarded child's intellectual capacity must be at least two standard deviations below the mean (Grossman, 1993). Thus, mentally retarded school-age children are classified according to expected achievement in the classroom. (There will be variations in classifications and nomenclature from state to state). They are usually classified as follows:

Educable: Expected achievement level 2nd to 5th grade.

Trainable: Some academic achievement but primary focus is upon self-help skills.

Custodial: Unable to care for their basic needs (Hardman, Drew, & Egan, 1993).

Readers should be aware that the above expected achievement levels are not intended to be used as ceilings for achievement among mentally retarded students. Some students in each category will exceed expectations–others may not reach the levels of expectations.

The social skills of the mentally retarded are evaluated as they relate to adaptive behavior. Adaptive behavior, which is included in the current definition of mental retardation, is defined as the ability to adapt to the environment, relate to others, and take care of personal needs (Henley, Ramsey, & Algozzine, 1993). In other words, impairments in maturation learning and social adjustment, in addition to other specified criteria, must be present in order to classify a student as mentally retarded.

In the classroom, mentally retarded children are socially immature. They usually have a poor self-concept and are thus susceptible to peer influence (Henley, Ramsey, & Algozzine, 1993). They are also rejected by their peers (Polloway, Patton, Epstein, & Luebke, 1986). Retarded children have inadequate attention levels, therefore, they experience difficulty in maintaining attention (Borkowski, Peck, & Damberg, 1983).

The dropout rate for mentally retarded children and youth is listed at 34 percent with behavior accounting for 13.6 percent of the rate. Using the educable, trainable and custodial classification, Hardman, Drew, Egan, and Wolf (1993) outline the social skill development of the mentally retarded as follows:

Educable: Social development will permit some degree of independence in the community.

Trainable: Social adjustment limited to the home and closely surrounding area.

Custodial: Need care and supervision throughout life.

Retarded children and youth may not be considered retarded in their home and community. Many mildly retarded adults (educable mentally retarded) achieve satisfactory adjustment in the community, marry and have children. They are, however, problems related to getting along with others, maintaining employment and personal frustration (Zetlin, 1988).

In spite of limited social skill development among the trainable, it is still necessary for them to develop appropriate social skills (Hardman, Drew, & Egan, 1993). It is important to recognize that the social needs of the mentally retarded may be overlooked because they are defined as having subaverage intellectual functioning. The emotions of the retarded are normal. They want to be accepted, liked and valued (Henley, Ramsey, & Algozzine, 1993).

ORTHOPEDIC AND HEALTH IMPAIRMENTS

Students with orthopedic and health disabilities are a varied population (Heyward & Orlansky, 1993). Researchers use different classifications when referring to this group. For example, Haring and McCormick (1994) refer to this group of disabling conditions as crippled and other health impaired, physically handicapped and physically disabled. Blackhurst and Berdine (1993) group this category of the disabled according to three functional categories: ambulation and vitality; medical diagnosis; and, other disabling conditions. Meyen (1990) used etiology to establish three categories; neurologic, orthopedic and health conditions. Public law 94-142 used orthopedic and health impairments to describe this group of children and youth (Federal Register, 1997, p. 42478).

Children with orthopedic and health impairments include children with cerebral palsy, muscular dystrophy, spina bifida, juvenile rheumatoid arthritis and poliomyelitis. Health impairments include asthma, allergies, epilepsy, juvenile diabetes mellitus, hemophilia, cystic fibrosis, sickle cell anemia, cardiac conditions, cancer and aids. *The Individual with Disabilities Education Act*, P.L. 101-476 of 1990 added traumatic brain injury as a separate disability category.

Because this group of children and youth typically have characteristics that do not conform with societal standards for physical attractiveness, they may have problems with being accepted or difficulty with feeling that they are accepted by peers (Meyen, 1990). Antonello (1996) related secondary physical problems such as atypical mannerisms, self control, hyperactivity, diminished attention, poor concentration, and failure to recognize social boundaries as influential in social interactions.

Undesirable social characteristics such as drooling, incontinence and seizure activity can have a negative effect on the establishment of positive relations. Mobility devices, life sustaining equipment and prosthetics may interfere with the development of positive images (Meyen, 1990).

Research defines three limitations on learning with reference to children who have orthopedic and health disabilities. These include:

1. limitations on the ability to process information.
2. limitations on the ability to receive information through the senses.
3. limitation on the range and nature of interpersonal and environmental interactions (Meyen, 1990).

Children who have conditions that affect their motor skills should have the full range of cognitive abilities. Generally, this group of children encompass the full range of intellectual capacity. Finally, the graduation rates of this group are equal to the non-disabled peers (Butler-Nalin & Padilla, 1989).

Characteristics of specific types of disabilities under the mildly-to-moderately categories are overviewed. A general portrait is given with strategies for improving social skills development in the socialemotional and academic areas. Chapter 8 addresses these topics in greater detail.

LEARNING DISABILITIES

Although there is great controversy regarding the nature of children and youth with learning disabilities, there are some generalizable social and emotional characteristics. Researchers (Hallahan & Reeve, 1980; Lloyd, 1980; Loper, 1980; Torgesen, 1988) have documented numerous social processes including rejection, isolation and loneliness. All students with learning disabilities have subject-related problems. Additionally, learning disability affects many other areas of the lives of students including relationships with friends, role in family, self-image and confidence in the ability to handle social situations.

It is quiet apparent that students with learning disabilities display social skills problems in school, (Haagar & Vaughn, 1995). Their interaction with non-disabled peers is often repulsive and misunderstood. Research conducted by Stone and LaGreca (1990) indicates that students who are constantly isolated and ignored are more likely to be aggressive, hostile and socially anxious in their classes. These behaviors (emotional intelligence) interfere with the necessary skills and time students need to focus and concentrate on classwork successfully. Emotional intelligence (a concept elaborated on by Goldman, 1996) indicated that to perform at the level commensurate with society expectations requires the ability for one to exercise awareness of social deftness, good impulse control, self-motivation, persistence, and self-discipline.

Since many learning disabled students often show extraordinary abilities (Thomas Edison, Nelson Rockefeller, Albert Einstein, Pablo Picasso, and Hans Christian Anderson), perhaps educators should focus on these areas to provide for social acceptance, school success and relevant learning experiences since much of the rejection is due to poor school achievement. Many learning disabled students possess hobbies and areas of interest that are well respected by significant others. A program where students are exposed to a variety of intellectual, social and cultural perspectives, and reflects the students' background needs and interest (willing many instances) addresses the social skills problems of the learning disabled (Kaplan, 1996).

Students with learning disabilities also have low-self esteem, poor self-concept and very low motivation. They usually have little success at school, and feel that effort is not rewarded. In many cases, they apply the learned helplessness approach (even if I try hard, I am destined to fail) to school-related situations and tasks. Students with learning disabilities often rely on external locus of control. That position does not permit them to become self-directed learners (internal locus of control). The attitude of learned helplessness (Seligman, 1992; & Bender, 1995) impeded their social, cognitive, and emotional abilities.

Research has shown that 36 percent of these students drop out of school due to academic and social problems and 14.4 percent drop out because of behavioral problems. During the high school years, social and behavior problems often take precedence over academic problems. These students, usually at this point, have had repeated failures in school, little encouragement and little motivation, social rejection by peers and are viewed as troublemakers.

Kaplan (1996) detailed several studies that have been conducted and failed to demonstrate significant discrepancy between the classroom behavior of students with learning disabilities and those labeled as mild mental disabled, slow learners or other mild disabilities (Vaughn et al., 1992; Stone and LaGreca, 1990). These researchers concluded that there is little social difference in students who fall within the low-achieving category. This category, in many cases, is evident during the school hours where acceptable communication skills, acceptable class behaviors and acceptable social perceptions are part of the norm of the school climate.

Students with learning disabilities usually have a disorder in one or more of the basic psychological processes involved in understanding or in using language–spoken or written, which may manifest itself in an imperfect ability to listen, think, speak, read, write, spell or to do mathematical calculations (Kaplan, 1996).

Students with learning disabilities tend to vary from average to above average intellectually. The range is 90-130 or two or more standard deviations above the mean. That range includes students who are classified as gifted and talented with learning disabilities. Many of these students do not differ from the average in terms of their characteristics.

A multiplicity of characteristics have been associated with the significant discrepancy between what a learning disabled student is capable of learning and academic achievement in reading, science, mathematics, social studies, vocabulary, and writing. Yet, there is immense confusion concerning a large number of the negative characteristics and traits these students receive. However, students with learning disabilities tend to demonstrate specific thinking deficits (cognition) more commonly than the average students.

Substantial evidence indicates that students with learning disabilities are very poor reflective thinkers. They also portray auditory and visual processing deficits. These difficulties often impede the smooth learning of classroom skills associated with school-related subjects.

Many of the strategies to succeed in school-related subjects require active participation and the employment of a host of problem solving, and critical thinking skills. Students with learning disabilities experience difficulty in the application and strategies necessary for memorization and generalization of these skills. However, when memory strategies are taught and apply in meaningful learning situations, learning disabled students perform as well as others in reading, writing, and other communication skills.

The academic performance of such students is poor. They usually possess problems in reading and writing. Achievement in some subjects may be average, but achievement in others are below average, and in many cases at the failure level, which is not indicative of their potential. There is great variation among thin population, too, in school subjects. Many of these students perform quite successfully and are classified as having areas of gifts and talents, but a great percentage of them possess basic academic and social problems.

Generally, students with learning disabilities experience severe problems in reading. Commonly noted observational characteristics include: accuracy, fluency, and normal rate in reading; omissions, substitutions and mispronunciations of words; inadequate auditory closure and sound blending skills; a deficit in phoneme-grapheme relationships; poor decoding and comprehension skills; vocabulary deficits, poor spelling skills and inferential reading skills. Reading skills are necessary for success in all aspects of school life and are correlated with psychological success (Norris, Haring, & Haring, 1994).

Difficulties with language is also common among the learning disabled population. They frequently have problems with impaired discrimination of auditory stimuli; slow language development; difficulty imitating statements; a mastery of automatic rules of language; difficulty in expressive and receptive language and problems with phonological production or speech. Learning disabled children and youth with oral language problems often manifest these problems in written assignments in all subjects.

THE VISUALLY IMPAIRED

The development and embellishing of social skills are very much dependent upon vision. Children and youth with limited vision find it difficult to rely on visual cues or signals to communicate with significant others in the social environment (Sacks & Reaedon, 1989). In a research study conducted by Kekelis and Sacks (1992) and MacCuspie (1992) on the social interaction of children who were blind and their non-disabled peers, it was pointed out that the behaviors of these children were void of creativity, flexibility, and elaboration. Visually disabled children and youth with severe visual loss, or the non-existence of vision are deprived of the opportunities to emulate social role models and engage in meaningful social interactive experiences (Haring & McCormick, 1990). These situations may cause social isolation, negative attitudes, and school anxiety (Leonhardt, 1990). These behaviors can have a significant impact on social and academic learning.

The self-esteem of visually impaired learners is not significantly different than that of their sighted peers (Ubiakor & Stile, 1990). "If learners with visual impairments have had significant verbal interaction with others, such as participating in games and friendships, they are not different from their sighted peers in social cognitive tasks" (Schwartz, 1983).

The classroom teacher plays an important role in helping the visually impaired students to develop good self-esteem and to feel good about their setting. Tuttle (1984) concluded from his analysis that the lack of self-confidence in the visually impaired is due to their limited interaction and attitudes of sighted people. The positive interaction of sighted others will provide a sense of confidence and further opportunities to develop social competencies for school, home and community independence.

The difference between the development of language in children who are visually disabled compared to sighted children is not significant. Research (Civelli, 1983; Matsuda, 1984) into the language of the visually impaired indicated that these students do not differ from their sighted peers on verbally-related activities. The visually impaired students may even have a higher auditory acuity then the non-disabled visual peers. The auditory channel is the major link between the visually impaired student's language and the outside world, and many researchers have highlighted its importance.

Studies highlighting the impact of this missing sense with the visually impaired have indicated that the quality of word meaning is deficit due to the lack of or an impairment of vision. Gallagher and Ansastasiow (1993) indicated that visually impaired students had less understanding of words as vehicles and were slower to form hypotheses about word meaning. Warren (1984) after studying the literature on the language of the visually impaired concluded:

> The new work of the past several years strongly suggests that, while blind children may use words with the same frequency count as sighted children, the meanings of words for the blind are not as rich or as elaborated. (p. 278)

Research also shows that there is much variation among the cognitive development of children and youth with visual impairments when compared to their non-disabled peers (Matsuda, 1984; Civelli, 1983). Because of the absence of visual information and experience, visually impaired students generally have difficulty with projecting positions in space, including recognition of shapes, construction of a projected straight line conceptualization of right and left in absolute and mirror image orientation.

Learners with visual impairments have difficulty in determining and relating right to left toward others although they are able to discriminate orientation to themselves. The concepts of spatial relationships is particularly important to the visually impaired due to personal mobility.

The development of concepts for the visually impaired student is quite different since many of them are learned through the visual modality. Researchers (Davidson, Dunn, Wiles-Kettermann, & Appelle, 1981; Stephens & Grube, 1982) using concepts based on the developmental theory have concluded that children who are blind lag behind their sighted peers. The tactual and auditory channels assist the visually impaired students in seeing the world. They must take great care in focusing their mental attention to gain the most from their social interaction environment and their experiences with significant others (Groenveld & Jan, 1992).

SPEECH AND LANGUAGE IMPAIRED

Speech, language, and communication problems may result from a variety of problems—including hearing and visual disabilities; problems related to the central nervous system; cleft palate disorders that appear single or in clusters, from articulation, voice, and fluency disorders.

When a child fails to acquire the semantic aspects of language, this interferes greatly with communicative skill and can result in acquiring other components. Children with language difficulties in semantics either do not learn the meaning of words or are unable to interpret the meaning of a series of words collectively or convey meaning. Expressive language problems may result from semantic difficulties from lack of symbols to partial deficits.

Pragmatism involves the functional use of language as a social tool for communication, learning, directing behavior, or generating new ideas. As children master the structural and content component of language, they also must learn to use language in appropriate and functional ways in various contexts. A great percentage of children with language disorders lack skills in pragmatic or language use (Haring & McCormick, 1990). Problems in expressive intentions and difficulties in maintaining a flow of conversations are the most common difficulties children experience. Some children are restricted communicatively because they use language in limited ways.

Communication disorders may interfere with the social interaction and cognitive development of language disabled learners throughout the school day. However, research indicates that it is important that learners with speech and language deficits be educated in settings with non-disabled peers (Schiefelbush & McCormick, 1981). Many language delayed children do not understand how to take turns or engage in reciprocal interactions necessary for conversation. Still others, may not attend to the contents of the speaker's remarks or understand their role in continuing the discussion. The context in which the disabled students must function is the best place to practice the art of communication.

A few states use generic classifications. The State of Maryland is one state employing this classification system. The State frequently categorizes disabled individuals as mildly to moderately or severely to profoundly and by age levels, regardless of their disabling conditions.

Regardless of the classification system in use, all disabled individuals can profit from training and intervention.

MILDLY TO MODERATELY DISABLED

This group of disabled individuals consist of the largest group of disabled individuals. They make up approximately 90 percent of all students with disabilities based on the federal categories. This large group include students who have disabilities in the following areas: (1) speech and language; (2) learning disabilities; (3) emotional disturbed; (4) mental retardation; (5) hearing impairments; (6) orthopedic impairments; (7) other health impairments; (8) visual impairments; and (9) deaf-blindness.

These children are very similar to their normal peers, displaying a variety of behaviors, social, physical, motor and academic and learning problems. A highly structured and functional program is needed in order to reduce and minimize their disabling conditions. Many of their educational needs can be met in the regular classroom, providing adaptations and modifications are made in their school program. Early identification and assessment and curriculum adaptations for mildly to moderately disabled children appear to be key elements in successful school experiences. If properly instructed, many mildly to moderately disabled individuals can become independent and productive adults in our society. Detail classification and characteristics of mildly to moderately disabled children are beyond the scope of this text. The reader is referred to any basic textbook in exceptionality.

SEVERELY TO PROFOUNDLY DISABLED

Students who are classified as severe to profound make up approximately 10 percent of all students with disabilities. Collectively, these students have wide and diverse abilities. Most of them can profit best from highly structured and individualized programs. Many skilled professionals are required to attend to many disabling conditions in the cognitive, physical, mental and social areas. Frequently, related services are needed to provide the most basic services.

Children classified as mildly to moderately disabled, if conditions are severe enough, may be classified as severe to profound. Appropriate assessment will determine the classification. In addition, PL 101476 lists autism and traumatic brain injury under the severely to profoundly disabled.

These children are markedly different from their normal peers, displaying noticeable differences in mental, physical, and social characteristics. Many of their needs cannot be successfully met in the regular classroom. Special placements and treatment are needed for many of them. Many of them will need adult supervision for all of their lives, they seldom will be independent adults.

COMMONALITY AMONG EXCEPTIONAL INDIVIDUALS

Characteristics attributed to most exceptional individuals seem to overlap. Regardless of how exceptional individuals are classified, they cannot really be described in neatly self-contained compartments without some overlapping. For example, impaired communication is recognized as a characteristic of individuals with sensory impairment or speech disorders. However, communication impairment is being increasingly recognized as a common element in the assessment and remediation of learning disabilities, emotional disturbance, and mental retardation.

Perceptual disorders are identified as important characteristics frequently attributed to individuals with learning disorders. The same characteristics of perceptual disorders are also seen among some individuals with cerebral palsy, mental retardation, hearing handicaps, and others. It seems reasonable to state that with few major exceptions most exceptional children have in common many similar characteristics.

Characteristics that differentiate exceptional individuals from each other are directly related to categorical classifications. Retardates have problems chiefly in the area of cognitive development; the crippled in motor development; the blind and deaf in sensory deficiencies. The majority of exceptional individuals not only have primary disabilities but also associated secondary disabilities that may contribute significantly to their disabling conditions.

HANDICAPS VERSUS DISABILITIES

Exceptional individuals may have disabilities in several areas of functioning, such as hearing and speech. Most authorities agree that the impairment of structure or function is a disability. A disability does not necessarily denote a handicap. A handicap is a social phenomenon. Handicaps arise when standards instituted by society make a person stand out or draw attention to his/her disability.

Special education exists mainly because society chooses to treat exceptional individuals differently. Special classes, treatment, labeling, and attitudes displayed by society combine to single out individuals as exceptional. These factors operate to remove exceptional individuals further from the mainstream of society and pinpoint their disabilities. Minimal adaptations are usually enough to help some exceptional individuals overcome the negative effects of their disabilities.

A handicap should be defined in terms of the situation or condition. An exceptional individual who is crippled should not be classified as disabled if he/she can perform a task that does not require excessive movement or locomotion. On the other hand, blindness should not constitute a disability if vision is not required to perform the task. These examples may be generalized to most areas of exceptionality. If exceptional individuals can perform as normal under certain conditions, their disabilities should not be classified as disabling conditions. In essence, simply because an individual is blind, his disability should not be equated with a global disability. He/she might be able to operate within normal ranges on certain tasks if society provides the opportunities for him to demonstrate his skills.

LEARNING STYLES OF EXCEPTIONAL INDIVIDUALS

A review of the research indicated very few studies in the area of learning styles. The styles which are recognized as being acceptable in the classroom are limited. Some pupils learn most readily by reading, some by listening, and others by means of physical doing. Styles are used in a variety of ways by individuals to suit their unique needs. Learning styles may be classified as a combination of sensory orientation, responsive mode, and thinking pattern. Sensory orientation describes whether the learner depends primarily on sensory contact with his environment; responsive mode was concerned with whether one works best alone or in a group; thinking pattern was referred to as whether one learns best by first getting many details and then organizing them into a pattern.

ADJUSTMENT AND THE EXCEPTIONAL

The severity of the disabling conditions of some exceptional individuals may not be the critical factor in their adjustment. Although it would appear that individuals with non-ambulatory disabilities would suffer more anguish than individuals with mild limps, some research results and reports clearly demonstrate that there is not a 100 percent positive relationship between severity of disability and the resultant educational, social, and vocational adjustment. Enough examples exist to demonstrate this view, namely Helen Keller, Charles Steinmetz, and Louis Braille. Such factors as school and community support, family concerns and initiatives, self-motivation, personality, and drives collectively affect the way individuals perform regardless of the severity of their disabilities.

One of the considerations that must be recognized when working with exceptional individuals is to discover what procedures or techniques can improve behaviors most effectively. Change in behavior may be the result of an altered or more favorable attitude by the teacher. Expectancy of good performance, comfortableness with the individual, and acceptance generate better performance on the part of exceptional individuals rather than attitudes of denigration, non-expectancy of performance, uncomfortableness, and lack of acceptance (Taylor, 2000).

Another aspect involves feelings and attitudes relating to the segregation and integration of exceptional individuals in regular classes. When individuals are segregated, a two-way process is created. Not only are the exceptional cut off from the normal, but also the normal from the exceptional. This may have the effect of making it more difficult for the normal to accept the exceptional on more or less equal terms. Thus, the effect of segregated special classes tends to create social handicaps over and above the actual effect of the original handicap. It seems more realistic for exceptional individuals to learn to live with their disabilities in normal surroundings.

SUMMARY

The history of educating children with exceptionalities does not reflect equality of education opportunities. Since the early nineteen century, some progress has been made. Recognition of the educational rights of children with exceptionalities was not completed in insolation. A variety of forces, such as parental groups, national associations representing the various exceptionalities, and federal and state laws have been instrumental in bringing about change. Changes have been slow, but constant. Today, all children with exceptionalities have the right to a free and appropriate education.

In spite of the various federal laws, school districts throughout the country have not performed a satisfactory job in providing quality education for children with exceptionalities. In order for the schools to come into compliance with the law, they must use the various amount of research and resources present and experiment with radical intervention models which address the needs of children with exceptionalities as reflected throughout this text.

As a practical guide to understanding and helping exceptional individuals, the following suggestions are made:

1. Individuals with exceptionalities, with rare exceptions, basically are more like other individuals than they are different, and areas of similarity and strengths should not be neglected.
2. Acceptance is of paramount importance to exceptional individuals. When acceptance is clearly communicated, exceptional individuals see themselves as important, unique, and useful.
3. Exceptional individuals are likely to have more difficulties than their normal peers, thus, extra effort must be devoted to provide strategies, materials, adaptations, and assistance in overcoming their difficulties.
4. Individuals, regardless of their exceptionalities, have highly individual learning and personality patterns. No two individuals learn in exactly the same manner or at the same speed. Therefore, lockstep methods are usually not desirable and are often ineffectual for exceptional individuals. The strengths and weaknesses of individuals, learning styles and modalities, task analyses, and other factors need to be considered in planning learning activities and individualized instruction.
5. Some individuals considered severely disabled seem to require specific instruction in highly structured settings.
6. Academic skills are part of what exceptional individuals need to acquire. Developing adequate self-concept, a sense of worth, coping with skills, and appropriate attitudes are also essential for many exceptional individuals.
7. Research findings have consistently showed that categorical labels

have little significance for educational intervention.

8. The major task of special education should be focused on providing services for individuals who have special needs, in most instances, through innovating programs in the regular classroom.

REFERENCES

Adelman, H. S., & Taylor, L. (1983). Enhancing motivation for overcoming learning and behavior problems. *Journal of Learning Disabilities, 16,* 384-392.

Agran, M., Salzberg, C., & Stowitschek, J. (1987). An analysis of a social skills training program using self-instructions on the acquisition and generalization of two social behaviors in a work setting. *Journal of the Association of Severe Handicaps, 12,* 131-139.

Antonello, S. (1996). *Social skill development: Practical strategies for adolescents and adults with developmental disabilities.* Boston: Allyn & Bacon.

Baron, C., Trickette, E., Schmid, K., & Leone, P. (1993). Transition tasks and resources: An ecological approach to life after high school. *Prevention in Human Services, 10* (2), 179-204.

Bender, W. (1995). Teachers' attitudes toward increased mainstreaming: Implementing effective instruction for students with learning disabilities. *Journal of Learning Disabilities, 28,* 87-94.

Bigge, J., & O'Donnell (1976). *Teaching individuals with physical and multiple disabilities.* Columbus, OH: Charles E. Merrill.

Blackhurst, A. E., & Berdine, W. H. (1993). *An introduction to special education* (3rd ed.). Lexington: Harper Collins College Publishers.

Borkowski, J., Peck, V., & Damberg, P. (1983). Attention, memory, and cognition. In J. L. Matson and J. L. Milich, *Handbook of Mental Retardation,* p. 479.

Butler-Nalin, P., & Padilla, C. (1989). *Dropouts: The relationship of student characteristics, behaviors, and performance for special education students.* Washington, DC: U. S. Department of Education, Office of Special Education Programs.

Carr, S., & Pungo, R. (1993). The effects of self-monitoring of academic accuracy and productivity on the performance of students with behavior disorders. *Behavior Disorders, 18*(4), 241-250.

Civelli, E. (1983). Verbalism in young children. *Journal of Visual Impairment and Blindness, 77* (3), 61-66.

Cole, P. R. (1987). Recognizing language disorders. In F. N. Martin (Ed.), *Hearing disorders in children.* Austin, TX: Pro-ed.

Davidson, P. W., Dunn, G., Wiles-Kettenman, M., & Appelle, S. (1981). Haptic conversation of amount in blind and sighted children: Exploratory movement effects. *Journal of Pediatric Psychology, 6,* 191-200.

Farmer, T., & Farmer, E. (1986). Social relationships of students with exceptionalities in mainstream classrooms: Social networks and hemophile. *Exceptional Children, 62* (5), 431-450.

Federal Register. (1977). 42 (163) 42474-42518.

Feldhusen, J. F. (1966). How to identify and develop special talents. *Educational Leadership, 53,* 66-69.

Forness, S. R., & Kavale, K. A. (1991). Social skills deficits as primary learning disabilities: A note on problems with the ICLO diagnostic criteria. *Learning Disabilities Research & Practice, 6,* 44-49.

Gallagher, K., & Ansastasiow, N. (1993). *Educating exceptional children.* Boston: Houghton Mifflin.

Geers, A. (1985). Assessment of hearing impaired children: Determining typical and optimal levels of performance. In F. Powell, T. Finitzo-Heiber, S., Friel-Patti & D. Henderson (Eds.). *Education of the hearing impaired child* (pp. 57-83). San Diego: College Hill.

Glassberg, L. (1994). Students with behavior disorders: Determinants of placement outcomes. *Behavior Disorders, 19* (3), 181-191.

Goldman, D. (1995). *Emotional intelligence: Why it can matter more than IQ.* New York: Bantam Books.

Greenberg, M. T., & Kusche, C. A. (1989). Cognitive, personal, and social development of deaf children and adolescents. In M. Wang, M. Reynolds, & H. Walberg (Eds), *Handbook of Special Education: Research and Practice,* pp. 95-129.

Groenveld, M., & Jan, J. E. (1992). Intelligence profiles of low vision and blind children. *Journal of Visual Impairment & Blindness, 86* (1), 68-71.

Grossman, H. (1993). Manual of classification of mental retardation. Washington: American Association of Mental Deficiency.

Gross-Tsur-Varda. (1995). Developmental right-hemisphere syndrome: Clinical spectrum of the non-verbal learning disability. *Journal of Learning Disabilities, 28,* 80-86.

Haager, D., & Vaughn, S. (1995). Parents, teachers, peers, self-reports to the social competence of students with learning disabilities. *Journal of Learning Disabilities, 28,* 205-215, 231.

Hardman, M. L., Drew, C. J., Egan, M. W., & Wolf, B. (1993). *Human exceptionality: Society, school, and family.* Needham Heights, MA: Allyn & Bacon.

Hallahan, D. P., & Reeve, R. E. (1980). Selective attention and distractibility. In B. K. Keogh (Ed). Advances in special education: Vol. 1. *Basic constructs and theoretical orientations* (pp. 141-181). Greenwich, CT: JAJ Press.

Haring, N., & McCormick, L. (1990). *Exceptional children and youth* (5th ed.). Columbus: Merrill.

Henley, M., Ramsey, R., & Algozzine, R. (1993). *Characteristics of and strategies for teaching students with mild disabilities.* Needham Heights, MA: Allyn & Bacon.

Heyward, W., & Orlansky, D. (1992). *Exceptional children* (4th ed.). New York: Merrill.

Higgins, D. (1990). *The challenge of educating together deaf and hearing youth: Making mainstreaming work.* Springfield: Charles C Thomas.

Kaufman, J., Cullinan, D., & Epstein, M. (1987). Characteristics of students placed in programs for the seriously emotional disturbed. *Behavior Disorders, 12,* 175-184.

Kaufman, J. (1989). *Characteristics of behavior disorders of children and youth* (4th ed.). Columbus: Merrill.

Kaplan, P. (1996). *Pathways for exceptional children.* Minneapolis: West Publishing (pp. 504-505).

Kekelis, L., & Sacks, S. Z. (1992). The effects of visual impairment on children's social interactions in regular education programs. In S. Z. Sacks, L. Kekelism and R. J. Gaylord Ross (Eds). *The development of social skills by blind and visually impaired students: Exploratory studies and strategies* (pp. 59-82). New York: American Foundation for the Blind.

Kirkcaldy, B. D., & Mooshage, B. (1993). Personality profiles of conduct and emotional disordered adolescents. *Personality and Individual Differences, 15* (1), 95-96.

Leonhardt, M. (1990). Stereotypes: A preliminary report on mannerisms and blindness, 78, 54-55.

Lloyd, J. (1980). Academic instruction and cognitive techniques: The need for attack strategy training. *Exceptional Education Quarterly, 1,* 1-8.

Loper, A. B. (1980). Metacognitive development: Implications for cognitive training of exceptional children. *Exceptional Education Quarterly, 1,* 1-8.

MacCuspie, A. P. (1992). The social acceptance and integration of visually impaired children in integrated settings. In S. Z. Sacks, L. Kekelism and R. J. Gaylord Ross (Eds.). *The development of social skills by blind and visually impaired students: Exploratory studies and strategies* (pp. 83-102). New York: American Foundation for the Blind.

Matsuda, M. (1984). A comparative analysis of blind and sighted children's communication skills. *Journal of Visual Impairment and Blindness, 78* (1), 1-4.

Merrell, K., Merz, J., Johnson, E., Ring, E. (1992). Social competence of students with mild handicaps and low achievement: A comparative study. *School Psychology Review, 21* (1), 125-137.

Meyen, E. (1990). *Exceptional children in today's schools.* Denver: Love.

Milich, R., McAnnich, C., & Harris, M. (1992). Effects of stigmatizing information on children peer relations: Believing is seeing. *School Psychology Review, 21* (3), 400-409.

Moore, D. M. (1987). *Educating the deaf: Psychology, principles and practices* (3rd ed.). Boston: Houghton Mifflin.

Nelson, C. M. (1988). Social skills training for handicapped students. *Teaching Exceptional Children, 20* (4), 19-23.

Norris, G., Haring, L., & Haring, T. (1994). *Exceptional children and youth* (6th ed.). New York: MacMillan.

Polloway, E., Patton, J., Epstein, M., Cullinan, D., & Luebke, J. (1986). Demographic, social and behavioral characteristics of students with educable mental retardation. *Education and Training of the Mentally Retarded, 21,* 27-34.

Raine, A., Hulme, C., Chadderton, H., & Bailey, P. (1991). Verbal short-term memory span in speech-disordered children: Implications for articulatory coding in short-term memory. *Journal of Child Development, 62,* 415-423.

Roberts, C., & Zubrick, S. (1992). Factors influencing the social status of children with mild academic disabilities in regular classrooms. *Exceptional Children, 59* (3), 192-202.

Sacks, S., & Reaedon, M. (1989). Maximizing social integration for visually handicapped students: Applications and practice. In R. Gaylord Ross (Ed). *Integration strategies for students with handicaps* (pp. 77-104), Baltimore, MD: Paul H. Bookes Publishing Co.

Sacks, S. Z., & Wolf, K. (1992). The importance of social skills training in the transition process for students with visual impairment. *Journal of Vocational Rehabilitation, 2* (1), 46-55.

Schiefelbush, R. L., & McCormick, L. (1981). Language and speech disorders. In J. Kaufman and D. Hallahan (Eds.). *Handbook of Special Education.* Englewood Cliffs, NJ: Prentice Hall.

Schwartz, T. (1983). Social cognition in visually and sighted children. *Journal of Visual Impairment and Blindness, 77,* 377-381.

Seligman, M. E. (1992). *Helplessness: On depression, development and death.* San Francisco: W. H. Freeman.

Silverman, F. (1995). *Speech, language, and hearing disorders.* Needham Heights, MA: Allyn & Bacon.

Sirvis, B. O., & Carpignanoi, J. (1976). Psychosocial aspects of disability. In J.L. Bigge (Eds). *Teaching individuals with physical and multiple disabilities.* Columbus, OH: Charles E. Merrill.

Stephens, B., & Grube, C. (1982). Development of Piagetian reasoning in congenitally blind children. *Journal of Visual Impairment and Blindness, 76,* 133-143.

Stewart, D. (1994). Distinguishing learning disabilities from learning disabilities in postsecondary settings. *Guidance and Counseling, (1994-95), 52,* 12-17.

Stone, W. L., & LaGreca, A. M. (1980). The social status of children with learning disabilities: A reexamination. *Journal of Learning Disabilities, 23,* 32-47.

Sullivan, C. A., Vitello, S., & Foster, W. (1988). Adaptive behavior of adults with mental retardation in a group home: An intensive case study. *Education & Training in Mental Retardation, 23,* 76-81.

Taylor, G. R. (2000). Curriculum models and strategies for educating individuals with disabilities. Springfield, IL: Charles C Thomas.

Torgesen, J. K. (1988). Studies of children with learning disabilities who perform poorly on memory span tasks. *Journal of Learning Disabilities.*

Tuttle, D. (1984). *Self-esteem and adjusting to blindness.* Springfield, IL: Charles C Thomas.

Ubiakor, F., & Stile, O. (1990). The self-concepts of visually impaired and normally sighted middle school children. *Journal of Psychology, 124,* 190-200.

USA Today (April, 1994). *Fostering creativity in youngsters,* v.114 (12).

U.S. Department of Education (1988). *To assure the free appropriate public education of all handicapped children.* Ninth annual report to congress on the implementation of the education of the handicapped act. Washington: DC.

Vaughn, S., Hogan, A., Kouzekanani, K., & Shapiro, S. (1990). Peer acceptance, self-perception, and social skills of LD students prior to identification. *Journal of Education Psychology, 82,* 101-106.

Warren, D. (1984). *Blindness and early childhood development.* New York: American Foundation for the Blind.

Whemeyer, M. (1995). A career education approach: Self-determination for your child with mild cognitive disabilities. *Intervention-in-school-and-clinic, 30,* 157-63.

Ysseldyke, J., & Alozzine, B. (1990). *Introduction to special education* (pp 132-145). Boston: Houghton Mifflin.

Ysseldyke, J., Alozzine, B., & Thurlow, M. (1992). *Critical issues in special education.* Dallas: Houghton Mifflin.

Zargota, N., Vaughn, S., & McIntosh, R. (1991). Social skills interventions and children with behavior problems: A review. *Behavior Disorder, 16* (4), 260-275.

Zetlin, A. (1988). Adult development of mildly retarded students: Implications for educational programs in M.C. Wang, M.C. Reynolds & H.J. Walberg (Eds.). *Handbook of special education research and practice vol. 2 mildly handicapped condition.* New York: Pergamon, pp. 77-90.

Zetlin, A. G., & Hosseini, A. (1989). Six post-school case studies of mildly handicapped young adults. *Exceptional Children, 55,* 405-411.

Chapter 4

TRENDS IN SPECIAL EDUCATION

GEORGE R. TAYLOR AND LORETTA MACKENNEY

INTRODUCTION

EXPERIMENTATIONS AND RESEARCH FINDINGS in the behavioral sciences, technological devices, and education have had a significant impact upon the field of special education. Application of these techniques and devices have improved the educational, social, and physical opportunities for children with exceptionalities.

A variety of trends and developments in computer technology, adaptive devices, transitional services, and the Internet and media integration constitute the major trend in special education during the past decade. Technology-assisted devices such as ventilators for breathing, urinary catheters and colostomy bags for bowel and bladder care, trachea colostomy tubes for supplying oxygen-enriched air to congested lungs, or suctioning equipment for treatment of mucus from airways. These devices are operated and controlled by computers. Specific use of technology-assisted devices are beyond the scope of this chapter. The reader is referred to physical exceptionalities in any basic exceptional children's book. This chapter is designed to give an overview of the application of computer technology in developing trends in educating children with exceptionalities.

INCLUSION

Inclusion is an important issue because it affects virtually all stakeholders in education, including children with and without exceptionalities and their families, special and general education teachers, administrators, related services personnel, school staff, and the general public (Alper, Schloss, Etscheidt, & MacFarlane, 1996). Inclusion, a grassroots movement driven by parental dissatisfaction with the current delivery system and the conviction

58

that all children should be educated together, has captured the attention of educators and the general public alike. According to Aefsky (1995), inclusion is turning the tables after 15 unsuccessful years of teaching children in a fragmented school setting. She stated we are asking professionals, teachers, administrators, and support staff to change their roles.

A preponderance of literature attests to the fact that most children with exceptionalities should be placed in inclusive classrooms. This position has created some controversy regarding inclusive versus special class placement as noted by (Baker, Wang, & Walberg, 1994-1995; Waldron & McLeskey, 1995-1998; Banerji & Daily, 1995; Bear & Proctor, 1990; Zigmond et al., 1995; Borthwick-Duffy et al., 1996; Fuchs & Fuchs, 1994; Rogers, 1993; Waldron & McLesky, 1998). The common consensus of these researchers indicated that the concept of inclusion is an excellent idea, however, it may not work for all children all of the time.

Historically, this issue was discussed in the 1970s. This issue was whether exceptional children learned best in integrated or segregated classes. Most of the research indicate that prior to 1975, most exceptional children with mild exceptionalities were educated in integrated classes, those with severe to profound exceptionalities were educated in segregated classes. Federal legislation, PL 94.142 changed this concept and gave all children with exceptionalities equality of educational opportunities with the concept of the least restricted environment (LRE) which provided all exceptional children opportunities to be educated with their peers (Taylor, 1999). The law provided for both types of placements, integration and segregation. Assessment data used in completing the IEP are used to determine the LRE for exceptional children. In comparing the research over the last two decades, data still support that inclusion placement is no panacea for educating all exceptional individuals. The public school record on behalf of students with exceptionalities is best characterized as one of exclusion, separation, and absence of services. In growing numbers, exceptional learners are receiving at least a portion of their instruction alongside their classmates.

During the present decade the schools have made significant progress toward including exceptional children in the regular classroom. This move has resulted in fewer exceptional children being placed in special schools and classes. Data from reports to Congress support this trend. Table 4 provides data regarding the percentage of students in each disability category who were served in each of four placement settings in 1988-89, and the percentage of students who were served in these settings in 1994-95. Data in Table 4 identify exceptional individuals across all disabilities categories in the least restricted environment.

Figure 2 reflects the changes in the percentage of exceptional children in each category who were served in the least restricted environment. Bars in

Educational Interventions and Services

TABLE 4

Percentage of Children with Various Disabilities by Setting 1988-89 and 1994-95

Specific Learning Disabilities	1988-89	19.6	58.0	21.0	1.4
Mentally Retarded	1988-89	6.2	23.1	60.4	10.3
Serious Emotional Disturbances	1988-89	14.2	36.2	36.4	19.2
Speech/Language Impairments	1988-89	75.9	19.9	3.7	1.5
Other Health Impairments	1988-89	31.0	20.8	19.3	28.9
Orthopedic Impairments	1988-89	30.4	18.8	33.1	25.5
Multiple Disabilities	1988-89	7.5	15.1	47.3	36.1
Visual Impairments	1988-89	40.8	25.8	29.3	13.1
Hearing Impairments	1988-89	27.7	21.0	34.0	17.3
Deaf-Blindness	1988-89	13.3	6.1	31.5	49.1

Percentages of school day apart in separate, special education setting.

FIGURE 2

Change in the Percentage of Students Served in Separate School Settings by
Disability Category Between 1988-89 and 1994-95

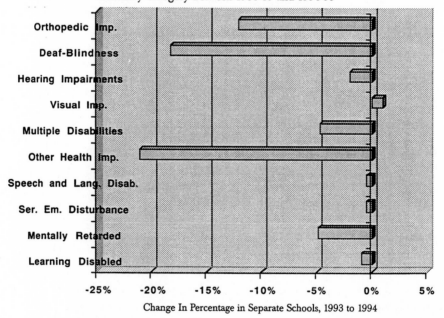

Change In Percentage in Separate Schools, 1993 to 1994

Source: Annual Reports to Congress on the Implementation of the Individuals with Disabilities Education Act, 1991 and 1997, by the Office of Special Education Programs, Washington, DC: U.S. Department of Education.

the negative range indicate decreases in separate school placements, while bars in the positive range indicate increases. As this figure illustrates, each disability category experienced a decrease in the percentage of students who were served in separate school settings, with the exception of the visual impairment category. The categories that experienced the largest percentage of students moving out of separate school settings were other health impairments (-21.1%), deaf-blindness (-18.3%), and orthopedic impairments (-12.1%).

Figure 3 shows data regarding the overall percentage of students in each disability category who were educated in separate school settings in 1994-95. It is obvious from Figure 3 that students in the deaf-blind, multiple disabilities, and serious emotional disturbed categories represented the largest disability categories served in separate school settings. This figure illustrates that large percentages of students from some disability categories continue to be educated in separate schools. These categories include deaf-blindness

FIGURE 3

Percentage of Students Educated in Separate School Settings by Disability Category: 1994-95

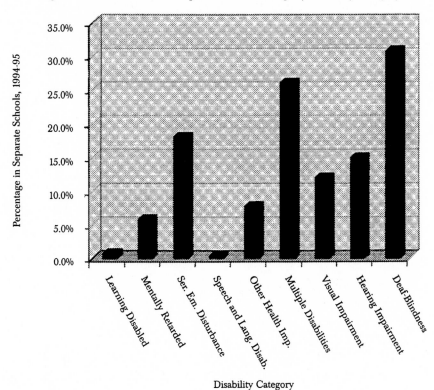

Source: Annual Reports to Congress on the Implementation of the Individuals with Disabilities Education Act, 1991 and 1997, by the Office of Special Education Programs, Washington, DC: U.S. Department of Education.

(30.8%), multiple disabilities (26.1%), and serious emotional disturbance (18.1%). In contrast, several categories include small percentages of students in separate school settings. These categories are speech/language impairments (.4%), learning disability (.8%), mental retardation (5.9%), and other health impairments(7.8%). Thus, categories that include students with more substantial needs continue to have a higher proportion of students in separate school settings than do categories that include students with milder disabilities.

Data in Figure 4 pinpoint changes in the percentage of students served in general education classrooms by disability categories between 1988-89 and 1994-95.

FIGURE 4

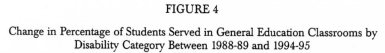

Change in Percentage of Students Served in General Education Classrooms by
Disability Category Between 1988-89 and 1994-95

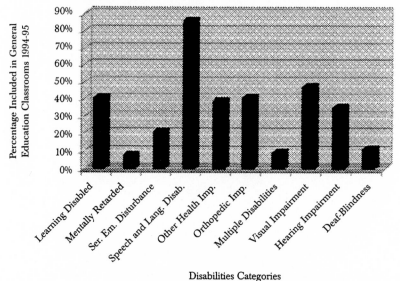

Disabilities Categories

Source: Annual Reports to Congress on the Implementation of the Individuals with Disabilities Education Act, 1991 and 1997, by the Office of Special Education Programs, Washington, DC: U.S. Department of Education.

Data in Figure 4 shows that students with speech and language disabilities showed the greatest increase of exceptional children being served in the regular classroom. Bars in the positive range indicate increases in general education classroom placements, while bars in the negative range indicate decreases. The trend that is illustrated in this figure is in the inverse of the trend in Figure 1; that is, every category with the exception of deaf-blindness showed an increase in the percentage of students who were served in general education classrooms. The categories that experienced the largest increases were learning disabilities (21.5%), speech/language impairments (11.6%), orthopedic impairments (8.0%), and visual impairments (6.5%). The only category that experienced a decrease in the percentage of students served in general education classrooms was deaf-blindness (-1.2%).

Figure 5 reflects the percentage of students educated in general education classrooms for 80 percent or more of the school day during the 1994-95 school year.

FIGURE 5

Percentage of Students Educated in General Education Classrooms
by Disability Category: 1994-95

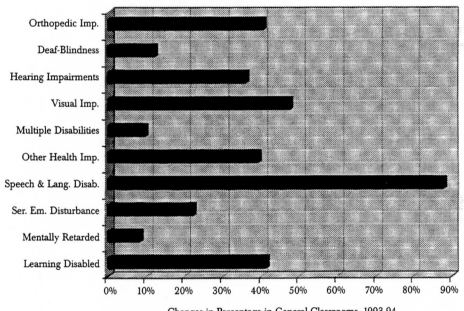

Changes in Percentage in General Classrooms, 1993-94

Source: Annual Reports to Congress on the Implementation of the Individuals with Disabilities Education Act, 1991 and 1997, by the Office of Special Education Programs, Washington, DC: U.S. Department of Education.

Statistics in Figure 5 reveals that students with speech/language impairment comprise the largest group. This figure reveals that a large percentage of some disability categories are served in general classrooms for 80 percent or more of the school day, including speech/language impairments (87.5%), visual impairments (47.3%), learning disabilities (41.1%), orthopedic impairments (40.3%), other health impairments (39.0%), and hearing impairments (35.9%). In contrast, several categories have a relatively small proportion of students who are educated in general education classrooms for most of the school day. These categories include mental retardation (8.2%), multiple disabilities (9.6%), deaf- blindness (12.1%), and serious emotional disturbance (22%). Thus, categories that include students with milder disabilities have a higher proportion of students in general education classrooms than do categories that include students with more substantial needs.

Data provided by the Office of Special Education programs clearly show that:

1. There has been a steady increase in the number of exceptional children served in inclusive settings.
2. Exceptional children having serious types of exceptionalities such as emotional disturbance, visual impairments, hearing impairments, mental retardation, and the deaf-blindness have been educated in inclusive settings to some degree, however, most of them are educated in separate school settings.
3. Exceptional children having multiple disabilities show the poorest record for being educated in inclusive classrooms.

Nationally, the schools are making significant progress in educating exceptional children in inclusive settings. Those trends are not universal across all states, they vary significantly from state to state. These data also show that exceptional children receive services outside of the regular classroom less than 21% of the school day. The percentages significantly increased from 21% to 60% in the resource room. Students in special classes receive more than 60% of their service outside of the regular class. Students in special classes receive 50% of the school day in separate day schools, and the same percentage was listed for residential facilities and homebound/hospital settings (Office of Special Education Programs, 1991 and 1997).

Most educators believe that exceptional children and their peers can be taught together. Isolating exceptional children may cause them to suffer from low self-esteem and may reduce their ability to deal with other people. In addition, non-exceptional children can learn much about personal courage and perseverance from exceptional children.

Inclusion Defined

Inclusion education has been defined in as many ways as there are attitudes toward this educational concept. For instance, Roach (1995), defined the term as serving students with a full range of abilities and exceptionalities in the general education classroom, with appropriate in-class support.

Written in the opinion of Brown, Schwarz, Udvari-Solner, Kampschroer, Johnson, Jorgensen, and Greenwald (1991), inclusion is a way to implement least restricted environment (LRE), however, it is not necessarily the regular education classroom. According to Bennett, Duluca, and Bruns (1997), Scruggs and Mastropieri (1991), the concept of inclusion is the integration of students with exceptionalities into a heterogeneous classroom for the entire school day, in which special education services would be received.

It is the attitudes of those involved in, or affected by, inclusive education that define and determine the impact of this practice on the individuals who will be placed in this setting. For example, Barry (1995), asserted that the process of including individuals with exceptional needs into the mainstream classroom has become a pressing issue among those in administration responsible for the education of these individuals.

Teaching students with exceptionalities in inclusive settings is a multifaceted task that cannot be accomplished by just one person. Inclusive education happens when a team of mutually supportive players pledges to provide best practices for a student with exceptionalities. Inclusive education focuses on a combination of best practices in education, including cooperative learning, peer tutoring, and community building in classrooms and schools. Teaching strategies for inclusive settings are synonymous with effective teaching strategies used in any area of education (Aefsky, 1995; Jones & Carlier, 1995). Depending on the exceptionality and level of student need, a team with unique but complementary skills should be consulted to guide, advocate for, and implement this student's educational program. More than any other element, the need for team effort to manage, deliver, and support a student's inclusive education is a drastic change for regular educators. Educators must develop a plan to integrate the lifelong goals and special needs of students with exceptionalities within the context of the regular classroom (Filbin, 1996; Jones & Carlier, 1995).

Collectively, research in support of inclusion is based upon:
1. Federal legislation in support of educating exceptional individuals in regular classes. The reader is referred to Chapter 2 for a comprehensive review of the impact of federal legislation on inclusion.
2. Research findings tend to support that exceptional children perform academically as well in inclusive classes as separate classes.
3. When provided with support, many exceptional children are able to succeed in regular education classrooms.
4. The continuum of service model is not needed in inclusive settings, exceptional children should be placed in regular classes on a full-time basis.
5. Exceptional children will benefit from associating with their normal peers.

6. Inclusion will reduce labeling of exceptional children.
7. Inclusion tends to increase interaction between exceptional children and their peers.

SOME KEY CONTROVERSIAL ISSUES IN INCLUSION

Integration of exceptional children into the regular classroom and elimination of separate education classrooms have been issues of major concern in the field of special education for well over two decades (Katsigannis, Conderman, & Franks, 1995; Swayer, McLaughlin, & Winglee, 1994; Baker, Wang, & Walberg, 1994-1995; Borthwick-Duffy, Palmer, & Lane, 1996; Fuchs & Fuchs, 1994). A multitude of conditions and trends have attributed to the controversy. As indicated, federal legislation generally supports educating exceptional children in the regular class, however; there is a provision in the *Individuals With Exceptionalities Education Act* which indicates that students with exceptionalities should be removed from regular education only when the nature and severity of the disability is such that education in regular classes with the use of supplementary aides and services cannot be successfully achieved (Taylor, 1999).

Data from the seventeenth Annual Report to Congress on the implementation of IDEA (1995), does not support that school districts are not generally following the least restrictive mandate (LRE). The percentage of learning exceptional children educated in regular class ranged from a low of 20% to a high of 35%. These percentages represent an increase in the number of learning exceptional children educated in regular classes in comparison to 1979 (McLeskey & Pacchiano, 1994; McLeskey & Waldron, 1995).

Research results in the field have endorsed both educating exceptional children in both inclusive and separate special classes. The preponderance of research tends to support placing exceptional children in inclusive settings (Banerji & Daily, 1995; Bear & Proctor, 1990; Giangreco, Dennis, Cloninger, Edelman, & Schattman, 1993; Sharpe, York, Knight, 1994; Staub & Hunt, 1993; Roberts & Mather, 1995; Alper, 1995; Mills & Bulach, 1996).

Inclusion offers the non-exceptional student an opportunity to develop an appreciation for the complexity of human characteristics as well as an appreciation for individual differences. Students who have not had these experiences may be surprised to learn that, for example, speech problems that accompany cerebral palsy do not necessarily indicate limited intelligence, cognitive impairment need not affect social development, and sensory impairment need not interfere with skill in motor activity. Additionally, students with exceptionalities may teach non-exceptional learners to go beyond dysfunctional stereotypes. All students with behavior disorders are not aggressive, and students with learning exceptionalities can be highly capable in some academic areas.

Advocates for full inclusion of exceptional children indicate that it is their democratic right to be educated with their peers, integration of exceptional children with non-exceptional children enhances interpersonal skills. Other studies indicate that curricula in inclusive schools should be appropriate for different levels of exceptionalities and sensory acuity. There is no separate knowledge base for teaching exceptional children. Teachers must be innovated and employ creative teaching strategies, such as learning centers, cooperative learning, concept teaching, directed teaching, and team teaching. Many adaptations and modifications will be needed in the instructional process, depending upon the amount and degree of disabling conditions present. The use of computer technology has been addressed later in the chapter. To the extent possible, exceptional children should be included in the regular learning process (Barry, 1995; Wang, Reynolds, & Walberg, 1995; Baker, Wang, Walberg, 1995; Staub & Peck, 1995; Johnston, Proctor, Corey, 1995; Jorgensen, 1995).

ASSESSING AND EVALUATING INCLUSION PROGRAMS

Vaughn, Schumm, and Brick (1998), developed and field tested a rating scale for educators to employ in rating the effectiveness of inclusion programs. This comprehensive rating scale was divided into 12 major categories ranging from assessing needs of exceptional individuals, competencies, and responsibilities of teachers both regular resources and special resources, curriculum innovations, parental involvement, evaluation of delivery models, professional development, and statements on a philosophy of inclusion. Teachers were requested to rate each of the individual 47 items using the following scale: 3=implements, 2=implements partially, and 1=does not implement or implements poorly. Data from the rating scale were used for program development, monitoring and evaluation of the school's inclusion program. Teachers voiced that the instrument was useful in assisting them in understanding what is needed and expected in order to conduct a successful inclusion program.

Proponents of full inclusion believe that a one-size-fits-all approach will be disastrous for exceptional children, it is not only unrealistic but also unjust. To correct this injustice according to Shanker (1995), public laws addressing inclusion will need to be rewritten to fund the cost of inclusion, provide adequate training for all teachers, to give equal weight to requests from parents and referrals by teachers, teachers must be totally involved in writing the IEP, and alternative arrangements should be made to temporarily place exceptional children who are violent or disruptive in secure settings. The National Association of State Boards of Education voiced that many special education programs are superior to regular classrooms for some types of exceptional children. Baker and Zigmond (1990), and Fuchs, Fuchs, and Bishop (1992), and Fuchs and Fuchs (1995) reported that individualizing strategies employed in special classes and superior to one-size-fit-all approach was observed in many regular classrooms. They supported the view that separate is better for some exceptional children, and to abolish special education placement in the names of full inclusion is to deprive many exceptional children of an appropriate education.

Although the preponderance of research supports the concept of inclusion, some researchers question whether or not children with exceptionalities can receive an adequate education in a regular classroom setting (Fuchs, 1994; Borthwick-Duffy, Plamer, & Lane, 1996).

In summary, most of the research in opposition to inclusion stated that inclusion will not work for exceptional children due to the following:

1. Children with exceptionalities with serious problems tend to perform better in separate classes.
2. There is a need to preserve the continuum of specialized programs and placement options.
3. Exceptional children enrolled in special classes performed as well as those in regular classes on curriculum-based measures.
4. Exceptional children will interfere with the progress of regular students.
5. Placing children with exceptionalities in regular classes can lead to stigmatized labels.
6. Some regular students may begin to mimic inappropriate behaviors of some exceptional children, thus affecting learning.
7. Some parents fear that services for their exceptional children will not be available under inclusion.
8. Parents of non-exceptional children fear that their children would be neglected in the classroom due to special attention required for exceptional children.
9. Segregated schools are considered safe havens for some parents because they provide the specialized services need for their exceptional children. (Taylor, 1999)

CRITICAL ISSUES TO BE CONSIDERED IN INCLUSION

Inclusion has proved to be a powerful tool in the education of children with exceptionalities. This trend is supported by the voluminous research reviewed in this chapter. The authors of this text support the notion that inclusion versus special placement is not the critical issue facing educators, rather, there are well-defined goals and objectives, instructional strategies, competent personnel, supportive services, related resources, community and parental support, successful delivery models, and positive attitudes of staff members toward children with exceptionalities. Specific examples and factors to consider relevant to inclusion are found in Appendices B, C, D, & E.

When there is no consensus on goals or objectives, there is no logical means for choosing one approach over another, one kind of staff over another, one program component over another. It would not make sense to initiate an experimental effort unless goals or objectives were made explicit and a set or priorities were chosen. Clearly stated, educational goals for exceptional children would minimize the conflict in the field. On the other hand, when an avoidance of clearly stated goals allows educators beneficial objectives that are unique for a particular exceptionality but cannot be identified, then the exceptional group in question should not be segregated from normal society or regular classes. It is true that while behavioral objectives of classroom instruction have been fairly well-defined in most exceptional areas with the exception of the retarded and learning exceptional, clearly defined objectives will emphasize expected behaviors of children as well as skills and activities needed to reach the objectives (Taylor, 1999).

To achieve these goals for exceptional children, educators should have scientific objectives in mind as well as a plan for sequencing steps or tasks that will lead to desired behaviors (Jones & Carlier, 1995). Steps that educators may take to assume that objectives and goals are met are as follows:

1. Understanding and categorizing the objectives of the school's curriculum.
2. Defining the objectives or goals in terms of expected behaviors, based upon observable and measurable data.
3. Developing instruments, materials and activities to assess or determine if desired behaviors have been met.
4. Instituting changes at any point in the instructional process if it appears that objectives are not being achieved.
5. Sequencing tasks where exceptional children can experience success. This will involve moving from known to unknown experiences, from concrete to abstract levels.

By defining goals on a continuum of levels of difficulty, a two-fold purpose is accomplished. First, the teacher is assisted in establishing objectives for each class in such a way that they are sequential in an ascending order of difficulty, and they are also achievable in a foreseeable future; second, because individual capabilities and competencies vary among children with comparable measurable abilities, such as sequence permits some to advance more rapidly than others in a single class.

Since some goals for exceptional children are essentially short-range in contrast with the traditional concept of short-and long-range plans, it becomes increasingly important for the stated objectives to be precise and clear-cut. In addition, there is a need for frequent evaluation of progress made, together with a review of an estimation of the child's potential in relation to his or her attainment. Finally, it is important that the limited capacity in mental, physical, and social growth not be dissipated in meaningless-unproductive activity.

Another crucial problem that communities and educators must face before they elect to choose a plan for their exceptional children is that of sequencing instructional tasks. Special educators must consider life adjustment out of school—in essence, what will the final product be. Before a plan is adopted, however, those behaviors which the pupil must master for successful living must be identified and programmed in sequential steps for the goals and instruction to be useful. These procedural changes should take priority over the inclusion versus special class placement controversy (Taylor, 1999).

More effective tools and new curricula to measure the characteristics of exceptional pupils must be developed, emphasizing needs and characteristics, rather than placement. The curriculum for exceptional children should be based upon realistic goals and approaches. These approaches in turn should be formulated on the basis of needs, capacities, and interests. Refer to Chapter 11 for curriculum strategies.

Individual differences and program scope must be recognized when planning an instructional program for exceptional children. Program scope includes the totality of experiences and activities to which an individual is exposed during a specified period of time. Therefore, teachers must be skilled in informal assessment procedures so that both the general and specific characteristics of the children can be described and reacted to in the instructional program. The evaluation of an instructional program includes evidence that the program has or has not reached its objectives; it should also provide the basis for conclusions and recommendations for improving the program. All relevant data should be matched or developed to meet the program's objectives; data and information not germane to the objectives should not be included in the instructional process.

Recognition by the school of the exceptional child as a whole, from the time of his or her identification to the time of discharge, would seem to warrant methods of instruction that take into account all of his or her general and specific behaviors. These behaviors would include the development of desirable general personality characteristics and the acquisition of specific knowledge and skills that should emulate from the instructional program. In essence, the instructional program should be directly associated with the goals and objectives set forth. The instructional program should be functional and include both literacy skills, problem solving techniques, and communication skills.

Professional preparation of school personnel is desperately needed. High standards are needed for the selection of directors, supervisors, and teachers of exceptional children to achieve stated goals. Ideally, before placing a special child into any class, the training, attitudes, and values of the teacher should be carefully and precisely delineated. Discovering a pupil's characteristics, which a given teacher will accept or reject, becomes a critical administrative duty. The nature of the teacher's response to expressed hostility, physical attributes, and academic skills should be included in the placement decision. Questions of this nature are critical and have more relevancy than inclusion versus special class placement. Solutions are not easy, but revisions in teaching training are evident; teachers must be trained to seek, identify, and demand the assistance needed to educate exceptional children.

Teachers must be trained to employ new teaching strategies, as well as cooperating with other teachers, parents, and the community. As much as their mental, physical, and social exceptionalities will permit, teachers should actively involve exceptional children in the instructional process. Collaboration among teachers is necessary in order to provide the best possible education for exceptional children. Joint planning, modifications, and adaptation in the instruction program are essential to assure equality of education opportunities for children with exceptionalities.

If proper supportive services are not provided for exceptional children, no degree of placement will be successful. Special helping teachers, itinerant, or school-based, a resource room, and other well-known educational manipulations are needed if any plan is to be successful. Exceptional children generally have many handicaps that the school cannot manage alone—speech disorders, defective hearing, poor reading ability, weak vision, and behavioral maladjustment—conversely, the services of many specialists will be needed to promote better pupil growth and adjustment. Refer to Chapter 1 for specific characteristics.

A desirable relationship between school and community is marked by a strong bond of understanding and cooperation between parents and school personnel. Parents should have a direct share in deciding what plan of placement appears to service their children's needs best. Parents should be made to feel free to make suggestions for the guidance of their children, and should be actively involved in all aspects of the planning process in a direct constructive way. Educators recognize the positive contributions that many parents of exceptional children can make, such as resource individuals, guest speakers, consultants, volunteers, substitute teachers, assisting on field trips, and other school-related activities. However, this important resource is frequently overlooked by educators. The issue at hand is now whether a particular school district has selected inclusion over special placement or vice versa, but whether there is mutual support and acceptance of the plan advanced. Without this agreement, it is doubtful whether any plan could be successful.

TRANSITIONAL SERVICES

If exceptional individuals are to make adequate adjustment in society as adults, appropriate transitional services must be undertaken to assist them in transferring from school to work (Telepak, 1995). Recognizing this fact, the schools, the community, business participation, and parents, need to address some of the issues facing individuals with exceptionalities as they prepare to leave school.

The Telepak (1995) view is that adequate preparation should be made to prepare children with exceptionalities to participate in the world of work. Factors such as age, nature, and type of disability, schedule at school, tasks to be performed, level of career awareness needed, and business accessibility are important. Students 14 to 21 years of age receive prevocational services. Older students are given priority placement in community work training projects which integrates education with a hands-on approach. The work skills and behaviors that are acquired through this work experience, application and interview, observation and hands-on learning, student reporting, evaluation and follow-up, better prepare students for vocational training or future employment.

ROLE OF THE FEDERAL GOVERNMENT

Public Law 94-142, PL 101-476, PL 98-524, and PL 105-17 all address in some detail, this important issue of transitional services for exceptional individuals. All of the components of the federal laws were summarized in Chapter 2. The impact on transition services was clearly articulated.

The requirements for providing transition services for youth with exceptionalities have been modified in IDEA 97. While the definition of transition services remains the same, two notable changes have been made to IEP requirements:
* beginning when a student is 14, and annually thereafter, the student's IEP must contain a statement of his or her transition service needs under the various components of the IEP that focuses upon the student's courses of study (e.g., vocational education or advanced placement); and

- beginning at least one year before the student reaches the age of majority under State law, the IEP must contain a statement that the student has been informed of the rights under the law that will transfer to him or her upon reaching the age of majority.

The new law maintains 16 as the age when student's IEPs must contain statements of needed transition services. These two requirements; one for students aged 14 and older, and one for students aged 16 and older seem confusingly similar. However, the purpose of including certain statements for students beginning at age 14, according to the Committee on Labor and Human Resource's Report (1997), "is to focus attention on how the child's educational program can be planned . . . [and] the provision is designed to augment, and not replace, the separate transition services requirement, under which children with exceptionalities [who are 16 or older] receive transition services."

In spite of federal laws, parental input and efforts instituted by the schools, many exceptional individuals leaving school are not prepared for employment or to enroll in postsecondary education (Bursuck & Rose, 1992; Florian & West, 1991; Nisbet, 1992).

It is generally agreed by most professionals involved with transitional services, that it is a complex and ongoing process that should begin as early as possible. The authors' view is that the process should begin at the end of the elementary grades, reinforced in middle schools, and be refined at the end of secondary school. In the authors' opinion, this strategy would better equip exceptional individuals to prepare for the adult world.

Public Law 98-524 is the vocational act which provides services through rehabilitation counseling in several areas related to employment and training for the world of work in high skill, high salaried careers and postsecondary education. With PL 105-17, greater coordination between education and vocational rehabilitation is mandated. We are optimistic that the future outlook for exceptional individuals in the area of improved transitional services will significantly improve when the full impact of PL 105-17 is achieved.

As indicated, preparation for the world of work should begin in the elementary grades for exceptional individuals. In secondary school, the roles of counselors and educators should be to assess the skills, abilities, job requirements, functional levels, and employment outlook. Resulting data from assessment should be used to develop a transitional plan. The plan should involve exceptional individuals to the extent of their abilities, and of equal importance will be the coordination of the transitional plan with parents and community agencies. The plan should be revised as needed, depending upon developmental physical, social, and academic changes which may occur in exceptional individuals as they progress through school.

ADAPTIVE SKILLS

Adaptive skills in the basic areas of social and interpersonal skills must be an integral part of any model of training for children with exceptionalities. Research has constantly documented that many exceptional individuals fail because of personal appearance, poor personal hygiene, and lack of appropriate decision skills (Taylor, 1997; Taylor, 1998). The school must provide appropriate social skills activities to improve interpersonal skills of exceptional individuals through activities designed to develop positive interpersonal relationship and to teach exceptional children how to internalize feelings and behaviors.

SOME CONCLUDING REMARKS

Transitional planning for children with exceptionalities is not only necessary for their future survival in the world of work, but it is mandated by federal law. The law requires that a statement relevant to transitional services be included in the IEP. The statement should include a description of how interagency coordination will be established to provide services and how these proposed services will be associated with high school experiences. Timelines for achieving services provided by agencies in the community as well as responsibilities should also be delineated (McDonnel, 1995). Integrated media and computer technology can be a significant influence on exceptional children making a smooth transition by providing useful information needed to transit from school to college or the workplace (Bader, 1998).

The transition from middle to high school and from high school and beyond is a focus that is taking on greater significance as time goes on. Computer training is seen as a transition tool for high school students planning to attend college or to enter the workplace. Therefore, the computer laboratory is emphasized as an important part of the students' curriculum, be it special education or regular education.

TECHNOLOGICAL SERVICES

Today, computers are widely used in educating individuals (Pena, 1995; Fraiser, 1995). According to Papert (1996) the new technologies have helped create a culture for learning. Rather than students listening to a teacher regurgitate facts and theories, they discuss ideas and learning from one another, while the teacher acts as a participant in the learning process. The digital media is causing educators and students to consider other ways of promoting learning.

According to Tapscott (1999) there are eight shifts of interactive learning. Educators should shift:

1. From linear to hypermedia learning. Most textbooks are linear in nature. TV and instructional videos provide a hypermedia or non-linear approach to learning. Non-linear is more interactive and non-sequential than linear materials.

2. From instruction to construction. The Internet can provide a shift from the tradition paradigm of teaching to a more innovative approach by teachers planning the curriculum with children. Constructivists argue that people learn best when they have center to learner-centered education.

3. From teacher-center to learner-centered education. The new technology focuses on the learning experience of the individual rather than the teacher learner-centered education and improves the child's motivation to learn by stimulating students discussion, debates, research, and collaborating on projects with themselves and the teacher.

4. From absorbing materials to learning how to navigate and how to learn. This implies that the student should know how to synthesize, not just analyze. The net provides opportunities and information for children to synthesize and evaluate, thus, promoting the use of higher level thinking skills.

5. From school to lifelong learning. Learning has become a continuous, lifelong process. The Internet can provide massive and detailed information to assist in updating new developments in various fields which will promote lifelong learning.

6. From one-size-fits-all to customized learning. The new technology permits individualization of instruction by providing highly customized learning experiences based upon the unique needs of the individual. According to Paper (1996), the new technology will make it possible to individualize instruction for every learner in the future.

7. From learning as a fortune to learning as fun. The new media can make learning pleasurable for learners by providing activities they like and which entertains them, thus, increasing motivation for learning.

8. From the teacher as a transmitter to the teacher as a facilitator. Learning is becoming a society activity, whereby children conduct their own learning experiences, facilitated by the teacher.

Many computer software programs teach exceptional children a variety of skills. Other programs are used to develop social and emotional skills. Instructional units can be facilitated through the use of computer software. Computer software has the potentiality of remediating skills in any content area (Choate, 1997; Latham, 1999). Computers have the ability of presenting information in a multisensory mode (Bakken & Aloia, 1998; Goldstein, 1998).

COMPUTER ASSISTED INSTRUCTION
FOR THE EXCEPTIONAL

Computer-based learning can be used to supplement skills and heighten interest in content areas such as math, reading, and writing (Latham, 1999). Effective use of technology, such as interactive videos to embellish lessons, video conferencing, or word processors to facilitate performance, may spark interest of children with exceptionalities (Choate, 1997). The technology can assist children with exceptionalities to develop appropriate prosocial and interpersonal skills, as well as academic skills through self-modeling to reinforce skills (Salend, 1995).

The use of video technology empowers the teachers of students with exceptionalities to strengthen his or her assessment, management, and instructional program in the classroom. Broom and White (1995) wrote that behavioral disorders are reduced when students can view videotapes of their behaviors as many times as they wish. Self-recording and peer evaluations are highly recommended strategies. Thomas and Knezek (1999) wrote that unleashing the power of technology has the potential to change how students acquire and demonstrate knowledge, how teachers facilitate learning, and even where better learning takes place.

The National Educational standards project is attempting to provide a national consensus on what students should know in content areas proposed standards:

1. Technology Foundation Standards for Students;
2. Standards for Using Technology in Learning and Teaching;
3. Educational Technology Support Standards; and
4. Standards for Student Assessment and Evaluation of Technology Use.

Only the first standards have been addressed, other standards will be addressed in the future. The initial standards and student performance indicators extend knowing content to include the application of knowledge in the context of learning, living, and working. The technology foundation standards for all students are divided into six broad standard categories:

1. Basic operations and concepts;
2. Social, ethnical, and human issues;
3. Technology productivity tools;
4. Technology communication tools;
5. Technology research tools; and

6. Technology problem-solving and decision making tools.

In addition to these students, profiles describing the technology competencies that students should exhibit upon the completion of four grade ranges are presently being developed (Thomas & Knezek, 1991). Benefits from the use of microcomputers in improving the performance of children with exceptionalities in the contact areas have been well-documented (Hughes, 1996; Frazier, 1995; Walters, 1998; Fodi, 1996; Bader, 1998; Lester, 1996, Polloway, 1993).

One of the major reasons why computers and other technological devices are not in great supply in many classrooms is due to expense. Many school districts simply do not have the funds to equip their classrooms. To assist school districts, the Clinton Administration has proposed increased spending for computer technology (Hughes, 1996). Subsequently, the passage of the Telecommunications Act (1996) includes goals and provisions to network classroom to the Internet by the year 2000. January 1, 1998, approximately $2.3 billion of annual, additional funding was made available to schools to offset connectivity costs. This law will enable school districts to use technology to enhance their instruction program by having access to the World Wide Web. The North Carolina Department of Public Instruction appears to be in the forefront by profiting from the new federal regulation. The department has advanced a plan to have computers in every classroom by the next decade.

The Telecommunication Act of 1996 will permit schools in need to apply for funds to improve telecommunications services through the Universal Service Fund for Schools and Libraries, commonly known as the "E-rate." It is a system of discounts that make telecommunication services affordable to schools and libraries. Virtually every school and library in the country is eligible to participate in the program, excluding profit-making schools with endowments of more than 50 million dollars. There is a sliding scale developed based upon social and economical factors of the student body which applies for the fund, students must develop a technology plan which fit with the mission statement of the school. For additional information on the plan go to SLC website (*www.slsfund.org*) or call the toll-free help line (888-203-8100) to find detailed information relevant to the plan (Revenaugh, 1999).

ADVANTAGES OF USING COMPUTERS AND OTHER TECHNOLOGICAL DEVICES

Generally, in computer technology, the drill-and-practice type programs lend themselves nicely to developing fluency on a skill. Currently, the best research suggests that when a student is in the fluency stage of learning, the use of drill-and-practice software will result in very positive student gains. Perhaps the best example of why these features are necessary can be seen in the area of mathematics (Polloway, et al. 1993). Bolger (1996) wrote that students choose the computer to complete assignments when they are functional and real. Students who have difficulty in any area can spend time looking at the very creative artwork on the introductory screen while they gather their thoughts. This is considered to be a constructive use of learning time in both inclusive and special education classrooms.

Prior to starting to use the computer, the teacher may wish to introduce computer-based vocabulary words to the students. Words such as information highway, on board, user-friendly, or e-mail, help the student become familiar with some computer terminology. A vocabulary list that is user-friendly to the student can be a source on which the teacher can motivate students' interests. The computer can offer a slow student an opportunity to slow down and repeat the correct answer as many times as needed to master the concept (Polloway, 1993).

The impact of the computer and other technological devices have been well entrenched into the American culture. Computers have impacted upon all aspects of cooperative planning and curriculum integration. Technology can transform school by improving tests scores, motivating students to achieve, creating a high level of student excitement, and renewing staff enthusiasm. While at one sitting, the student can literally visit a Web Site in virtually any country, or research a topic anywhere in the city, state, country or world (Lester, 1996).

AUDIOVISUAL MEDIA INTEGRATION

The integration of integrated technologies such as computers and telephones combined, VCR's and computers combined, and other assistive devices can open a source of information to children with exceptionalities, which have historically been denied to them (Lester, 1996). Computer lab teachers are better able to teach classes of students with divergent abilities. Individual needs of exceptional children can be successfully met through use of integrated media systems (Cornish, 1996; Burtch, 1999, Thoman, 1999). Elias and Taylor (1995) reported on an innovated approach using television and other audiovisual media with children in special education programs. The program is called (TVDRP) and refers to television or other audiovisual media, discussions conducted with open-ended questions designed to stimulate critical thinking, and rehearsal and guided practice. The program is designed to improve social awareness and techniques for solving social problems. Activities involve role-playing and a variety of practical and hands-on activities to make learning more concretely combining all three instructional approaches. TVDRP has proven to be successful used with diverse groups of children in multiple grade levels, including children with severe emotional and perceptual disabilities.

The affects of TVDRP on social skills development are numerous and include:

1. Improving attention and promoting a relaxing and calming effect.
2. Stimulating of thinking and problem solving skills employing open-ended questions and dialoguing.
3. Using guided practice and role-playing in solving interpersonal problems and ways for transferring positive interpersonal behaviors outside of the instructional setting by using a series of discussion questions and activities that indirectly build interpersonal skills. Essential to the process is adapting strategies to meet the individual needs of individuals with exceptionalities.

VIDEO TECHNOLOGY

The application of video technology in the classroom has many applications. Video conferencing can be used in one class in another wing of the school or with another school a conference via camera and computer screen (Choate, 1997). Video technology improves the academic and social skills development of children with exceptionalities by preparing them for inclusion, improving study skills, improving interpersonal skills, improving physical skills, and assisting teachers in evaluating performance. Children with exceptionalities can self model physical academic skills on videos and later watch the videotapes to reinforce the skills. Teachers may use video portfolios to report students' progress to parents, to evaluate students' strengths and weaknesses in selected areas, to provide motivation, to reinforce shared experiences, to build cooperation and trust. Successful use of video technology will depend upon adapting and modifying strategies to meet the unique needs of children with exceptionalities (Salend, 1995; Broome &White, 1995).

Some teachers have successfully used video technology in their classroom management program. Videos can be used to teach appropriate interpersonal skills, students can view and observe appropriate and inappropriate ways of behaving, as an instructional technique by the teacher posing specific questions to students relevant to the video observed. The enjoyment factor should not be ignored when designing students' curricula. This is often an overlooked aspect of special education. Use of the computer can be used as a reward for positive behavior.

COMPUTER-BASED INSTRUCTION
FOR THE EXCEPTIONAL

As indicated, computer-based learning can be used to supplement skills and heighten interest in content areas such as math, reading, and writing. Effective use of technology, such as interactive videos to embellish lessons, video conferencing, or word processors to facilitate performance, may spark interest of exceptional children (Choate, 1997).

Computer laboratory offers students fun to look forward to in a busy day. Fun activities include asking students to create computer-generated formats, analogies or crossword puzzles for independent practice. Computer-assisted instruction can be successfully used for most children with exceptionalities. Their abilities and exceptionalities must be appropriately assessed and modification and adaptations made in the software. Numerous software packages are available for many instructional programs. Technology can augment the instructional process by providing one-to-one instructions on a variety of instructional strategies for exceptional individuals. Necessary and Parish (1996) demonstrated that a positive relationship exists between student's experience levels with computers and favorable attitudes toward their use. Premised upon the above, exceptional children should be exposed to computerized instruction as soon as possible.

A commonly used computer-based program used with cerebral palsy children is the "Touch Talker with Minispeak." This electronic device uses symbols to relate to children. When these symbols are pressed in sequence, they produce audio output which can be easily understood by the teacher (Bigge, 1991).

An advantage of computer usage is with exceptional children who have poor motor control; the method of entering information through the oversized keyboard pad may make accessing the microcomputer more possible. Poor motor control might also be accessed with heated keyboard or voice response keyboards. Movable control stations where adjustments are made to fit the student would be most useful for many physically exceptional students (Ryba, 1995). The literacy-poor student, visually impaired or not, can expand his or her vocabulary with related services offered by the microcomputer. The active learner and the overactive user may, through consistent persistence with the computer, become literacy proficient. Using the example set by the piano and the manual typewriter, the microcomputer helps develop fine motor exercises of particular importance for some mentally and physically exceptional students. Adaptations can be made to microprocessors for physically exceptional students in the keyboard and physical arrangement in computer classes.

Lester (1996) contended that computers and high technologies offer exceptional children the ability to access databases. Ryba (1995) remarked that adaptations of computers enable many exceptional children full access to them. Adaptation of other technological devices such as laser-scanners, alternative keyboards and voice recognition allow exceptional children to achieve their optimal level of growth.

Cornish (1996) predicts that by the year 2025 teachers will be better able to handle classes of students with widely different abilities. Children with exceptionalities will be the beneficiaries of infotech-based education by having equipment that offsets their exceptionalities. The assistance computers offer special education children is little short of miraculous. Many exceptional children may possess writing or math blocks or unable to produce even one neat page of handwritten text, often discover the labor-saving faculty of word processing programs. Computers can give independence, employment; knowledge and accessibility to the outside world for exceptional children. Additionally, they promote individualization of instruction and have high interest values for exceptional children, however, computers alone cannot educate individuals with exceptionalities, the human element must always be present.

THE INTERNET

The Internet can serve as a lure or a magnet to attract children to the computer and make them work. The attraction of the Internet for children with exceptionalities has been discussed widely on television and radio and while all the material obtained via the Internet cannot be validated, the informational and research use of the Internet cannot be denied.

Technology is a tool, which can assist the special education teacher by providing exceptional children with a multisensory environment. The Internet can provide information in the major curriculum areas so children can make associations between information and transfer information in the major to solve problems (Doyle, 1999; Lewin, 1999; Drier, Dawson, & Garofalo, 1999; Leamon, 1999). The Internet appeals to all of the senses because it incorporates sight, sound, and touch. The Internet arranges information hierarchically. Broad topics are presented first, information is narrowed down by requesting more specific facts. This process enables children with exceptionalities to employ critical thinking skills to solve problems. Additionally, working on the Internet can give exceptional children the opportunity to work at their own pace. By the school providing early Internet training to exceptional children, it is equipping them to prepare for the challenges they will face in competing for employment in the job market of the future (Goldstein, 1998).

According to Andrews and Jordan (1998) multimedia technology allows one to develop stories in two or more languages, or present information in different formats. This technology has many benefits for instructing deaf children because video dictionaries of sign language can be built right into the stories. The technology allows an exceptional child to explore information at his or her own pace. It combines printed text, narration, words, sound, music, graphics, photos, movies, and animation on one computer page.

Many exceptional children have difficulties accessing information over the Internet due to poor Web Site designs (Walters, 1998). Many of the Web Sites create barriers for some exceptional children. Children who have vision problems have difficulties accessing the Web because the Web requires a degree of vision acuity. Students who have reading problems will not be able to access the Web appropriately because information is in a text format. Children with attention deficit disorders will have problems accessing the Web due to their short attention span and the inability to stay focused for an extended time. Other exceptional children without the aforementioned exceptionalities can easily access the Web. Specific modifications and adaptations have been recommended by the author for Web designers to implement so that the Web can be accessible for all exceptional children (Necessary & Parish, 1996; Bigge, 1991). The reader is referred to the source below for additional information modification and adaptation of Web Sites designs for exceptional children.

SUMMARY

Due to recent trends in special education, the future for exceptional children is positive. These trends and innovations have enabled many children with exceptionalities to become self sufficient and more independent. Direct results of the interventions have enabled many of them to be successful in inclusive classrooms and have made transition from school to the world of work a reality. Digital technology has the potential for making presentations in research finding by exceptional children. Digital technology will aid many children with exceptionalities to find practical solutions to many problems they face (Fodi, 1996).

Legal laws and mandates are reinforcing the rights of exceptional individuals in all segments of society, including placement in the public schools, rehabilitation training, and equal employment opportunities are to name but a few. Medical, psychological, and social services are being researched. Research findings from these disciplines have important implications for exceptional individuals in the future. The trends in special education will continue to reflect interest in the welfare of all children with exceptionalities by preparing them to become active participants and informed citizens in our society.

REFERENCES

Aefsky, F. (1995). *Inclusion confusion: A guide to educating students with exceptional needs.* Thousand Oaks, CA: Corwin Press, Inc.

Alper, S., Schloss, P. J., Etscheidt, S. K., & MacFarlane, C. A. (1995). *Inclusion: Are we abandoning or helping students?* Thousand Oaks, CA: Corwin Press, Inc.

Andrew, J., F., & Jordan, D. L. (1998). Multimedia stories for deaf children. *Teaching Children, 30* (6), 28-33.

Bader, B. (1998, April). Measuring progress of exceptional students. *American Teacher, 15,*

Baker, E. T., Wang, M., & Walberg, H. G. (1995). The effects of inclusion on learning. *Educational Leadership, 50* (4), 33-35.

Baker, J., & Zigmond, N. (1990). *Fall time mainstreaming: Arc learning exceptional students integrated into the instructional program?* Paper presented at the Annual Meeting of the American Educational Research Association, Boston, MS: ERIC Document Reproduction Service, NO. PD 320373.

Bakken, J. P., & Aloia (1998). Evaluating the world wide web. *Teaching Exceptional Children, 36* (6), 48-52.

Bannerji, M., & Dailey, R. (1995). A study of the effects of an inclusion model on students with specific learning exceptionalities. *Journal of Learning Exceptionalities, 28,* 511- 522.

Barry, A. L. (1995). Easing into inclusion classrooms. *Educational Leadership, 52* (4), 4-6.

Bear, G. G., & Proctor, W. A. (1990). Impact of full time integrated program on the achievement of non-handicapped and mildly handicapped children. *Journal of Exceptionality, 1,* 227-238.

Berger, S. (1995). Inclusion: A legal mandate: An educational dream. *Updating School Board Politics, 26* (4), 104.

Bennett, R., Deluca, D., & Burns, D. (1997). Putting inclusion into practice. *Exceptional Children, 64* (1), 115-131.

Bigge, J. L. (1991). *Teaching individuals with physical and multiple exceptionalities.* New York, NY: Macmillan Publishing Co.

Bolger, R. (1996, October 2). Learning with technology. *Teachwork, 1.*

Borthwick-Duffy, S. A., Palmer, D. S., & Lane, K. L. (1996). One size doesn't fit all: Full inclusion and individual differences. *Journal of Behavioral Education, 6,* 311-329.

Broome, S. & White, R. B. (1995). The many uses of video tape in classrooms serving youth with behavioral disorders. *Teaching Exceptional Children, 27,* 10-13.

Brown, L. P., Schwarz, A., Udvari-Solner, E. F., Kampschroer, F., Johnson, J., Jorgensen, J., & Greenwald, L. (1991). How much time should students with severe exceptionalities spend in regular classrooms and elsewhere? *Journal of the Association for Persons with Severe Exceptionalities, 16,* 39-47.

Bursuck, W. D., & Rose, E. C. (1992). *Community college options for students with mild exceptionalities.* In F. R. Rusch, L. Destefano, J. Chadsay-Rusch, L. A. Phillips, & E. Syzmanski. Transition from school to adults life (pp. 71-91). Sycamore, IL: Sycamore.

Burtch, J. A. (1999). Technology is for everyone. *Educational Leadership, 56* (5), 33- 34.

Choate, J. S. (1997). *Successful inclusion teaching.* Boston: Allyn and Bacon.

Clark, C., Dyson, A., & Millward, A. (1995). *Towards inclusive schools*. New Teachers College Press.

Committee on Labor and Human Resources (1997, May 9). Washington, DC: Government Printing Office.

Cornish, E. (1996, January-February). The cyber future: 92 ways our lives will change by the year 2025. *The Futurist, 6.*

Doyle, A. L. (1999). A practitioner's guide to sharing the net. *Educational Leadership, 56* (5), 12-15.

Drier, H. S., Dawson, K. M., & Garofalo, J. (1999). Not your typical math class. *Educational Leadership, 56* (5), 21-25.

Elias, M. J., & Taylor, M. (1995). Building social and academic skills via problem solving videos. *Teaching Exceptional Children, 27,* 13-17.

Filbin, J. et al. (1996). *Individualized learner outcome: Infusing student needs into the regular education curriculum.* (ERIC Document Reproduction Services NO. ED 400641.)

Florian, L., & West, J. (1991). Beyond access: Special education in America. *European Journal of Special Needs Education, 6* (2), 124-132.

Fodi, J. (1991, November). Kids communicate through adaptive technology. *Exceptional Parents, 36,*

Frank-Nachmias, C., & Machmias, D. (1996). *Research methods in the social sciences.* New York: St. Martin's Press.

Frazier, M. K. (1995). Caution: Students on board the Internet. *Educational Leadership, 53* (2), 26-27.

Fuchs, D. (1991). Toward a responsible reintegration of behaviorally disordered students. *Behavioral Disorders, 16* (2), 133-137. (ERIC Document Reproduction Service NO. EJ428534.)

Fuchs, L. D., Fuchs, S. D., & Bishop, N. (1992). Teacher planning for students with learning exceptionalities: Differences between general and special education. *Learning Exceptionalities Research and Practice, 7,* 120-128.

Fuchs, D. , & Fuchs, L. (1994). Inclusive schools movement and the radicalization of special education reform. *Exceptional Children, 60,* 294-309.

Fuchs, D., & Fuchs, L. (1995). Sometimes separate is better. *Educational Leadership, 50* (4), 22-26.

Gable, R. A., Hendrickson, J. M., & Rutherford, R. B. (1991). Strategies for integrating students with behavioral disorders into general education. *Severe Behavior Disorders Monograph, 14,* 18-32.

Giangreco, M., Dennis, R., Cloninger, C., Edelman, S., & Schattman, R. (1993). I've counted Jon: Transformation experiences of teachers educating students with exceptionalities. *Exceptional Children, 59,* 359-371.

Goldstein, C. (1998). Learning at cyber camp. *Teaching Exceptional Children, 30* (5), 16-26.

Hardman, M. L., Drew, C. J., & Egan, W. M. (1996). *Human exceptionality: Society, school, and family.* Boston: Allyn and Bacon.

Hughes, R. T. (1996, September-October). Computers in the classroom. *The Clearinghouse, 4.*

Johnston, D., Proctor, W., & Corey, S. (1995). Not a way out: A way in. *Educational Leadership, 50* (4), 46-49.

Jones, M. M., & Carlier, L. L. (1995). Creating inclusionary opportunities for learners with multiple disabilities: A team teaching approach. *Teaching Exceptional Children, 27,* 23-27.

Jorgensen, C. M. (1995). Essential questions—Inclusive answers. *Educational Leadership, 50* (4), 52-55.

Katsigannis, A., Conderman, G., & Franks, D. J. (1995). State practices on inclusion: A national review. *Remedial and Special Education, 16,* 279-287.

Latham, A. S. (1999). Computers and achievement. *Educational Leadership, 56* (5), 87- 88.

Leamon, P. (1999). Apples and arias in the language lab. *Educational Leadership, 56* (5), 28-31.

Lewin, L. (1999). Site reading: The world wide web. *Educational Leadership, 56* (5), 16-20.

Lester, M. P. (1996, November). Connecting to the world. *Exceptional Parents, 36.*

McDonnel, J., & Hardman, M. L. (1995). Planning the transition of severely handicapped youth from school to adult services: A framework for high school programs. *Educational and Training of the Mentally Retarded, 20* (4), 75-286.

McLeskey, J., & Pacchiano, D. (1994). Mainstreaming students with learning exceptionalities: Are we making progress? *Exceptional Children, 60,* 508-517.

McLeskey, J., & Waldron, N. (1995). Inclusive elementary programs: Must they cure students with learning exceptionalities to be effective? *Phi Delta Kappan, 77,* 300-302.

Meadows, N. B. (1991). Social competency, mainstreaming, and children with serious behavioral disorders. Severe Behavior Disorders of Children and Youth. *Monograph in Behavioral Disorders, 14.* (ERIC Document Reproduction Service NO ED341198.)

Mills, D., & Bulach, S. (1996). *Behavior disordered students in collaborative/cooperative classes: Does behavior improve?* Tampa, FL. (ERIC Document Reproduction Service NO. ED394224.)

National Association of State Board of Education. (1992). *Winners all: A call for inclusive schools.* Washington, DC: NASBE.

Necessary, J. R., & Parish, T. S. (1996, October). The relationship. *Education, 116,* 27.

Nisbet, J. (1992). *Introduction.* In J. Nisbet (Ed.). Natural support in school, at work, and in the community for people with exceptionalities. Baltimore: Paul H. Brookes.

Office of Special Education Programs. (1991). To assure the free appropriate public education of children with disabilities. Thirteenth annual report to Congress on the implementation of the Individuals with Disabilities Education Act. Washington, D.C.: ERIC Document Reproduction Service No. ED 332-488).

Office of Special Education Programs. (1997). To assure the free appropriate public education of children with disabilities. Thirteenth annual report to Congress on the implementation of the Individuals with Disabilities Education Act. Washington, D.C.: ERIC Document Reproduction Service No. ED 412-721).

Papert, S. (1996). *The connected family: Bridging the digital generation gap.* Mariette, GA: Longstress Press.

Pena, J. M. (1995). How K-12 teachers are using computer networks. *Educational Leadership, 53* (2), 18-25.

Polloway, E. A., & Patton, J. R. (1993). *Strategies for teaching learners with special needs.* New York: Merrill.

Reising, B. (1996, September-October). What's new. *The Clearinghouse,* p. 55.

Revenaugh, M. (1999). All about the E-Rate. *Educational Leadership, 56* (5), 36-38.

Roach, V. (1995). Beyond the rhetoric. *Phi Delta Kappan, 77,* 295-299.

Roberts, R., & Mather, N. (1995). The return of students with learning exceptionalities to regular classrooms: A sellout? *Learning Exceptionalities Research and Practice, 10* (6), 46- 58.

Rogers, J. (1993). The inclusion revolution. *Research Bulletin, 1* (11), 106.

Ryba, K., Selby, L., & Nolan, P. (1995, October). Computers empower students with special needs. *Educational Technology, 53,* 82.

Salend, S. J. (1995). Using videocassette recorder technology in special education classrooms. *Teaching Exceptional Children, 27,* 4-9.

Sawyer, R., McLaughlin, M., & Winglee, M. (1994). Is integration of students with exceptionalities happening? An analysis of national data trends over time. *Remedial and Special Education, 15,* 204-215.

Scruggs, T. E., & Mastropieri, M. A. (1958/1995). Teacher perceptions of mainstreaming/inclusion. A research synthesis. *Exceptional Children, 63* (1), 59-74.

Shanker, A. (1995). Full inclusion is neither free nor appropriate. *Educational Leadership, 50* (4), 18-21.

Sharpe, M. N., York, J. L., & Knight, J. (1994). Effects of inclusion on the academic performance of classmates without exceptionalities. *Remedial and Special Education, 15,* 281- 287.

Smith, T. E. C., Polloway, E. A., Patton, J. R., & Dowdy, C. A. (1995). *Teaching students with special needs in inclusive settings.* Boston, MA: Allyn and Bacon.

Staub, D., & Hunt, P. (1993). The effects of social interaction training on high school peer tutors of schoolmates with severe exceptionalities. *Exceptional Children, 60,* 41-57.

Staub, D., & Peck, C. A. (1995). What are the outcomes for non-exceptional students? *Educational Leadership, 50* (4), 36-39.

Strickland, B. B., & Turnbull, A. (1993). *Developing and implementing individual education programs.* Columbus, OH: Merrill.

Tapscott, D. (1999). Educating the new generation. *Educational Leadership, 56* (5), 7- 11.

Taylor, G. R. (1997). *Curriculum strategies: Social skills interventions for young African American males.* Westport, CT: Praeger Publisher.

Taylor, G. R. (1998). *Curriculum strategies for teaching social skills to the exceptional.* Springfield, IL: Charles C Thomas Publishers.

Taylor, G. R. (1999). *Inclusion: Panacea or delusion.* ERIC Clearing House for Teacher Education. ED 423225.

Telecommunication Act of 1996. (1996). Pub. LA. NO 104, 110 Stat. 56.

Telepak, T. A. (1995). The local business community: A natural resource for transition from school to work. *Teaching Exceptional Children, 27,* 61-64.

Thoman, E. (1999). Skills and strategies for media education. *Educational Leadership, 56* (5), 50-54.

Vaughn, S., Schumm, J. S., & Brick, J. B. (1998). Using a rating scale to design and evaluate inclusion programs. *Teaching Exceptional Children, 30* (4), 41-45.

Waldron, N. L., & McLeskey, J. (1998). The effects of an inclusive school program on students with mild and severe learning exceptionalities. *Exceptional Children, 64* (3), 395-405.

Walters, S. P. (1998). Accessible web site design. *Teaching Exceptional Children, 30* (6), 42-47.

Wang, M. C., Reynolds, M. C., & Walberg, H. J. (1995). Serving students at the margins. *Educational Leadership, 50* (4), 12-17.

Zigmond, N., Jenkins, J., Fuchs, L., Fuchs, D., Baker, J., Jenkins, L., & Couthino, M. (1995). Special education in restricted schools: Findings from three multiyear students. *Phi Delta Kappan, 76,* 531-540.

Chapter 5

BEHAVIORAL STYLES OF INDIVIDUALS WITH EXCEPTIONALITIES

GEORGE R. TAYLOR

INTRODUCTION

TEACHING SOCIAL SKILLS TO SOME individuals with exceptionalities is deemed not important or simply overlooked by many community agencies, including the schools. Social skills training is a prerequisite to the development of other skills and should be systematically taught to exceptional individuals in order to increase learning deficits in other cognitive and social areas (Taylor, 1998). Many exceptional individuals have not mastered the social skills needed to be successful at school within their ecological community. There are frequent conflicts between the children and school on what is considered to be appropriate behavior. Much of this confusion can be attributed to the school's lack of understanding specific characteristics of individuals with exceptionalities, as outlined in Chapter 1, as well as the value and impact of various cultural styles on learning. Cultural values influences the behavior of these individuals. Hyun and Fowler (1995) wrote that culture understanding and awareness may be expedited by employing the following strategies: (1) Exploring one's own culture heritage, and (2) Understanding and examining the attitudes and values associated with one's cultures.

Specific strategies were outlined to improve culture awareness, such as interviewing family members, examining official records, clarifying one's attitudes toward diverse cultures, reading and reviewing resources about various cultures, and associating with various groups and members of diverse culture groups.

The powerful influence of cultural systems on cognitive style and behavior should be recognized and integrated into the instructional program of exceptional individuals. Curriculum planners must be cognizant of the fact that no one behavioral instructional strategy will be appropriate for inter-

87

vention. Rather, strategies selected should be based upon children's abilities and assessed needs.

The teacher's reaction to certain behaviors can significantly influence the instructional process in a negative or positive way. The teacher, by recognizing his/her biases, can assist in promoting a positive classroom environment by recognizing pupils who may influence his/her ability to properly instruct the class. The key individual in the classroom is the teacher. The teacher's behavior can advance or retard the learning process.

Consideration should be given to cultural factors when planning instructional programs for exceptional individuals. Each cultural style is different, however, there are similar characteristics which operate across specific cultures. It is essential that the school recognize cultural styles and how styles impact and influence learning. All curricula should reflect the richness and contribution of each culture, thus, promoting the self-perception of exceptional individuals.

THE IMPORTANCE OF BEHAVIORAL STYLES AND ADJUSTMENT

Style is learned, learned patterns can be either changed or augmented, but cannot be ignored. Style tends to be rooted at a deep cultural level and is largely determined by prior experiences and motivation. Hilliard's (1989) research indicated that educational dialogue in recent years has given substantial attention to the question of the importance and precise meaning of style in teaching and learning, particularly for minority groups. Style differences between teachers and students and between students and the curriculum have been cited as explanations for the low academic performance of some exceptional individuals.

Misunderstanding of behavioral style can lead to misjudging exceptional students' language abilities and intelligence. Style is directly associated with cultural values. Modifying style is a slow and arduous process, and may never be fully realized. A proper sensitivity to style can provide a perspective for the enrichment of instruction of all children for the improvement both of teacher-student communication and of the systematic assessment of students. The schools must become more sensitive to style out of basic respect for children, and for their tremendous potential for learning (Hilliard, 1989). Additionally, a person can use more than one style and can be taught to switch styles when appropriate. A climate for growth depends upon healthy, fertile, social relationships where the styles and experiences of exceptional individuals are recognized and respected. The notion that each culture has made significant contributions to mankind should be highlighted by the school and integrated into the curriculum (Bennet, 1986; Bank, 1991; Obiakor, 1990).

COLLABORATIVE SCHOOL ACTIVITIES

Upon entering school, children are regimented and required to follow specific school rules, which often conflicts with their styles and modes of learning. In many instances, the child and school conceive learning differently. The school is mostly concerned with verbal and written expressions and standardized tests results. Accordingly, many of these activities are strange to some individuals with exceptionalities and many have not developed sufficient background or skills to master them. Consequently, behavior problems frequently occur when different standards of behaviors are expected between the children's abilities and the expectations imposed by the school. If the school is to be successful in meeting the needs of children, especially exceptional individuals, children and their parents must be given an active role in their own learning by structuring activities which are relevant and meaningful to them. Additionally, teachers must be free to experiment with various models of instruction which works best for the children (Taylor, 1992).

The role of the school should not be to fill exceptional children with irrelevant information, but to help them construct understanding about what they are doing. Exceptional children's competence, their ability to make meaning from their environments to construct knowledge to form generations, to solve problems and to associate and transfer knowledge, is seldom encouraged by the school.

The concept that style requires a pedagogical response, especially at the point of applying special teaching strategies, appears to be a sound approach. It is widely believed that such an approach ought to be attempted and that when they are made, teaching and learning will be more successful. Student's cultural and learning styles appear to be inseparable, therefore, matching these styles with appropriate instruction appears to be a sound instructional strategy for exceptional individuals.

LEARNING STYLES

Children receive and order information differently and through a variety of dimensions and channels. Mason and Egel (1995) implied that teachers frequently find it difficult to assess an individual's learning style preference. Making sense out of the world is a very real and active process. During early childhood, children master complex tasks according to their own schedules without formal training or intervention, the structured environment of the school appears to impede the personal learning styles of many exceptional individuals.

There is no *one* common definition of learning styles, however, researchers have considered learning styles from four dimensions: cognitive, affective, physiological, and psychological.

COGNITIVE DIMENSION

The cognitive dimension of learning styles refers to the different ways that children mentally perceive and order information and ideas.

AFFECTIVE DIMENSION

Affective dimension refers to how students' personality traits–both social and emotional–affect their learning. This dimension refers to how the student feels about himself/herself? What way can be found to build his/her self-esteem? These research findings tend to indicate that learning styles are functions of both nature and nurture. Learning style development starts at a very early age.

PHYSIOLOGICAL DIMENSION

The physiological dimension of learning involves the interaction of the senses and the environment. There are several channels under the psychological dimension and they are: visual, auditory, tactile/kinesthetic, and a mixed combination of the five senses. The physiological dimension involves the senses and the environment. Does the student learn better through auditory, visual, or tactile/kinesthetic means? And how is he/she affected by such factors as light, temperature, and room design?

EVALUATING LEARNING STYLES

Pupils learn through a variety of sensory channels and have individual patterns of sensory strengths and weaknesses. Teachers should capitalize on using the learning styles of pupils in their academic programs. Exceptional individuals go through the same development sequence, however, due to developmental problems, some progress at a slower rate. Several aspects are recommended in considering factors characterizing a pupil's learning style:

1. The speed at which a pupil learns. This is an important aspect to consider. A pupil's learning rate is not as obvious as it may appear. Frequently, a learner's characteristics interfere with his/her natural learning rate. Although the learning rate is more observable than other characteristics, it does not necessarily relate to the quality of a learner's performance. Therefore, it is of prime importance for the teacher to know as much as possible about all of a learner's characteristics.

2. The techniques the pupil uses to organize materials he/she plans to learn. Individuals organize materials they expect to learn information from by remembering the broad ideas. These broad ideas trigger the details in the pupil's memory. This method of proceeding from the general to the specific is referred as deductive style of organization. Application of this principle may be applied in many situations. Other pupils prefer to remember the smaller components which then remind them of the broader concept, an indicative style of organization. In utilizing inductive organization, the pupil may look at several items or objectives and form specific characteristics, and develop general principles or concepts. Knowing an exceptional individual's style of organization can assist the teacher to effectively guide the learning process by presenting materials as close as possible to his/her preferred style of organization (Mason & Egel, 1995).

3. The pupil's need for reinforcement and students in the learning situation. All learners need some structure and reinforcement to their learning, this process may be facilitated through a pupil's preferred channels of input and output.

4. Input involves using the five sensory channels–auditory, tactile, kinesthetic, olfactory and gustatory. These stimuli are transmitted to the brain. In the brain, the sensory stimuli are organized into cognitive patterns referred to as perception. The input channel through which the person readily processes stimuli is referred to as his/her preferred mode of modality.

5. Similar differences are also evident in output which may be expressed verbally or non-verbally. Verbal output uses the fine motor activity of

the speech mechanism to express oral language. Non-verbal output uses both fine and gross motor activities. Fine motor skills may include gesture and demonstration. Pupils usually prefer to express themselves through one of these outputs.

6. A pupil's preferred model of input is not necessarily his strongest acuity channel. Sometimes a pupil will transfer information received through one channel into another which he/she is more comfortable. This process is called internodal transfer. Failure to perform this task effectively may impede learning.

The differences in learning styles and patterns of some pupils almost assures rewarding educational achievement for successful completion of tasks. This is, unfortunately, not true for many exceptional individuals. The differences reflected in learning can cause interferences with the exceptional individual's achievement. The educational environment of exceptional individuals is a critical factor. The early identification, assessment, and management of exceptional individual's learning differences by the teacher can prevent more serious learning problems from occurring.

Children display diverse skills in learning. This necessitates proven knowledge as well as sound theories for teaching. Some educators who are interested in the development of children often lack the necessary understanding of how children learn, what they are interested in, and how to put these two together. Due to wide individual differences among exceptional individuals, instructional techniques must vary. Individuals with exceptionalities need special attention; their teachers need special orientation to meet their special needs. The teacher must know what can be expected of them, and then try to adapt the activities to their capabilities.

It has been voiced that no activity provides a greater variety of opportunities for learning than creative dramatics. Children are given a rationale for creative dramatics with specific objectives and values, exercises in pantomime, improvisation, play structure, and procedures involved in preparing a play. Creative dramatics and play are not meant to be modes of learning styles, but rather, as more is discovered about learning and in particular the variety of ways certain exceptional individuals learn, they add immeasurable knowledge to the development of a theoretical construct for various types of learning styles. Equally important, these techniques may lead to the discovery of different learning styles at various developmental levels (Taylor, 1998).

In spite of the paucity of research studies in the area of learning styles, it is generally recognized that individuals learn through a variety of sensory channels and have individual patterns of sensory strengths and weaknesses. It then becomes tantamount to discover techniques for assessing the individual's sensory strengths and weaknesses, and to identify ways that materials can be presented to capitalize on sensory strengths and/or weaknesses. This does not mean that materials should be presented to the pupil via his preferred style, but it would mean that credit would be given for his/her strength (e.g., hearing) while he/she worked to overcome his/her weakness (e.g., vision). Basic to the concept of learning styles is the recognition to initiate and sustain the learning process. Some exceptional individuals seem to have adequate sensory acuity, but are unable to utilize their sensory channels effectively.

A major concern of all education is to assist individuals in realizing their full learning potentialities. Educational services should be designed to take into account individual learning behavior and style. To be able to accomplish this task it will be required that we know something about the pupil as a learner. The Maryland State Department of Education's Division of Instructional Television (1973) has listed several ways to characterize a pupil's learning style: (1) the speed at which a pupil learns, (2) the techniques the pupil uses to organize materials he hopes to learn, (3) the pupil's need for reinforcement and structure in the learning situation, (4) the channels of input through which the pupil's mind proceeds, and (5) the channels of output through which the pupil best shows us how much he/she has learned.

The speed at which a pupil learns is important for individualizing instruction. Observations of the learner's characteristics will facilitate planning for his individual needs. A keen observer should be cognizant of the various ways an individual organizes materials. Some children learn best by proceeding from general to specific details, others from specific to general details. Knowing a pupil's style of organization can assist the teacher in individualizing his/her instruction. All learners need some structure and reinforcement in their learning. Pupils who have had successful experiences tend to repeat them. Proceeding from simple to complex, or from known to unknown principles provides opportunities for successful experiences for children.

The senses provide the only contact that any individual has with his environment. Sensory stimulations are received through the five sensory channels: auditory, visual, tactile, olfactory, and gustatory. These stimuli are organized into cognitive patterns called perceptions. Chapter 9 addressed cognitive patterns at length. The input channel through which the person readily processes stimuli is referred to as his preferred modality. The one through which he processes stimuli less readily is the weaker modality. Similar differences are also apparent in output which may be expressed verbally or non-verbally. Individuals usually prefer to express themselves through one of these channels.

A pupil's preferred mode of input is not necessarily related to his/her strongest acuity channel. Individuals with impaired vision may still process the vision stimuli they receive more efficiently than they do auditory stimuli. Sometimes a pupil will transfer information received through one channel into another with which he/she is more comfortable. This process is called intermodal transfer. An example of intermodal transfer might be the pupil who whispers each word as he/she reads it. The pupil is attempting to convert the visual stimuli (the printed word) into auditory stimuli (the whispering). Pupils differ in their ability to perform the intermodal transfer. For many exceptional individuals, failure to perform the intermodal transfer may hamper learning.

Many exceptional individuals might be using their preferred channels of input, which could be their weakest modality. Therefore, it is essential that the pupil's preferred mode of input and output be assessed. A variety of formal or informal techniques may be employed. Differentiation of instructional techniques based on assessment will improve the pupil's efficiency as a learner.

The following Tables 5, 6, and 7 have been prepared to provide some possible behaviors, assessment techniques, and instructional procedures to assist the teacher working with exceptional individuals. These tables describe three basic modalities: auditory, visual, and tactile kinesthetic. The olfactory and the gustatory modalities are not included in the tables because they constitute detailed medical and psychological insight that are outside the realm of education. Specific behaviors that are characteristic for auditory, visual, and tactile kinesthetic modalities are given, with suggestions for

TABLE 5

The Auditory Modality*

Possible Behaviors		*Possible Techniques*		
Pupil who is strong auditorily MAY:		The teacher may utilize these:		
SHOW THE FOLLOWING STRENGTHS	SHOW THE FOLLOWING WEAKNESS	FORMAL ASSESSMENT TECHNIQUES	INFORMAL ASSESSMENT TECHNIQUES	INSTRUCTIONAL TECHNIQUES
Follow oral instructions very easily.	Lose place in visual activities	Present statement verbally; ask pupil to repeat.	Observe pupil reading with the use of finger or pencil as a marker.	Reading: Stress phonetic analysis; avoid emphasis on sight vocabulary or fast reading. Allow pupils to use markers, fingers, etc., to keep their place.
Do well in tasks sequencing phonetic analysis.	Read word by word.	Tap auditory pattern beyond pupil's point of vision. Ask pupil to repeat pattern.	Observe whether pupil whispers or barely produces sounds to correspond to his/her reading task.	
Appear brighter than tests show him/her to be.	Reverse words when reading.			
	Make visual discrimination errors.	Provide pupil with several words in a rhyming family. Ask pupil to add more.	Observe pupil who has difficulty following purely visual directions.	Arithmetic: Provide audiotapes of story problems. Verbally explain arithmetic processes as well as demonstrate.
Sequence speech sounds with facility.	Have difficulty with written work; poor motor skill.			
Perform well verbally.				
	Have difficulty copying from the chalkboard.	Present pupil with sounds produced out of his/her field of vision. Ask him/her if they are the same or different.		Spelling: Build on syllabication skills; utilize sound clues.
				Generally: Utilize work sheets with large unhampered areas. Use lined wide-spaced paper. Allow for verbal rather than written responses.

* Reprinted with permission of Maryland State Department of Education, Division of Instructional Television.

TABLE 6

The Visual Modality*

Possible Behaviors		*Possible Techniques*		
Pupil who is strong visually MAY:		The teacher may utilize these:		
SHOW THE FOLLOWING STRENGTHS	SHOW THE FOLLOWING WEAKNESS	FORMAL ASSESSMENT TECHNIQUES	INFORMAL ASSESSMENT TECHNIQUES	INSTRUCTIONAL TECHNIQUES
Possess good sight vocabulary.	Have difficulty with oral directions.	Give lists of words that sound alike. Ask pupil to indicate if they are the same or different.	Observe pupil in tasks requiring sound discrimination, i.e., rhyming, sound blending.	Reading: Avoid phonetic emphasis; stress sight vocabulary, configuration, clues, context clues.
Demonstrate rapid reading skills.	Ask, "what are we supposed to do" immediately after oral instructions are given.	Ask pupil to follow specific instructions. Begin with one direction and continue with multiple instructions.	Observe pupil's sight vocabulary skills. Pupil should exhibit good sight vocabulary skills.	Arithmetic: Show examples of arithmetic function.
Skim reading materials.				
Read well from picture clues.	Appear confused with great deal of auditory stimuli.			
Follow visual diagrams and other visual instructions well.	Have difficulty discriminating between words with similar sounds.	Show pupil visually similar pictures. Ask him/her to indicate whether they are the same or different.	Observe to determine if the pupil performs better when he/she can see the stimulus.	Spelling: Avoid phonetic analysis; stress structural clues, configuration clues.
Score well on group tests.				Generally: Allow a pupil with strong auditory skills to act as another child's partner. Allow for written rather than verbal responses.
Perform nonverbal tasks well.		Show pupil a visual pattern, i.e., block design or pegboard. Ask pupil to duplicate.		

* Reprinted with permission of Maryland State Department of Education, Division of Instructional Television.

TABLE 7

The Tactile Kinesthetic Modality*

Possible Behaviors		*Possible Techniques*		
Pupil who is strong tactile kinesthetically MAY:		The teacher may utilize these:		
SHOW THE FOLLOWING STRENGTHS	SHOW THE FOLLOWING WEAKNESS	FORMAL ASSESSMENT TECHNIQUES	INFORMAL ASSESSMENT TECHNIQUES	INSTRUCTIONAL TECHNIQUES
Exhibit good fine and gross motor balance.	Depends on the "guiding" modality or preferred modality since tactile kinesthetic is usually a secondary modality. Weaknesses may be in either the visual or auditory mode.	Ask pupil to walk balance beam or along a painted line.	Observe pupil in athletic tasks.	Reading: Stress the shape and structure of a word; use configuration clues, sandpaper letters; have pupil trace the letters and/or words.
Exhibit good rhythmic movement.			Observe pupil maneuvering in classroom space.	
Demonstrate neat handwriting skills.		Set up obstacle course involving gross motor manipulation.	Observe pupil's spacing of written work on a paper.	Arithmetic: Utilize objects in performing the arithmetic functions; provide buttons, packages of sticks, etc.
Demonstrate good cutting skills.		Have pupil cut along straight, angled, and curved lines.	Observe pupil's selection of activities during free play, i.e., does he/she select puzzles or blocks as opposed to records or picture books.	
Manipulate puzzles and other materials well.		Ask child to color find areas.		Spelling: Have pupil write the word in large movements, i.e., air, on chalkboard, on newsprint, utilize manipulative letters to spell the word. Call pupil's attention to the feel of the word. Have pupil write word in cursive to get feel of the whole word by flowing motion.
Identify and match objects easily.				

* Reprinted with permission of Maryland State Department of Education, Division of Instructional Television.

possible techniques that might be employed.

It appears to be psychologically sound that exceptional individuals should be introduced to new tasks through their strongest input channels and review tasks presented to the weak channels. The concept of learning styles holds great promises for facilitating the achievement of exceptional individuals. As further investigations are conducted in relationship to specific exceptional individuals, more will be discovered about sensory acuity and the inability of some individuals to use their sense modalities effectively. Some children are concrete learners while others are abstract learners, others focus on global aspects of the problem, while others focus on specific points. Since schools traditionally give more weight to analytical approaches than to holistic approaches, the teacher who does not manifest analytical habits is at a decided disadvantage (Hilliard, 1989).

ASSESSMENT INSTRUMENTS

Assessment, the pupils preferred mode of input and output, may be conducted through formal and informal techniques. A commonly used instrument is "The Learning Channel Preference Checklist." This checklist is divided into three major sections as outlined.

THE LEARNING CHANNEL PREFERENCE CHECKLIST

The learning channel preference checklist is designed for assessing learning styles. Teachers can administer this checklist and follow up with interpretive discussions. Some modification and adaptation will be needed for exceptional individuals depending upon their disabilities.

Students are asked to rank each statement as it relates to them. There are no right or wrong answers. Students rate each item often (3), sometimes (2), and never (1), on three broad categories: visual, auditory, and haptic. The highest score indicated preferred learning style is the aforementioned categories.

AUDITORY LEARNING STYLE

This is the least developed learning channel for most children, including exceptional individuals. Most children do not report this channel as their strongest, using the checklist.

VISUAL LEARNING STYLE

Many children learn best when they can see information. High scores in this area denotes that they prefer textbooks over lectures and rely on lists, graphs, charts, pictures, notes, and taking notes. Significantly, a higher number of children rate this area higher than the auditory channel.

HAPTIC LEARNING STYLE

This is the high learning channel reported by children. In essence, most children prefer this style. Haptic students show a cluster of right-brained characteristics. They learn best from experimenting rather than from textbooks and reading textbooks.

The combined scores in the three areas usually range from 10 to 30. Usually two areas will be close. Scores in the high 20s indicate that the student has satisfactorily developed all three channels and is able to use the modality that best fit the task. Scores below 20 indicate that the student has not yet developed a strong learning channel preference.

Usually students scoring in the 20s have great difficulty with school because they do not have a clearly defined method for processing information. These students should be treated as haptic learners because the haptic style is much easier to develop than the others.

According to O'Brien (1989), the checklist will indicate areas of strengths and weaknesses in sensory acuity. Teachers can then adapt or modify the instructional program to include activities to support the strongest modality. Information from the checklist should be shared with the student. O'Brien (1989) stated that, "All students benefit from knowing their learning styles, as well as how to use and manipulate them in the learning process."

Another well-known instrument for assessing learning styles is the Myers-Briggs Type Indicator. Learning styles are assessed from basic perceptual and judging traits. The Swassing-Barbe Modality Index assess auditory, visual, and tactile acuity by asking individuals to repeat patterns using the above modalities. Results also show differences in cognitive strengths, such as holistic and global learning in contrast to analytical, part, and the whole approach (Guild, 1994).

These tests are culture and language specific. Individuals respond and interpret self-reporting instruments through their cultural experiences. These responses may be in conflict with established norms and yield conflicting results. Consequently, caution is needed when interpreting results, especially from exceptional individuals.

THE RELATIONSHIP OF CULTURE TO LEARNING STYLE

Individuals from certain cultures have a preference for specific learning styles and this preference may effect classroom performance. Schools must also recognize that exceptional students from diverse backgrounds have a favored learning style which may affect academic performance. When teachers fail to accommodate students' favored learning style in their instructional delivery, they may not meet the individual's needs (Guild, 1994).

Hilliard's (1989) point of view supported the above analysis. He indicated that the lack of matching cultural and learning styles in teaching younger students is the explanation for low performance of culturally different minority group students. He contended that children, no matter with their styles, are failing primarily because of systematic inequities in the delivery of whatever pedagogical approach the teachers claim to master—not because students cannot learn from teachers whose styles do not match their own.

Guild (1994) provided us with three cautions to observe when attempting to match learning styles with cultural styles:

1. Do students of the same culture have common learning styles? If so, how do we know it? What are the implications for instructional intervention and individual student learning? Care should be taken when matching learning and cultural styles; not to make generalizations about a particular group based upon culture and learning styles. An example would be to conclude that most exceptional individuals have the same traits as the targeted group.

2. Caution should be taken in attempting to explain the achievement differences between exceptional individuals and their peers; this being especially true when academic differences are used to explain deficits.

3. There is some controversy between the relationship of learning and cultural styles due chiefly to philosophical beliefs and issues. Such issues and philosophical beliefs such as instructional equity versus educational equity and the major purpose of education, all combine to confuse the controversy. The relationship between learning style and culture may prove to be divisive, especially as related to students in elementary and secondary schools. It may result in generalizations about culture and style and result in discrimination in treatment. It may be used as an excuse for student failure. There is also an implication that some styles are more valuable than others even though learning style should be neutral. Properly used, matching learning and cultural styles can be an effective tool for improving learning of exceptional individuals.

THE RELATIONSHIP BETWEEN LEARNING
AND INSTRUCTIONAL STYLES

There is some indication that teachers choose instructional styles closely approximating their learning preferences. The key to the learning/instructional style theory is that students will learn more effectively through the use of their preference in learning styles (Hilliard, 1989).

The matching of instructional style and learning style may also have implications for student achievement. The best way for schools to adapt to individual differences is to increase their effect by differentiated instructional techniques (Guild, 1994). According to Hilliard (1989), learning styles and instructional styles matching may not be the only factor in student achievement. The reason younger students do not learn may not be because students cannot learn from their instructors with styles that do not match their learning styles. Additionally, he articulated there is not sufficient research or models to relate specific pedagogy to learning styles. He concluded by stating that a better perspective may be for teachers to provide more sensitivity to learning styles in the instructional programs until appropriate instructional models are developed.

IMPLICATIONS FOR EDUCATION

By keying teaching and assessment techniques to the diverse ways people think and learn, teachers will be surprised at how much smarter their students get. Traditionally, teachers teach and assess students in ways that benefit those with certain learning styles, but place many other children at a marked disadvantage.

Exceptional individuals, as well as all individuals, favor a preferred style, however, they may vary their styles, depending upon the situation. Teachers should be flexible in their teaching and use a variety of styles to assure all students' needs are met. Teachers are generally best at instructing children who match their own style of learning. Consequently, the more students differ from the cultural, socioeconomic, or ethical values of the teacher, the more likely that the learning needs will not be met. Studies have shown that students receive higher grades and more favorable evaluations when their learning styles more closely match those of their teachers. Most students begin to experience success when they are permitted to pursue an interest in their preferred learning style.

SUMMARY

The preponderance of research on cultural and learning styles of exceptional individuals, has demonstrated the value of matching these two styles in order to facilitate the learning process. There is widespread belief that this matching can facilitate classroom instruction and provide exceptional individuals with the skills necessary to succeed in cultural, learning, and teaching styles when applied to educating exceptional individuals. However, there is little disagreement in the professional literature concerning the relationship between learning and cultural styles and their impact on academic and social success in school.

Research conducted over the last decade has revealed certain learning patterns characteristic of certain exceptional and diverse groups (Hilliard, 1989; Shade, 1989; Vasques, 1989; Bert & Bert, 1992; Hyun, Jinhee, & Fowler, 1995). Some cultural groups emphasize unique patterns and relationships. The implications for instructional intervention for these individuals should be self-evident.

As indicated earlier, there is no universal agreement relevant to the application of cultural and learning styles to instruction. Some advocate the application of cultural and learning styles to the instructional process will enable educators to be more sensitive toward cultural differences. Others maintain that to pinpoint cultural values will lead to stereotyping (Guild, 1994). Another controversy revolves around what extent does culture and learning affect achievement. Research findings have consistently shown that there are serious inequities when the school does not value or accept certain cultural values. Other studies have shown that by incorporating cultural and learning styles in the learning process will not significantly increase achievement, unless inequities in delivery/instructional procedures are improved (Hilliard, 1989; Bennett, 1986, 1988).

A third controversy centers around how teachers operating from their own cultural and learning styles can successfully teach diverse and exceptional populations. Most of the research show that the day-to-day rapport, caring teachers who provide opportunities for children to learn are more valuable than matching teaching and learning styles (Taylor, 1992; Guild, 1994).

The major issue at hand in this controversy is not whether learning and cultural styles should be incorporated in the instructional plan for exceptional individuals, but whether using cultural and learning styles information will assist teachers in recognizing diversity and improve delivery of educational services for them.

REFERENCES

Bank, J. A. (1991). Multicultural education. For freedom's sake. *Educational Leadership, 49,* 22-25.

Bennett, C. (1986). *Comprehensive multicultural education. Theory and practice.* Boston, MA: Allyn and Bacon.

Bennett, C. (1988). Assessing teacher's abilities for educating multicultural students: The need for conceptual models in teacher education. In C. Heid (Ed.). *Multicultural education: Knowledge and perceptions.* Indianapolis, IN: University Center for Urban Education.

Bert, C. R., & Bert, M. (1992). *The Native American: An exceptionality in education and counseling.* ERIC. 351168.

Guild, P. (1994). The cultural learning style connection. *Educational Leadership, 51,* 16- 21.

Hilliard, A. G. (1989). Teachers and culture styles in a pluralistic society. *NEA Today, 7,* 65-69.

Hyun, K. K., & Fowler, S. A. (1995). Respect cultural sensitivity and communicating. *Teaching Exceptional Children, 28,* 25-28.

Maryland State Department of Education. (1973). *Teaching children with special needs.* Baltimore, MD: Division of Instructional Television.

Mason, S., & Egel, A. L. (1995). What does Amy like? Using a mini-reinforcer in instructional activities. *Teaching Exceptional Children, 28,* 42-45.

Meyers, I. B. (1990). *Gifts differing* (2nd ed.). Palo Alto, Ca: Consulting Psychologists Press.

Obiakor, F. E. (1990). Development of self-concept: Impact on student's learning. *The Journal of the Southeastern Association of Educational Opportunity Program Personnel, 9,* 16-23.

Obiakor, F. E. (1992). Self-concept of African American students: An operational model for special education. *Exceptional Children, 59,* 160-167.

O'Brien, L. (1989). Learning styles: Make the student aware. *NASSP Bulletin.* October, 85-89.

Shade, B. J. (1989). The influence of perceptual development on cognitive styles: Cross ethnic comparison. *Early Childhood Development and Care, 51,* 137-155.

Taylor, G. (1992). Impact of social learning theory on educating deprived/minority children. *Clearinghouse for Teacher Education.* ERIC. 349260.

Taylor, G. (1998). *Curriculum strategies for educating disabled individuals.* Springfield, IL: Charles C Thomas.

Vasques, J. A. (1991). *Cognitive style and academic achievement in cultural diversity and the schools: Consensus and controversy.* Edited by J. Lynch, C. Modgil, and S. Modgil. London: Falconer Press.

Chapter 6

INTERVENTION STRATEGIES

HELEN BRANTLEY

OVERVIEW

FOR EACH EXCEPTIONAL GROUP mentioned, there are several types and degrees of disabilities and each type will require a different type of assessment and intervention strategy, as reflected under the short portrait for each group. Detail analysis of each group of exceptional individuals have been reported in Chapter 3. This chapter will also indicate specific strategies to employ in reducing, minimizing, or eradicating maladaptive behaviors.

BEHAVIOR DISORDERS

Portraits of Behavior Disordered Students

In a self-contained multihandicapped class in a primary school, three boys diagnosed as behavior disordered enter the classroom with the teacher assistant. One of the boys (Student A) yells, "Good morning everybody," while he throws his backpack onto the floor. The teacher directs the class to begin their seat work and the boys to put their things away, have a seat, and likewise, get started with their morning work. Student A, removes his paper from his desktop, rolls it into a ball, and throws it and hits Student B on the side of his face. Student B, runs toward Student A and the two begin an altercation. The teacher immediately intervenes while directing Student C to leave for his mainstreaming class. Specific strategies will need to be in place to deal with maladaptive behaviors in the classroom.

Social-Emotional Characteristics

Children with behavior disorders are more likely than any other category of disabled youth to drop out of school. Dropout rates are reported at 55% with nearly half of the dropout rate, 26.8%, due to behavior problems (Butler-Nalin & Padilla, 1989). The behaviors observed interfere with the establishing and maintaining positive relations with others (Zargota, Vaughn, & McIntosh, 1991). Problems in adapting to the school environment, relating socially, and responsibly to teachers and authority figures are evident.

In addition, behavior disordered students are skilled at eliciting emotional, responses to others (Henley, Ramsey, & Algozzine, 1993). These behaviors affect the social climate of the classroom and are of particular concern to the teacher because they require the teacher to take time to arbitrate disputes and encourage appropriate social interaction. Defiance, aggression, and non-compliance toward authority figures are likely to alarm the teachers and other school officials (Carr & Pungo, 1993; Blackhurst & Berdine, 1993).

Behavior disordered children and youth are also characterized by distractibility and impulsivity (Carr & Pungo, 1993). Frequently, there are difficulties in listening, asking for teacher assistance, bringing materials to class, following directions, and completing assignments. Many behavior disordered students are unable to ignore distractions and often cannot deal with anger and frustration. Introducing oneself, beginning and ending a conversation, sharing social problems, solving problems, and apologizing are generally difficult social skills for behavior disordered students to master (Hardman, Drew, Egan, & Wolf, 1993).

Some children with behavior problems avoid peer and social relationships (Glassberg, 1994; Henley, Ramsey, & Algozzine, 1993). They withdraw and isolate themselves. Others have engaged in social behaviors that are unacceptable to their peers and are, thereby, rejected by their peers (Kirkcaldy & Mooshage, 1993). Older behavior disordered students are described as destructive and intractable (Glassberg, 1994).

Zargota, Vaughn, and McIntosh (1991) reviewed 27 studies that examined social skills interventions for behavior disordered youth. These studies validate the behaviors discussed previously. The independent variables in the research included: nine studies used interpersonal problem solving;– smiling, conversation skills; following instructions, and joining a group were targeted in ten; one study addressed coping with anger, two included one or more of social cognition, coping with conflicts and forming friendships; three addressed peer interactions; one examined moral development, choice, perspective taking and consequences; and finally, a study addressed on self-control and coping behaviors.

Academic Characteristics

It becomes obvious from the prior discussion that behavior disordered children will most likely experience academic deficits as an indirect result of their behaviors. According to Heyward and Orlansky (1992) many more children than normal score in the slow learner or mildly retarded range on IQ tests. These authors define a score of about 90–95 as the average score for behavior disordered children and youth. Kaufman (1989) concurred, but used a range of 80–100. He also cited the average IQ score for children who are severely disturbed at around 50.

DEAF AND HARD-OF-HEARING

Portrait of a Deaf Individual

Student E is deaf as a result of a hereditary neurological impairment. She is 18, a senior in high school, and lost her hearing around the age of three. Her younger brother who is two, also appears to be affected. She is an A student enrolled in regular education. Student E sits in the front of the class and is an avid lip reader. She reads the lips of the speaker and responds verbally. Her voice is soft with a slight foreign accent. She has a driver's license and works as Santa's helper during Christmas. A two-year follow-up of Student E revealed that she was in college, still an A student, and engaged to marry a hearing male.

Student E, along with many other deaf individuals cast doubt into much of the research regarding deaf individuals. Student E; however, came from a middle to upper income family and was enrolled in an enrichment preschool program for the deaf.

Social-Emotional Characteristics

The social-emotional development of children with hearing impairments follows the same basic pattern found among non-disabled peers (Meyen, 1990). Young deaf children are like hearing children in many ways–few differences exist. In language development, the deaf and the hearing child coo, gurgle, and babble. However, within eight to 12 months of age, vocalizations cease for deaf children and they withdraw and become silent. Children who are hard-of-hearing continue to vocalize (Moore, 1987). During the next few years of the child's life, parents become concerned and realize that something is wrong. The child, thus, becomes confused and frustrated (Bigge &

O'Donnell, 1976). The beginning of school may involve the deaf and hard-of-hearing in mutual play interests that are not impeded by communication differences (Meyen, 1990). However, the social interactions of the deaf and hard-of-hearing child may, because of social immaturity, result in impulsivity (Haring & McCormick, 1990; Greenberg & Kusche, 1990). Thus, children who are deaf and hard-of-hearing may be characterized by isolation and peer rejection, passive inferiority, and egocentrism (Greenberg & Kusche, 1989). In addition, deaf children may be less capable of interpreting emotional states and situations due to limited opportunities for social interaction (Cole, 1987).

Although the graduation rates of deaf and hard-of-hearing children–school age youth approach the rate of the non-disabled (Butler-Nalin & Padilla, 1989), their estimated rate of behavior problems is high (Greenberg & Kusche, 1989). The social environment of deaf children and youth is dependent upon whether the deaf child has deaf or hearing parents, severity of the loss (severity of the hearing loss is positively correlated with social adjustment), and the family climate (Hardman, Drew, Egan, & Wolf, 1993; Greenberg & Kusche, 1989).

MENTAL RETARDATION

Portrait of Mentally Retarded Students

Student G is a 12-year-old mildly retarded Down Syndrome female. She had surgery at an early age that removed much of the visible effects of the syndrome. She is enrolled in regular education but has speech and occupational therapy twice a week. She spent two years in the kindergarten and 1st grade in self-contained classes with resource support. From 2nd grade she has been in regular classes with related services. Student G maintains a "C" average.

Student H is 15 and severely retarded. Additionally, he has cerebral palsy. He is non-ambulatory and is non-verbal. He is enrolled in an Severe Profound Handicapped class (SPH). He performs at about the 3 year age range. He is enrolled in alternative communication classes. This wide deviation in mental retardation will require alternative instructional strategies.

Academic Characteristics

According to the American Association of Mental Deficiency, mental retardation refers to subaverage general intellectual functioning . . . which interpreted means that a retarded child's intellectual capacity must be at least two standard deviations below the mean (Grossman, 1993). Thus, mentally retarded school age children are classified according to expected achievement in the classroom. (There will be variations in classifications and nomenclature from state to state). They are usually classified as follows:

Educable– Expected achievement level 2nd to 5th grade.

Trainable– Some academic achievement but primary focus is upon self-help skills.

Custodial– Unable to care for their basic needs (Hardman, Drew, & Egan , 1993).

Readers should be aware that the above expected achievement levels are not intended to be used as ceilings for achievement among mentally retarded students. Some students in each category will exceed expectations–others may not reach the levels of expectations.

Social-Emotional Characteristics

The social skills of the mentally retarded are evaluated as they relate to adaptive behavior. Adaptive behavior, which is included in the current definition of mental retardation, is defined as the ability to adapt to the environment, relate to others, and take care of personal needs (Henley, Ramsey, & Algozzine, 1993). In other words, impairments in maturation, learning, and social adjustment, in addition to other specified criteria must be present in order to classify a student as mentally retarded.

In the classroom, mentally retarded children are socially immature. They usually have a poor self-concept, and are thus susceptible to peer influence (Henley, Ramsey, & Algozzine, 1993). They are also rejected by their peers (Polloway, Patton, Epstein, & Luebke, 1986). Retarded children have inadequate attention levels, therefore, they experience difficulty in maintaining attention (Borkowski, Peck, & Damberg, 1983).

The dropout rate for mentally retarded children and youth is listed at 34 percent with behavior accounting for 13.6 percent of the rate. Using the educable, trainable and custodial classification, Hardman, Drew, Egan, and Wolf (1993) outlined the social skill development of the mentally retarded as follows:

Educable– Social development will permit some degree of independence in the community.

Trainable– Social adjustment limited to the home and closely surrounding area.

Custodial– Need care and supervision throughout life.

Retarded children and youth may not be considered retarded in their home and community environments. Many mildly retarded adults (educable mentally retarded) achieve satisfactory adjustment in the community, marry, and have children. They are, however, problems related to getting along with others, maintaining employment and personal frustration (Zetlin, 1988).

In spite of limited social skill development among the trainable, it is still necessary for them to develop appropriate social skills (Hardman, Drew, & Egan, 1993).

It is important to recognize that the social needs of the mentally retarded may be overlooked because they are defined as having subaverage intellectual functioning. The emotions of the retarded are normal. They want to be accepted, liked and valued (Henley, Ramsey, & Algozzine, 1993).

ORTHOPEDIC AND HEALTH IMPAIRMENT

Student G is 12 years of age and has spina bifida. He is non-ambulatory and is incontinent. His IQ is in the normal range of intelligence. He is well-liked by his peers because of his attractiveness. Student G is in a self-contained classroom setting, and he is mainstreamed for a part of the school day.

Student K has cerebral palsy. She is hemiplegic. Her speech is slurred and she functions well within the normal range of intelligence. She has speech therapy and one hour of resource assistance. As much as possible, these children should be included with their normal peers.

Academic Characteristics

Research defines three limitations on learning with reference to children who have orthopedic and health disabilities. These include:
1. limitations on the ability to process information.
2. limitations on the ability to receive through the senses.
3. limitations on the range and nature of interpersonal and environmental interactions (Meyen, 1990).

Children who have conditions that affect their motor skills, should have the full range of cognitive abilities. Generally, this group of children encompass the full range of intellectual capacity. Finally, the graduation rates of this group are equal to their non-disabled peers (Butler-Nalin & Padilla, 1989).

Characteristics of specific types of disabilities under the mildly to moderately categories are overviewed. A general portrait is given with strategies for improving social skills development in the social-emotional and academic areas. Chapter 8 addresses these topics in greater detail.

Social-Emotional Characteristics

Students with orthopedic and health disabilities are a varied population (Heyward & Orlansky, 1993). Researchers use different classifications when referring to this group. For example, Haring and McCormick (1994) refer to this group of disabling conditions as crippled and other health impaired, physically handicapped and physically disabled. Blackhurst and Berdine (1993) group this category of the disabled according to three functional categories: ambulation and vitality; medical diagnosis; and, other disabling conditions. Meyen (1990) used etiology to establish three categories; neurologic, orthopedic and health conditions. Public law 94-142 used orthopedic and health impairments to describe this group of children and youth (Federal Register, 1997, p. 42478).

Children with orthopedic and health impairments include children with cerebral palsy, muscular dystrophy, spina bifida, juvenile rheumatoid arthritis and poliomyelitis. Health impairments include asthma, allergies, epilepsy, juvenile diabetes mellitus, hemophilia, cystic fibrosis, sickle cell anemia, cardiac conditions, cancer and aids. The Individual with Disabilities Education Act, PL 101-476 of 1990 added traumatic brain injury as a separate disability category.

Because this group of children and youth typically have characteristics that do not conform with societal standards for physical attractiveness, they may have problems with being accepted or difficulty with feeling that they are accepted by peers (Meyen, 1990). Antonello (1996) related secondary physical problems such as atypical mannerisms, self control, hyperactivity, diminished attention, poor concentration, and failure to recognize social boundaries as influential in social interactions.

Undesirable social characteristics such as drooling, incontinence and seizure activity can have a negative effect on the establishment of positive relations. Mobility devices, life-sustaining equipment and prosthetics may interfere with the development of positive images (Meyen, 1990).

LEARNING DISABILITIES

Portraits of Learning Disabled Students

Franklin is a 14-year-old adolescent who enjoys sharing and discussing articles of interest from the *New York Times* with his teacher. In reading, Franklin reads "was" for "Saw," "on" for "no" and "b" for "d." He appears quiet and withdrawn at times, highly distractible, and awkward during his gym classes. He also has low frustration tolerance and negative impulse control. His cursive writing consists of large letters that overlap the lines on his paper. However, he thinks critically and engages in complex problem solving activities.

Loretta is a 12-year-old who daydreams in her math class and works laboriously through her class assignments. She is inattentive, unmotivated, and shows no interest in classwork. Her school assignments are below grade level, and she performs poorly in all academic subjects. Her creative skills are two grade levels above her current grade placement, and she enjoys working alone. As indicated, there are wide deviations among and between learning disabled individuals.

Academic Characteristics

Students with learning disabilities usually have a disorder in one or more of the basic psychological processes involved in understanding or in using language-spoken or written, which may manifest itself in an imperfect ability to listen, think, speak, read, write, spell or to do mathematical calculations (Kaplan, 1996).

Students with learning disabilities tend to vary from average to above average intellectually. The range is 90–130 or two or more standard deviations above the mean. That range includes those students who are classified as gifted and talented with learning disabilities. Many of these students do not differ from the average in terms of their characteristics.

A multiplicity of characteristics have been associated with the significant discrepancy between what a learning disabled student is capable of learning and academic achievement in reading, science, mathematics, social studies, vocabulary, and writing. Yet, there is great confusion concerning a great number of the negative characteristics and traits these students receive. However, students with learning disabilities tend to demonstrate specific thinking deficits (cognition) more commonly than the average students. Substantial evidence indicates that students with learning disabilities are very poor reflective thinkers. They also portray auditory and visual processing deficits. These difficulties often impede the smooth learning of classroom skills associated with school-related subjects.

Many of the strategies to succeed in school-related subjects require active participation and the employment of a host of problem-solving, and critical thinking skills. Students with learning disabilities experience difficulty in the application and strategies necessary for memorization and generalization of these skills. However, when memory strategies are taught and apply in meaningful learning situations, learning disabled students perform as well as others in reading, writing, and other communication skills.

The academic performance of such students is poor. They usually possess problems in reading and writing. Achievement in some subjects may be average, but achievement in others are below-average, and in many cases at the failure level, which is not indicative of their potentials. There is great variation among this population, too, in school subjects. Many of these students perform quite successfully and are classified as having areas of gifts and talents, but a great percentage of them possess basic academic and social problems.

Generally, students with learning disabilities experience severe problems in reading. Commonly noted observational characteristics include: accuracy, fluency, and normal rate in reading; omissions, substitutions and mispronunciations of words; inadequate auditory closure and sound blending skills; a deficit in phoneme-grapheme relationships; poor decoding and comprehension skills; vocabulary deficits, poor spelling skills and inferential reading skills. Reading skills are necessary for success in all aspects of school's life and are correlated with psychological success (Norris, Haring, & McCormick, 1994).

Difficulties with language is also common among the learning disabled population. They frequently have problems with impaired discrimination of auditory stimuli; slow language development; difficulty imitating statements; a mastery of automatic rules of language; difficulty in expressive and receptive language and problems with phonological production or speech. Learning disabled children and youth with oral language problems often manifest these problems in written assignments in all subjects.

Social-Emotional Characteristics

Although there is great controversy regarding the nature of children and youth with learning disabilities, there are some generalizable social and emotional characteristics. Researchers (Hallahan & Reeve, 1980; Lloyd, 1980; Loper, 1980; Torgesen, 1988) have documented numerous social processes including rejection, isolation and loneliness. All students with learning disabilities have subject-related problems. Franklin and Loretta experience social relations problems. Additionally, learning disability affects many other areas of the lives of students including relationships with friends, role in family, self-image and confidence in the ability to handle social situations.

It is quiet apparent that students with learning disabilities display social skills problems in school, (Haagar & Vaughn, 1995). Their interaction with non-disabled peers is often repulsive and misunderstood. Research conducted by Stone and LaGreca (1990) showed that students who are constantly isolated and ignored are more likely to be aggressive, hostile and socially anxious in their classes. These behaviors (emotional intelligence) interfere with the necessary skills and time students need to focus and concentrate on classwork successfully. Emotional intelligence (a concept elaborated on by Goldman, 1995) indicated that to perform at the level commensurate with one's ability requires them to exercise awareness of social deftness, good impulse control, self-motivation, persistence, and self-discipline.

Since many learning disabled students often show extraordinary abilities (Thomas Edison, Nelson Rockefeller, Albert Einstein, Pablo Picasso, and Hans Christian Anderson), perhaps educators should focus on these areas to provide for social acceptance, school success and relevant learning experiences since much of the rejection is due to poor school achievement. Many learning disabled students possess hobbies and areas of interest that are well respected by significant others. A program where students are exposed to a variety of intellectual, social and cultural perspectives, and reflective of students' background needs and interest, willing many instances, address the social skills problems of the learning disabled (Kaplan, 1996).

Students with learning disabilities also have low self-esteem, poor self-concept and very low motivation. They usually have little success at school, and feel that effort is not rewarded. In many cases, they apply the learned helplessness approach (even if I try hard, I am destined to fail) to school-related situations and tasks. Students with learning disabilities often rely on external locus of control. That position does not permit them to become self-directed learners (internal locus of control). The attitude of learned helplessness (Seligman, 1992; & Bender, 1995) impeded their social, cognitive, and emotional abilities.

Research showed that 36 percent of these students dropout of school due to academic and social problems and 14.4 percent dropout because of behavioral problems. During the high school years, social and behavior problems often take precedence over academic problems. These students, usually at this point, have had repeated failures in school, little encouragement and little motivation, social rejection by peers and viewed as troublemakers.

Kaplan (1996) detailed several studies that have been conducted failing to demonstrate significant discrepancy between the classroom behavior of students with learning disabilities and those labeled as mild mental disabled, slow learners or other mild disabilities (Vaughn et al., 1990). These researchers concluded that the social difference in learning disabled students may be a pattern that occurs in students who fall within the low-achieving category. This category, in many cases are evidenced during the school hours where acceptable communication skills, acceptable class behaviors and acceptable social perceptions are part of the norm of the school climate.

THE VISUALLY IMPAIRED

Portraits of Visually Impaired Students

Ashanti was born with a moderate visual impairment. She is now 14 and will be attending high school in a regular class setting. Ashanti reads braille fluently, but is not performing well in reading-related classes. She loves math and science, enjoys solving complicated math problems and conducting science experiments. Her attitude toward school work is positive, but she is constantly alone and is very unsure of herself.

Wander is a blind 13-year-old who is in a regular class placement and receiving assistance from the resource room. She is intellectually above average and demonstrates academic subjects, she cries frequently and cannot sustain her ability in completing many of the class assignments. Wander is very withdrawn and finds it difficult to interact with her sighted peers.

Academic Characteristics

The difference between the development of language of children who are visually disabled compared to sighted children is not significant. Research (Civelli, 1983; Matsuda, 1984) into the language of the visually impaired indicated that these students do not differ from their sighted peers on verbally-related activities. The visually impaired students may even have a higher auditory acuity then the non-disabled visual peers. The auditory channel is the major link between the visually impaired student's language and the outside world, and many researchers have highlighted its importance.

Studies highlighting the impact of this missing sense with the visually impaired have indicated that the quality of word meaning is deficit due to the lack of or an impairment of vision. Gallagher and Ansastasiow (1993) indicated that visually impaired students had less understanding of words as vehicles and were slower to form hypotheses about word meaning. Warren (1984) after studying the literature on the language of the visually impaired concluded:

> The new work of the past several years strongly suggests that, while blind children may use words with the same frequency count as sighted children, the meanings of words for the blind are not as rich or as elaborated. (p. 278)

Research, also shows that there is much variation among the cognitive development of children and youth with visual impairments when compared to their non-disabled peers . Because of the absence of visual information and experience, visually impaired students generally have difficulty with projecting positions in space, including recognition of shapes, construction of a projected straight line conceptualization of right and left in absolute and mirror image orientation (MacCuspie, 1992).

Learners with visual impairments have difficulty in determining and relating right to left to others although they are able to discriminate orientation to themselves. The concepts of spatial relationships is particularly important to the visually impaired due to personal mobility.

The development of concepts for the visually impaired student is quite different since many of them are learned through the visual modality. Researchers (Davidson, Dunn, Wiles-Ketterman, & Appelle, 1981; Stephens & Grube, 1982) using concepts based on the developmental theory have concluded that children who are blind lag behind their sighted peers. The tactual and auditory channels assist the visually impaired students in seeing the world. They must take great care in focusing their mental attention to gain the most from their social interaction environment and their experiences with significant others (Groenveld & Jan, 1992).

The classroom teacher plays an important role in helping the visually impaired students to develop good self-esteem and to feel good about their setting. Tuttle (1984) concluded from his analysis that the lack of self-confidence in the visually impaired is due to their limited interaction and attitudes of sighted people. The positive interaction of sighted others will provide a sense of confidence and further opportunities to develop social competencies for school, home and community independence.

Social-Emotional Characteristics

The development and embellishing of social skills are very much dependent upon vision. Children and youth with limited vision find it difficult to rely on visual cues or signals to communicate with significant others in the social environment (Sacks & Reaedon, 1989). In a research study conducted by Ken of children who were blind and their non-disabled peers, it was pointed out that the behaviors of these children were void of creativity, flexibility, and elaboration. Visually disabled children and youth with severe visual loss, or the non-existence of vision are deprived of the opportunities to emulate social role models and engage in meaningful social interactive experiences (Norris & McCormick, 1990). These situations may cause social isolation, negative attitudes, and school anxiety. These behaviors can have a significant impact on social and academic learning.

The self-esteem of visually impaired learners is not significantly different than that of their sighted peers (Ubiakor & Stile, 1990). "If learners with visual impairments have had significant verbal interaction with others, such as participating in games and friendships, they are not different from their sighted peers in social cognitive tasks (Schwartz, 1983).

THE SPEECH AND LANGUAGE IMPAIRED

Portrait of a Language Impaired Student

Timothy says "Wabbit" for "rabbit" and "poch" for "porch." His articulation problems also interfere with his classwork. When he attempts to speak out in class, his peers tease and kid him. He has a difficult time making friends, and purposely stays away from girls. Since he has entered high school, he fights often and is constantly isolated because of his behavior.

Academic Characteristics

Speech, language, and communication problems may result from input problems–hearing, or visual disability; processing disability–problems related to central nervous system dysfunction; or output disability–cleft palate disorders appear single or in clusters. They may result from articulation, voice, and fluency which are the various types of speech disorders.

When a child fails to acquire the semantic aspects of language, this interferes greatly with communicative skill and can result in acquiring other components. Children with language difficulties in semantics either do not learn the meaning of words or are unable to interpret the meaning of a series of words collectively or convey meaning. Expressive language problems may result from semantic difficulties from lack of symbols to partial deficits.

Pragmatic involves the functional use of language as a social tool for communication, learning, directing behavior, or generating new ideas. As children master the structural and content component of language, they also must learn to use language in appropriate and functional ways in various contexts. A great percentage of children with language disorders lack skills in pragmatic or language use (Haring & McCormick, 1990). Problems in expressive intentions and difficulties in maintaining a flow of conversations are the most common difficulties children experience. Some children are restricted communicatively because they use language in limited ways.

Social-Emotional Characteristics

Communication disorders may interfere with the social interaction and cognitive development of language disabled learners throughout the school day. However, research indicates that it is important that learners with speech and language deficits be educated in settings with non-disabled peers (Schiefelbush & McCormick, 1981). Many language delayed children do not understand how to take turns or engage in reciprocal interactions necessary for conversation. Still others may not attend to the contents of the speaker's remarks or understand their role in continuing the discussion. The context in which the disabled students must function is the best place to practice the art of communication.

A few states use generic classifications. The State of Maryland is one state employing this classification system. The State frequently categorizes disabled individuals as mildly to moderately or severely to profoundly and by age levels, regardless of their disabling conditions. Regardless of the classification system in use, all disabled individuals can profit from training and intervention.

MILDLY TO MODERATELY DISABLED

This group of disabled individuals consist of the largest group of disabled individuals. They make up approximately 90 percent of all students with disabilities based on the federal categories. This large group include students who have disabilities in the following areas: (1) speech and language, (2) learning disabilities, (3) emotional disturbed, (4) mental retardation, (5) hearing impairments, (6) orthopedic impairments, (7) other health impairments, (8) visual impairments, and (9) deaf-blindness.

These children are very similar to their normal peers, displaying a variety of behaviors, social, physical, motor and academic and learning problems. A highly structured and functional program is needed in order to reduce and minimize their disabling conditions. Many of their educational needs can be met in the regular classroom, providing adaptations and modifications are made in their school program. Early identification and assessment and curriculum adaptations for mildly to moderately disabled children appear to be key elements in successful school experiences. If properly instructed, many mildly to moderately disabled individuals can become independent and productive adults in our society. Detail classification and characteristics of mildly to moderately disabled children are beyond the scope of this text. The reader is referred to any basic textbook in exceptionality.

SEVERELY TO PROFOUNDLY DISABLED

Students who are classified as severe to profound make up approximately 10 percent of all students with disabilities. Collectively, these students have wide and diverse abilities. Most of them can profit best from highly structured and individualized programs. Many skilled professionals are required to attend to many disabling conditions in the cognitive, physical, mental and social areas. Frequently, related services are needed to provide the most basic services.

Children classified as mildly to moderately disabled, if conditions are severe enough, may be classified as severe to profound. Appropriate assessment will determine the classification. In addition, PL 101-476 lists autism and traumatic brain injury under the severely to profoundly disabled.

These children are markedly different from their normal peers, displaying noticeable differences in mental, physical, and social characteristics. Many of their needs cannot be successfully met in the regular classroom. Special placements and treatment are needed for many of them. Many of them will need adult supervision for all of their lives, they seldom will be independent adults.

Detail classification and characteristics of severely to profoundly disabled children are beyond the scope of this text. The reader is referred to any basic book in exceptionality.

THE GIFTED AND TALENTED

Portraits of Two Gifted and Talented Individuals

When Laysalle was seven years old, he demonstrated delight in reading. He picked out a psychology textbook from the bookcase and began reading the words on the page. He played constantly with dinosaurs and could pronounce their multisyllabic names at the age of four.

Fitima is a 2 and a half year old who can read 35 books. She asked many questions and has the vocabulary of the adults in her immediate environment. She can write and spell her first name and identify the letters of the alphabet and the corresponding sounds.

Gifted and talented students come from all strata of society and encompass a multiplicity of area including intellectual, specific academic aptitude, creativity, leadership, talents, and psychomotor skills. This diverse population makes it difficult for identification and programs within many of our schools to meet their broad range of conglomerate needs.

Cognitive, gifted students are capable of engaging in complex activity, abstracting, generalizing quickly, and accurately at an early age (Blackhurst & Berdine, 1993). These important abilities allow them to link learning in the academic and social environments to everyday problems. Sternberg's (1985, 1991) definition of gifted and talented has provided a broader scope on the concept. He described giftedness as including intelligence in analytical, synthetic, and practical output.

An important part of giftedness is being able to coordinate these three aspects of abilities, and knowing when to use which. Giftedness is as much a well-managed balance of these three abilities as it is a high score on any one or more of them (Sternberg, 1985, 1991).

Gardner's multiple intelligence (1983, 1993b) viewed giftedness from a variety of perspectives as are shown in Table 1.

Additional research has attempted to delineate characteristics along physical education, social, and emotional lines (Ysseldyke & Algozzine, 1990). Many such researchers have attempted to list general characteristics of gifted/talented students. However, caution should be applied to any one list for several reasons. First, any listed behaviors can apply to any person depending on the activity and the environment. Second, some behaviors are learned, and many gifted and talented students soon learn how to display the expected behavior whether it is positive or negative. Third, a list of characteristics may not reflect those outstanding behaviors of students from different ethnic groups. Fourth, many of the behaviors are reflective of school-related tasks. In many cases, abilities in creative divergent thinking may not surface at school and may not be inclusive on any list (Clark, 1992; Jenkins-Friedman & Nelson, 1990; Roberts & Lovett, 1994; Van Tassell-Baska, 1995).

The need to view intelligence from a multidimensional and multifaceted perspective is a necessity to reach the variety of abilities, developmental levels, and learning styles which exist among the gifted and talented population. Females, those from culturally and linguistic backgrounds, those who are gifted with disabilities, and those who are underachievers, are also the nations' natural resources and worthy of differentiated school programs to meet their needs. All gifted and talented students possess extraordinary needs that require special attention. Differentiated activities should be made in terms of creating educational climates to capture talents and abilities early for those from special populations (Gearheart, Mullen, & Gearheart, 1993).

The integrative approach utilized by Clark (1992) for servicing the gifted and talented analyzes the characteristics and needs of this population into cognitive, effective, physical, intuitive, and social domains. They are organized to include suggested strategies to embellish and nurture the multiple "intelligence" and social abilities.

Academic Characteristics

Students who are gifted and talented possess a host of cognitive characteristics. Although many of these characteristics can be generalizable, many of them do vary because of the social and cultural contexts these diverse students experience.

Many researchers have stated that gifted and talented students display a high level of intellectual curiosity, inquisitive, and limitless supply of questions. They often have an unusual large vocabulary, greater comprehension of language, the ability to learn basic skills quicker with less practice, and a wide interest. Both receptive and expressive language are developmentally advanced, and provide fluency, flexibility, and elaboration of oral and spoken vernacle. Their great capacity for learning allow them to understand complex abstract concepts and enables them to portray and retain advanced conceptualization among ideas, topics, and content. Most of these students are persistent, imaginative, and can generate original and unique ideas, solutions, and answers to everyday and worldwide problems (Gearheart, Mullen, & Gearheart, 1993; Turnbull, Turnbull, Shank, & Leal, 1995).

Social-Emotional Characteristics

If the environment is stimulating and supportive, gifted and talented students usually prefer working alone. On the other hand, the environment can be very depressing and isolating. As these students progress through school, their advanced mental development sets them apart from their peers. However, many of them do assume leadership roles and are favored by their peers. They perceive themselves as positive role models and are concerned about interpersonal and intrapersonal ideas, issues, and events (Piechowski, 1997).

Clark (1992) described social/affective characteristics of gifted and talented to include high expectations of self and others, which often lead to high levels of frustration with self, others, and situations. Students who are gifted and talented are shown to be superior to average individuals in their awareness concerning social problems (Hallahan & Kaufman, 1994). Any definitions of giftedness will include people who are recognized as social and moral giants (Piechowski, 1997).

Gifted and talented students have a great need to be champions for the rights of mankind. Gifted and talented students in this area are those who are strongly motivated by self-actualization. They possess creative, effective, and cognitive capacity for conceptualizing advanced issues and ideas for solving worldly problems. The societal gifted and creative person differs from the average in their personal drive, optimism, initiative, imaginative, confidence, communicating the worthiness of justice, and truth in word and deed.

Another area of discussion includes gifted and talented underachievers who are often overlooked and often drop out of school or are placed in remedial settings. The characteristics of gifted underachievers often include aggressiveness, withdrawn, low self-esteem, poor study habits, rebellious, rejected by family, distrust of adults, weak motivation, and lacking skills (Clark, 1992). Research shows that many of these students avoid school-related tasks due to poor self-esteem. School is perceived as irrelevant and in many cases unchallenging.

In the schools where many students are viewed as underachievers, the level of academic futility present among students seems to be a major barometer for the zeal by which they pursue learning. A school climate where expectations are low reinforces the gifted and talented students' poor motivation. An environment conducive to counseling, guidance, facilitating, mentoring, and self-directness would help to alleviate some of the problems associated with this group and increase their chances of maintaining focus (Piechowski, 1997).

SOME CONCLUDING REMARKS

If successful, academic programs are to be realized for individuals with exceptionalities, the school must develop interpersonal and social skills strategies to enable them to feel better about themselves. Social skills should be taught to those individuals with exceptionalities who need them, and in some instances should supercede academic skills. Appropriate social skills must be taught and modeled for many of these children before a meaningful academic program can be pursued (Taylor, 1992).

PARENTAL INVOLVEMENT

Not only are social skills important in academic areas, but they are also related to socialization. Several behaviors are necessary in the socialization process, including the emergence of self-identify and self-concept. Social skills are developed through the interactions with family, school, and the community, but none as important as the role of the parents.

There has been strong support from the federal government to include the family in the early education process of the handicapped child. The passage of the Education of the Handicapped Act Amendments of 1986 (PL 99-

547) established guidelines for the relationship among federal, state, and local education agencies to provide professional resources to disabled children and their families. The federal government created guidelines for the educational community in developing and implementing a comprehensive, coordinate, multidisciplinary, interagency program of early intervention services for infants, toddlers, and their families (Gallagher, 1989).

The role of parental participation in education in general, in special education in particular, according to much of the research in the field, has shown limited participation. This view has been interpreted to imply that parents simply had no interest in the education of their children (Marion, 1981). Several factors may contribute to the lack of parental participation. Many parents do not feel welcome in the school. They believe that they have little to offer in educating their children. Cassidy (1988) reported that problems with scheduling, transportation, and knowledge of the individualized education program (IEP) and special education procedures were partly responsible for poor parental participation. Other researchers implied that many parents, especially minority parents, disagreed with the present classification system. Many believed that their children were misplaced, or rejected the diagnosis and assessment process used to place their children (Harry, 1992; Smith, Osborne, Crim, & Rhu, 1987).

The role of parents in the school must supersede the mandates of PL 94-142. Parents must feel that they are welcome in the school, and be given responsibilities concerned with planning, collaborating with teachers, made aware of the IEP and legal processes associated with special education, and involved in policy-making (Harry, 1992; Turnbull & Turnbull, 1990). Parents should have an active role in planning and instructing their children and function as advocates for them if children are to profit significantly from their school experiences. Schools should experiment with various ways of improving parental participation. Parents provide the model of self-acceptance and the feeling that life is worthwhile. Also, parents who demonstrate a positive self-concept and high self-esteem treat their children with respect and acceptance and provide them with support and encouragement.

A child's social skills are shaped by the reinforcement he or she receives as a result of an action in the environment (Wood, 1984). Lack of social development diminishes the social status within the group (Anita, 1992; Peck & Cooke, 1983). The predominant philosophy today is that all exceptional individuals should be educated in inclusive classrooms, where they will have adequate social models to emulate. Environmental conditions which nurture negative and aggressive behaviors must be transformed. Massive financial, social, and psychological support must be provided early. A coordinated holistic community effort is needed to offset the present conditions in many urban communities in this country.

REFERENCES

Antia, S. D., & Kreimeyer, K. (1992). Project interact: Interventions for social integration of young hearing-impaired children. *Office of Special Education and Rehabilitative Services, 414,* 14-20.

Antonello, S. (1996). *Social skill development: Practical strategies for adolescents and adults with developmental disabilities.* Boston: Allyn & Bacon.

Bender, W. (1995). Teachers' attitudes toward increased mainstreaming: Implementing effective instruction for students with learning disabilities. *Journal of Learning Disabilities, 28,* 87-94.

Blackhurst, A. E., & Berdine, W. H. (1993). *An introduction to special education* (3rd ed.). Lexington: Harper Collins College Publishers.

Bigge, J., & O'Donnell. (1976). *Teaching individuals with physical and multiple disabilities.* Columbus, OH: Charles E. Merrill.

Borkowski, J., Peck, V., & Damberg, P. (1983). Attention, memory, and cognition. In J. L. Matson and J. L. Milich, *Handbook of Mental Retardation,* p. 479.

Butler-Nalin, P., & Padilla, C. (1989). *Dropouts: The relationship of student characteristics, behaviors, and performance for special education students.* Washington, DC: U. S. Department of Education, Office of Special Education Programs.

Carr, S., & Pungo, R. (1993). The effects of self-monitoring of academic accuracy and productivity on the performance of students with behavior disorders. *Behavior Disorders, 18* (4), 241-250.

Cassidy, E. (1988). *Reaching and involving black parents of handicapped children in their child's education program.* Lansing, MI: Cause, Inc. ERIC 302982.

Civelli, E. (1983). Verbalism in young children. *Journal of Visual Impairment and Blindness, 77* (3), 61-66.

Clark, B. (1992). *Growing up gifted* (4th ed.). New York: Merrill MacMillan.

Cole, P. R. (1987). Recognizing language disorders. In F. N. Martin (Ed.), *Hearing disorders in children.* Austin, TX: Pro-ed.

Davidson, P. W., Dunn, G., Wiles-Kettenman, M., & Appelle, S. (1981). *Haptic conversation of amount in blind and sighted children: Exploratory movement effects.*

Federal Register. (1977). 42 (163) 42474-42518.

Gallagher, J. J. (1989). The impact of policies for handicapped children on future early education policy. *Phi Delta Kappan,* 121-124.

Gallagher, K., & Ansastasiow, N. (1993). *Educating exceptional children.* Boston: Houghton Mifflin.

Gardner, H. (1983). *Frames of mind: The theory of multiple intelligence.* New York: Basic Books.

Gardner, H. (1993b). *Multiple intelligence: The theory in practice.* New York: Basic Books.

Gearheart, B., Mullen, R., & Gearheart, C. (1993). *Exceptional individuals: An introduction.* Pacific Groups, CA: Brooks/Cole Publishing Company.

Geers, A. (1985). Assessment of hearing impaired children: Determining typical and optimal levels of performance. In F. Powell, T. Finitzo-Heiber, S., Friel-Patti & D. Henderson (Eds.), *Education of the hearing impaired child* (pp. 57-83). San Diego: College Hill.

Glassberg, L. (1994). Students with behavior disorders: Determinants of placement outcomes. *Behavior Disorders, 19* (3), 181-191.

Goldman, D. (1995). *Emotional intelligence: Why it can matter more than IQ.* New York: Bantam Books.

Greenberg, M. T., & Kusche, C. A. (1989). Cognitive, personal, and social development of deaf children and adolescents. In M. Wang, M. Reynolds, & H. Walberg (Eds), *Handbook of Special Education: Research and Practice*, p. 95-129.

Groenveld M., & Jan, J. E. (1992). Intelligence profiles of low vision and blind children. *Journal of Visual Impairment & Blindness, 86* (1), 68-71.

Grossman, H. (1993). Manual of classification of mental retardation. Washington, D.C.: American Association on Mental Deficiency.

Haager, D. & Vaughn, S. (1995). Parents, teachers, peers, self-reports to the social competence of students with learning disabilities. *Journal of Learning Disabilities, 28,* (5), 215, 231.

Hallahan, D. P., & Reeve, R. E. (1980). Selective attention and distractibility. In B. K. Keogh (Ed), Advances in Special Education: Vol 1. *Basic constructs and theoretical orientations* (pp 141-181). Greenwich, CT: JAJ Press.

Hardman, M. L., Drew, C. J., Egan, M. W., & Wolf, B. (1993). *Human exceptionality: Society, school, and family.* Needham Heights, MA: Allyn & Bacon.

Haring, N. & McCormick, L. (1990). *Exceptional children and youth* (5th ed.). Columbus: Merrill.

Harry, B. (1992). *Cultural diversity, families, and the special education system: Communication and empowerment.* New York: Teachers College Press.

Henley, M., Ramsey, R. & Algozzine, R. (1993). *Characteristics of and strategies for teaching students with mild disabilities.* Needham Heights, MA: Allyn & Bacon.

Heyward, W., & Orlansky, D. (1992). *Exceptional children* (4th ed.). New York: Merrill.

Higgins, D. (1990). *The challenge of educating together deaf and hearing youth: Making mainstreaming work.* Springfield, IL: Charles C Thomas.

Jenkins-Friedman, R., & Nielsen, M. E. (1990). Gifted and talented students. In E. L. Meyen (Ed.), *Exceptional children in today's school* (2nd ed.). Denver: Love Publishing Company.

Kaplan, P. (1996). *Pathways for exceptional children.* West Publishing Company: Minneapolis, MN: West Publishing Co. (pp. 504-505).

Kaufman, J. (1989). *Characteristics of behavior disorders of children and youth.* (4th ed.). Columbus: Merrill.

Kirkcaldy, B. D. & Mooshage, B. (1993). Personality profiles of conduct and emotional disordered adolescents. *Personality and Individual Differences, 15* (1), 95-96.

Lloyd, J. (1980). Academic instruction and cognitive techniques: The need for attack strategy training. *Exceptional Education Quarterly, 1,* 1-8.

Loper, A. B. (1980). Metacognitive development: Implications for cognitive training of exceptional children. *Exceptional Education Quarterly, 1,* 1-8.

MacCuspie, A. P. (1992). The social acceptance and integration of visually impaired children in integrated settings. In S. Z. Sacks, L. Kekelism and R. J. Gaylord Ross (Eds.), *The development of social skills by blind and visually impaired students: Exploratory studies and strategies* (pp. 83-102). New York: American Foundation for the Blind.

Marion, R. (1981). *Educators, parents, and exceptional children.* Rockville, MD: Aspen.

Matsuda, M. (1984). A comparative analysis of blind and sighted children's communication skills. *Journal of Visual Impairment and Blindness, 78* (1), 1-4.

Meyen, E. (1990). *Exceptional children in today's schools.* Denver: Love.

Moore, D. M. (1987). *Educating the deaf: psychology, principles and practices* (3rd ed.). Boston: Houghton Mifflin.

Norris, G., Haring, L., & Thomas Haring (1994). *Exceptional children and youth* (6th ed.). New York: MacMillan.

Peck, C. A., & Cooke, T. P. (1983). Benefits of mainstreaming at the early childhood level: How much can we expect? *Analysis and Intervention in Developmental Disabilities, 3,* 1-22.

Piechowski, M. (1997). Emotional giftedness: The measure of intraperson intelligence. In N. Colangelo and G. A. Davis (Eds.), *Handbook of gifted education* (2nd ed.). Boston: Allyn and Bacon.

Polloway, E., Patton, J., Epstein, M., Cullinan, D., & Luebke, J. (1986). Demographic, social and behavioral characteristics of students with educable mental retardation. *Education and Training of the Mentally Retarded, 21,* 27-34.

Roberts, S. M. & Lovett, S. B. (1994). Examining the "F" in gifted: Academically gifted adolescents' physiological and affective responses to scholastic failure. *Journal for the Education of the Gifted, 17,* 241-259.

Sacks, S., & Reaedon, M. (1989). Maximizing social integration for visually handicapped students: Applications and practice. In R. Gaylord Ross (Ed.), *Integration strategies for students with handicaps* (pp. 77-104), Baltimore, MD: Paul H. Bookes Publishing Co.

Schiefelbush, R. L., & McCormick, L. (1981). Language and speech disorders. In J. Kaufman and D. Hallahan (Eds.), *Handbook of Special Education.* Englewood Cliffs, NJ: Prentice Hall.

Schwartz, T. (1983). Social cognition in visually and sighted children. *Journal of Visual Impairment and Blindness, 77,* 377-381.

Seligman, M. E. (1992). *Helplessness: On depression, development and death.* San Francisco: W. H. Freeman.

Smith, R. W., Osborne, L. T., Crim, D., & Rhu, A. H. (1986). Labeling theory as applied to learning disabilities: Findings and policy suggestions. *Journal for Learning Disabilities, 19* (4), 195-202.

Stephens, B., & Grube, C. (1982). Development of Piagetian reasoning in congenitally blind children. *Journal of Visual Impairment and Blindness, 76,* 133-143.

Sternberg, R. (1985). *Beyond I.Q.: The triarchic theory of human intelligence.* New York: Cambridge University Press.

Sternberg, R. (1991). *Giftedness according to the triarchic theory of human intelligence.* New York: Cambridge University Press.

Stone, W. L., & LaGreca, A. M. (1980). The social status of children with learning disabilities: A reexamination. *Journal of Learning Disabilities, 23,* 32-47.

Taylor, G. (1992). Integrating social learning theory in educating the deprived. *ERIC Clearing House for Education.* ED. 349260

Torgesen, J. K. (1988). Studies of children with learning disabilities who perform poorly on memory span tasks. *Journal of Learning Disabilities, 21,* 484-486.

Turnbull, A. P., & Turnbull, H. R. (1990). *Families, professional, and exceptionality* (2nd ed.). Columbus, OH: Merrill.

Turnbull, A. P., Turnbull, H. R., Shank, M., & Leal, D. (1995). *Exceptional lives: Special education in today's schools.* New York: Englewood Cliffs.

Tuttle, D. (1984). *Self-esteem and adjusting to blindness.* Springfield, IL: Charles C Thomas.

Ubiakor, F., & Stile, O. (1990). The self-concepts of visually impaired and normally sighted middle school children. *Journal of Psychology, 124,* 190-200.

Van Tassell-Baska, J. (1995). The development of talent through curricular. *Roeper Review, 18,* 98-102.

Vaughn, S., Hogan, A., Kouzekanani, K., & Shapiro, S. (1990). Peer acceptance, self-perception, and social skills for LD students prior to identification. *Journal of Education Psychology, 82,* 101-106.

Warren, D. (1984). *Blindness and early childhood development.* New York: American Foundation for the Blind.

Wood, J. W. (1984). *Adapting instruction for the mainstream.* Columbus, OH: Charles E. Merrill.

Ysseldyke, J., & Algozzine, B. (1990). *Introduction to special education*. Boston: Houghton Mifflin.

Zargota, N., Vaughn, S., & Mcintosh, R. (1991). Social skills interventions and children with behavior problems: A review. *Behavior Disorder, 16* (4), 260-275.

Zetlin, A. (1988). Adult development of mildly retarded students. Implications for educational programs in M.C. Wang, M. C. Reynolds, & H. J. Walberg (Eds.), *Handbook of special education research and practice,* vol 2. New York: Pergamon, pp. 77-90.

Chapter 7

DIRECT INTERVENTION TECHNIQUES FOR TEACHING SOCIAL SKILLS TO INDIVIDUALS WITH EXCEPTIONALITIES

GEORGE R. TAYLOR

INTRODUCTION

DIRECT INSTRUCTIONAL TECHNIQUES according to Harris and Graham (1996) are based on behavioral principles. Direct instruction is commonly used by educators to provide direct instruction to many individuals with exceptionalities to support instructional activity. The technique may be employed to instruct individuals with exceptionalities in a variety of areas, including academic and social/emotional skills. Many individuals with exceptionalities will need explicit instruction, and guided practices in the academic, physical, and social/emotional domains, if they are to become productive members of society.

Goldstein and McGinnis (1984) supported the concept of direct instruction of social skills. These authors indicate that modeling, role playing, practice, and feedback are principal procedures and techniques used to teach and promote social skills. Additional instruction using the following techniques can facilitate the teaching of social skills through direct instruction.

Direct instruction implies that the teacher is directly intervening to bring about a desired change, by providing basic information for children to master the task, which is a prerequisite. Direct instruction may be used with any subject area to assist children in learning basic skills, as well as employing the concept of task analysis (step-by-step sequence of learning a task).

Bandura (1970) provided us with the conceptual framework for using direct instruction. Bandura advanced the concept of "Social Learning Theory" and "Behavioral Modeling." He advocated that much of what the student learns is through modeling from observing others. Carefully and systematically conducted information gained through modeling may be transferred to other academic, social, and non-academic functions. Social skills are prerequisite to the development of skills in other areas. Direct instruction is a strategy to use in developing prosocial skills. Intervention should reflect the assessed social needs of exceptional individuals. Specific techniques for using effective modeling strategies have been delineated later in this chapter.

SKILLSTREAMING

Skillstreaming is a comprehensive social skills program developed by Goldstein (1984). In this program, social skills are clustered in several categories with specific skills to be demonstrated. Clear directions are provided for forming the skillstreaming groups, group meetings, and rules. Activities include modeling, role playing, feedback, and transfer of training. The program is designed to foster human interaction skills needed to perform appropriate social acts. Feedback is received in the form of praise, encouragement, and constructive criticism. The feedback is designed to reinforce correct performance of the skills.

COGNITIVE BEHAVIOR MODIFICATION

These techniques focus on having exceptional individuals to think and internalize their feelings and behaviors before reacting. The process involves learning responses from the environment by listening, observing, and imitating others in their environments. Both cognition and language processes are mediated in solving problems and developing patterns of behaviors (Gresham, 1985).

Cognitive behavioral strategies are designed to increase self-control of behavior through self-monitoring, self-evaluation, and self-reinforcement. These strategies are designed to assist children in internalizing their behaviors, to compare their behaviors against predetermined standards, and for children to provide positive and negative feedback to themselves. Research findings indicate that there is a positive relationship between what individuals think about themselves, and the types of behaviors they display (Rizzo, 1988). Matching the cognitive and effective processes in designing learning experiences for exceptional individuals appears to be realistic and achievable within the school.

BEHAVIOR MODIFICATION TECHNIQUES

Behavioral modification techniques may provide the teacher with strategies for assisting exceptional individuals in performing desirable and appropriate behaviors, as well as promoting socially acceptable behaviors. Refer to Chapter 8 for recommended strategies to use. The technique is designed to provide teachers, educators, and parents with a method to modify exceptional individuals' behaviors to the extent that when they are emitted in a variety of situations, it is consistently more appropriate than inappropriate (Aksamit, 1990; Shores, Gunter, & Jack, 1993).

There are some cautions for teachers using behavioral strategies in the classroom. The chief purpose of the teacher using this technique is to change or modify behaviors. The teacher is not generally concerned with the cause of the behaviors, rather with observing and recording overt behaviors. These behavioral responses may be measured and quantified in any attempt to explain behaviors. Motivation and the dynamic causes of the behaviors are primary concerns for the teacher.

In spite of the cautions involving using behavioral modification techniques, most of the research supports its use (Salend, 1983; Lane, 1992; Rizzo, 1988; Katz, 1991; Taylor, 1992). The major concerns voiced were that the technique must be systematically employed, the environmental constraints must be considered, and teachers, educators, and parents are well-versed in using the technique.

There are many effective ways in which behavior can be modified. Contingency contracting, the task center approach, peer mediation, and proximity control are four of the promising techniques to employ.

CONTINGENCY CONTRACTING

This technique involves pupils in planning and executing contracts. Gradually, pupils take over recordkeeping, analyzing their own behavior, and even suggest the timing for cessation of contracts. Microcontracts are made with the pupil in which he/she agrees to execute some amount of low probability behavior after which he/she may engage immediately in some high probability behavior (Pre-mack Principle) for a specified time.

TASK-CENTERED APPROACH

The task-centered approach to learning is another approach for modifying behaviors of exceptional individuals. This system provides exceptional individuals a highly structured learning environment. Individuals may be experiencing difficulty because they cannot grasp certain social skill concepts. Behavioral problems may stem from the frustration of repeated failure, such as poor attention or the inability to work independently or in groups. Elements in the task-centered approach may include activities to promote:

1. Attention level tasks designed to gain and hold exceptional individuals' attention;
2. Development of visual and auditory discrimination activities as needed;
3. Interpretation and reaction to social level task emphasizing skill related to social interaction;
4. Limitation of social exchanges, the development of verbal and social courtesies, and group participation activities.

PEER MEDIATION STRATEGIES

Peer mediation strategies have been successfully employed to manage behavior. The model is student-driven and enables students to make decisions about issues and conflicts which have impact upon their lives. The model requires that students exercise self-regulation strategies which involves generating socially appropriate behavior in the absence of external control imposed by teachers or other authorities. To be effective, the concept must be practiced by exceptional individuals and frequently reinforced by the teachers through role models, and demonstrations of prosocial skills.

Several investigations have shown that negative behaviors and discipline problems decrease when using this strategy. There is an increase in cooperative relationships and academic achievement. Findings also show an increase in task behaviors (Salend, 1992; Lane, 1992). Implications for using this strategy with exceptional individuals may assist them in internalizing appropriate behaviors and significantly influence developing appropriate social skills (Storey, 1992; Odom, 1984).

Several studies have investigated the importance of using microcomputers to improve interpersonal skills of exceptional individuals. We have addressed this issue sufficiently in Chapter 4. Students tended to make less errors in subject areas when they worked in groups. Exceptional individuals' behaviors also improved. They tended to imitate the behaviors of their peers by increasing their personal and social awareness skills and competencies. Normal peers tended to accept exceptional individuals more readily with the use of computers (Hines, 1990; Hedley, 1987; Thorkildsen, 1985).

PROXIMITY CONTROL

Studies have shown that teacher movement in the class may provide effective control of student behaviors by bringing the teacher and student into closer proximity. It is believed that this close proximity will improve interaction between student and teacher (Shores, Gunter, & Jack 1993; Aksamit, 1990; Banbury & Herbert, 1992; Aksamit, 1990; Banbury & Herbert, 1992; Denny, Epstein, & Rose, 1992).

The technique is easily implemented. The teacher stands close to pupils or arranges desk close to their desk. It is believed that this close proximity provides an external type of control for the pupil. Findings by Denny, Epstein, and Rose (1992) found that teachers generally are not taking advantage of this technique. It was recommended that teachers move freely throughout the room and monitor activities.

COACHING

Appropriate coaching techniques may be employed by teachers to develop social skills for exceptional individuals. Some of the commonly known techniques include: (1) participation, (2) paying attention, (3) cooperation, (4) taking turns, (5) sharing, (6) communication, and (7) offering assistance and encouragement. These techniques are designed to make individuals cognizant of using alternative methods to solving problems; anticipating the consequences of their behaviors; and to develop plans for successfully coping with problems.

CUEING

Cueing is a technique employed to remind students to act appropriately just before the correct action is expected rather than after it is performed incorrectly. This technique is an excellent way of reminding students about prior standards and instruction. A major advantage of this technique is that it can be employed anywhere, using a variety of techniques such as glances, hand signals, painting, nodding or shaking the head and holding up the hand, are to name but a few.

Cueing can be utilized without interrupting the instructional program or planned activities for exceptional individuals. The technique assists in reducing negative practices and prevents students from performing inappropriate behaviors.

Successful implementation of this technique requires that students thoroughly understand the requirement, as well as recognizing the specific cue. Failure to employ the above may result in confused students, especially when they are held accountable for not responding appropriately to the intended cue.

MODELING

Modeling assumes that an individual will imitate the behaviors displayed by others. The process is considered important because exceptional, as well as all individuals, acquire social skills through replicating behaviors demonstrated by others. Educators and adults may employ modeling techniques to change and influence behaviors of children by demonstrating appropriate skills to model. The impact and importance of this valuable technique is frequently overlooked by teachers. Teachers frequently do not assess the impact of their behaviors on children.

Modeling, if used appropriately, may influence or change behaviors more effectively than positive behavior. This is promised upon the fact that once a behavior pattern is learned through imitation, it is maintained without employing positive reinforcement techniques. Teachers should be apprised and cognizant of the importance of modeling or promoting appropriate social skills of exceptional individuals. Additionally, they should be trained and exposed to various techniques to facilitate the process. Children do not automatically imitate models they see. Several factors are involved: (1) Rapport established between teachers and children; (2) The reinforcing consequences for demonstrating or not demonstrating the modeled behavior; and (3) Determining the appropriate setting for modeling certain behaviors.

Exceptional individuals should be taught how to show or demonstrate positive behaviors in structured situations. The technique provides for the structured learning of appropriate behaviors through examples and demonstration of others. Internal or incidental modeling may occur at any time, however, a regular structured time or period of day is recommended in order to develop structure in a variety of social conditions. Teaching behavioral skills through modeling is best accomplished by beginning with impersonal situations which most students encounter, such as the correct way to show respect to others. As exceptional individuals master the modeling process, additional behavioral problems may be emphasized.

Modeling activities may be infused throughout the curriculum at random, however, a specific time is recommended for modeling instruction. Activities should be planned based upon the assessed needs of the class and be flexible enough to allow for changes when situations dictate.

ROLE PLAYING

Role playing is an excellent technique for allowing exceptional individuals to act out both appropriate and inappropriate behaviors without embarrassment, or experiencing the consequences of their actions. It permits exceptional individuals to experience hypothetical conditions which may cause some anxiety or emotional responses in ways which may enable them to better understand themselves. Once entrenched, these activities may be transferred to real life experiences. Role playing may assist exceptional individuals in learning appropriate social skills through developing appropriate models by observing and discussing alternative behavioral approaches. Role playing may be conducted in any type of classroom structure, level, or group size. It may be individually or grouped induced. Through appropriate observations and assessment procedures, areas of intervention may be identified for role playing activities.

Role playing assists individuals identifying and solving problems within a group context. It is also beneficial to shy students. It encourages their interactions with classmates without aversive consequences. As with most group activities, role playing must be structured by the teacher. Activities should be designed to reduce, minimize, correct, or eliminate identified areas of deficits through the assessment process. Gills (1991) listed the following advantages of role playing:

1. Allows the student to express hidden feelings.
2. Is student-centered and addresses itself to the needs and concerns of the student.
3. Permits the group to control the content and pace.
4. Enables the student to empathize with others and understand their problems.
5. Portrays generalized social problems and dynamics of group interaction, formal and informal.
6. Gives more reality and immediacy to academic descriptive material (history, geography, social skills, English).

7. Enables the student to discuss private issues and problems.
8. Provides an opportunity for non-articulate students and emphasizes the importance of non-verbal and emotional responses.
9. Gives practice in various types of behavior.

Disadvantages listed include:

1. The teacher can lose control over what is learned and the order in which it is learned.
2. Simplifications can mislead.
3. It may dominate the learning experiences to the exclusion of solid theory and facts.
4. It is dependent upon the personality, quality, and mix of the teacher and students.
5. It may be seen as too entertaining and frivolous.

Gills (1991) investigated the effects of role playing, modeling, and videotape playback on the self-concept of elementary school children. The Piers-Harris children's self-concept scale was employed on a prepost test basis. Intervention was for a six-month period. Data showed that the combination of role playing, modeling, and videotape playback had some effect upon various dimensions of self-concept.

VIDEOTAPE MODELING

Videotape modeling is an effective measure to improve self-concept of exceptional individuals. They may be encouraged to analyze classroom behavior and patterns of interaction through reviewing videotapes. This technique can show exceptional individuals the behaviors expected before they are exposed to them in various settings. Videotape modeling affords the teachers the opportunity to reproduce the natural conditions of any behavior in the classroom setting. Videotape modeling may provide realistic training which can be transferred to real experiences inside and outside of the classroom (Banbury & Herbert;, 1992; Shores, Gunter, & Jack, 1993).

For exceptional learners, educators may employ this technique to bridge the gap between transferring modeling skills to real life situations. It has been proven as an effective tool to teach prosocial skills to this group.

COOPERATIVE LEARNING

A basic definition of cooperative learning is a method of learning through the use of groups. Five basic elements of cooperative learning are:

1. Positive interdependence.
2. Individual accountability.
3. Group processing.
4. Small group/social skills.
5. Face-to-face primitive interaction.

A cooperative learning group is one in which two or more students are working together toward a common goal in which every member of the group is included. Cooperative learning seems ideal for mainstreaming. Learning together in small groups has proven to provide a sense of responsibility and understanding regarding the importance of cooperation among youngsters. Exceptional individuals socialize and interact with each other (Adams, 1990; Slavin, 1984; Johnson, 1983; Gemma, 1989).

Cooperative learning strategies have the power to transform classrooms by encouraging communities of caring supportive students whose achievements improve and whose social skills grow. Harnessing and directing the power of cooperative learning strategies present a challenge to the classroom teacher. Decisions about the content, appropriateness of the structures, the necessary management routines, and the current social skill development of exceptional individuals call for special teacher preparation (Johnson, 1988). For successful outcomes with students, teachers also need the follow-up of peer coaches, administrative support, parent understanding, and time to adapt to the strategies (Slavin, 1991).

While cooperative models replace individual seat work, they continue to require individual accountability. Teachers who use cooperative structures recognize that it is important for students to both cooperate and compete.

Cooperative learning organizes students to work together in structured groups toward a common goal. Among the best known cooperative structures are Jigsaw, Student Teams Achievement Divisions (STAD), Think-Pair-Share, Group Investigation, Circle of Learning, and Simple Structures. To use a cooperative structure effectively, teachers need to make some preliminary decisions. According to Kagan (1990) the following questions should be asked:

1. What kind of cognitive and academic development does it foster?
2. What kind of social development does it foster?
3. Where in the lesson plan (content) does it best fit?

Teachers also need to examine what conditions increase the effect of cooperative strategies. Positive interdependence, face-to-face (primitive) interaction, individual accountability, and group processing affects cooperative learning outcomes.

The benefits of cooperative learning appear to be reflected in the following:

1. Academic gains, especially among disabled and low-achieving students.
2. Improved race relations among students in integrated classrooms.
3. Improved social and affective development among all students. (Kagan, 1990; Johnson, 1988; Slavin, 1991)

Cooperative learning practices vary tremendously. The models can be complex or simple. Whatever the design, cooperative strategies include:

1. A common goal.
2. A structured task.
3. A structured team.
4. Clear roles.
5. Designated time frame.
6. Individual accountability.
7. A structured process.

We need cooperative learning structures in our classrooms because many traditional socialization practices are absent. Not all students come to school with a social orientation, and students appear to master content more efficiently with these structures (Kagan, 1990; Cosden, 1985). The preponderance of research indicates that cooperative learning strategies motivate students to care about each other and to share responsibility in completing tasks. (Refer to Appendix F for some Cooperative Learning Strategies to use in the classroom.)

COOPERATIVE LEARNING VERSUS PEER TUTORING

It is frequently assumed by some parents that cooperative learning is another concept of peer tutoring, but there are many significant differences between cooperative learning and peer tutoring. In cooperative learning, everyone is responsible for learning and nobody is acting as a teacher or as a tutor. On the other hand, in peer tutoring, one child has the role of teacher and another of student or tutor. The tutor already knows that subject and material and teaches it to a peer who needs individualized remedial help to master a specific skill. In cooperative learning, the initial teaching comes not from a student but from the teacher, because all students grasp concepts quickly and some slowly. These students reinforce what they have just learned by explaining concepts and skills to teammates who need help (Slavin, 1991). Cooperative work puts a heterogeneous group of students together to share ideas and knowledge.

SPECIAL GROUP ACTIVITIES

In a paper presented at the annual meeting of the American Education Research Association, Dorr-Bremme (1992) advanced some unique techniques for improving social identity in kindergarten and first grade. Students sat in groups and planned daily activities; these activities were videotaped. Analysis of the videotapes revealed several dimensions of social identity to be important, such as academic capability; talkativeness; independence; aggressiveness; ability to follow through; and leadership ability. The teacher responded to students individually and as circle participants, depending upon how the behavior was viewed. Findings indicated that social identity was the combined responsibility of everyone in the classroom interacting to bring about the most positive social behavior. Interactions between individual students and the teacher were minimized.

GROUP PLAY ACTIVITIES

The values and benefits of group play therapy cannot be overemphasized when employed with many exceptional individuals. These activities may assist exceptional individuals in developing appropriate interpersonal skills and relationships. Many exceptional individuals tend to settle differences with peers by physical means. This trend may be attributed to poor impulse control, poor modeling and imitation strategies, and inability to internalize their behaviors (Coker & Thyer, 1990; Istre, 1993; Goldstein, 1990; Bratton, 1994).

In order for exceptional individuals to internalize their behaviors, activities must be designed to bring behaviors to the conscience level. Exceptional individuals frequently have problems in self-control which may be manifested in behavioral problems. Group play activities should be designed to enable them to cope with problems which may cause loss of control. Properly employed, these activities will assist exceptional individuals in understanding the consequences of their behaviors, they are moving toward self-management.

SOCIAL-COGNITIVE APPROACHES

These techniques are designed to instruct exceptional individuals to deal more effectively with social matters through self-correction and problem solving. Self-monitoring or instruction involves verbal prompting by the student concerning his/her social behavior. Verbal prompting may be overt or covert. The approach is designed to help students maintain better control over their behaviors.

MAKING BETTER CHOICES

This social-cognitive approach is designed to assist exceptional individuals in making better choices. Group lessons are developed around improving social skills. Lessons are designed to promote forethought before engaging in a behavior and to examine the consequences of the behavior. The major components of this program include the following cognitive sequence:

1. Stop (inhibit response);
2. Plan (behaviors leading to positive behaviors);
3. Do (follow plan and monitor behavior);
4. Check (evaluate the success of the plan).

The aforementioned steps should be practiced by exceptional individuals and reinforced by the teacher. Various social skills are identified by the teacher for the student to practice. Progress reports should be kept and assessed periodically by both teachers and students.

ROLE OF THE SCHOOL IN A BEHAVIOR SETTING

A meaningful course of action for dealing with negative behavior would be to isolate the behavior and then to quantify, record, and observe the number of acts involved. When this determination has been made, the teacher is equipped to undertake a course of action to change the negative behaviors. Social skills training is the technique advocate.

Exceptional individuals, as well as all children, enter school with a wide range of learning abilities, interest, motivation, personality, attitudes, cultural orientations, and social economic status. These traits and abilities must be recognized and incorporated into the instructional program. Promoting positive behavior may take several forms such as using praise frequently, eye contact, special signals, and having individual conferences with pupils.

Exceptional individuals enter school with set behavioral styles. Frequently, these styles are inappropriate for the school. Several techniques are recommended to change inappropriate behaviors in the classroom:

1. Have teachers to raise their tolerance levels. Teachers generally expect exceptional individuals to perform up to acceptable standards. Additionally, it is assumed that they have been taught appropriate

social skills at home. Whereas, the above premise may be true for most pupils, frequently, it is not true for pupils with exceptionalities. By the teacher recognizing casual factors, such as environment, culture, and value, tolerance levels may be raised.

2. Change teacher expectations for pupils. Pupils generally live up to expectations of teachers. Teachers should expect positive behaviors from children. To accomplish this goal, behaviors will sometimes have to be modeled. It is also recommended that individual time be allowed for certain pupils, through interviews and individual conferences where the teacher honestly relates how the child's behavior is objectionable.

SUMMARY

Most learning is social and is mediated by other people. Consequently, pupils with exceptionalities, as well as all children, profit when working in groups. Individual and group activities have proven to be successful in teaching appropriate social skills. Behavioral intervention techniques have proven to be equally successful. There are many individual and group experiences designed to promote social growth among and between children. One of the most promising technique is cooperative learning. It appears to be a promising technique for improving the social skills of exceptional individuals. As the term implies, students work together in groups, to help each other attain the behavioral objective when engaged in cooperative learning. Students benefit both socially and academically when participating in group activities. Therefore, the exceptional's social skills are being duly challenged and developed.

Although cooperative models call for group activities, they require individual accountability. And teachers who use such structures of cooperative learning recognize the need for reaching every student to cooperate and compete while working toward the group goal (Lyman, 1993). The most widely used cooperative learning programs are Jigsaw, Student Teams Achievement Divisions (STAD), Think-Pair-Share, Group Investigation, and Circle of Learning.

With the movements of mainstreaming and inclusion, more and more exceptional students will be interacting with their peers. Some of them may engage in offensive behaviors because of the inability to interact positively. Others have difficulties in communication, which may also result in integration failure (Kaplan, 1990). Teachers must recognize the importance and need for improved interpersonal relationships or increased interaction among all students.

Most exceptional learners do not meet academic success due partly to their inability to implement the above social skills or techniques. These techniques are designed to reduce student isolation and increase students' abilities to react and work with other students toward the solution of common problems. Teachers should experiment with various forms of individual, group, and behavioral intervention strategies to improve social skills of exceptional individuals (Taylor, 1992). Since most behaviors are learned, they can be changed through behavioral intervention strategies, and once social skills are learned through the application of these techniques, they become automatic.

Lutfiyya's (1991) approach outlined three strategies needed for successful group facilitation: (1) facilitation, (2) interpretation, and (3) accommodation. He concluded that all three approaches depend upon cooperation within the group. Roles are shared by all involved. Although this approach is primarily used to diagnose and evaluate exceptional individuals, implications for group planning are clear.

Social skills interventions are needed if exceptional individuals are to be successfully integrated into the mainstream. Activities such as greeting, sharing, cooperation, assisting, complementing, and inviting should be developed and modeled. Social skills development assist exceptional individuals in several ways:

1. Social competence helps compensate for academic deficits.
2. Social skills are needed for success in the mainstream and in employment.
3. Social skills training helps derive maximum benefit from academic and/or vocational instruction.
4. Social competence is fundamental to good interpersonal relationships and fosters improved leisure and recreational activities.

With these in mind, it is incumbent upon our educational systems to focus on designing social skills curricula in all exceptional students.

The teaching of social skills for the exceptional student can be as subtle as the teacher incidentally modeling the correct social behavior in a classroom situation to overt direct instruction in the form of approaches or techniques such as skillstreaming, coaching cooperative learning, structure modeling, role playing, or creative dramatics. The manner in which social skills are taught and the specific teacher characteristics can determine the quality of the entire educational experience for the exceptional youngster.

Positive behavior is a prerequisite for attaining the other skills necessary for school success. For whatever reason, social skills are a major deficit area for the exceptional student. Social skills include the ability to follow instruction, accept criticism, disagree appropriately, greet someone, make a request, reinforce and compliment others, as well as using acceptable ways of getting attention. Thus, activities should be infused throughout the curriculum (Anita, 1992).

REFERENCES

Adams, D. N. (1990). Involving students in cooperative learning. *Teaching Pre-K, 8,* 51-52.

Aksamit, D. L. (1990). Practicing teachers' perceptions of their pre-service preparation for mainstreaming. *Teacher Education and Special Education, 13,* 21-29.

Anita, S. D., & Kreimeyer, K. (1992). *Project interact: Intervention for social integration of young hearing-impaired children.* Office of Special Education and Rehabilitative Services.

Banbury, M., & Herbert, C. R. (1992). Do you see what I mean? *Teaching Exceptional Children, 24,* 34-48.

Bandura, A. (1970). *A social learning theory.* Englewood Cliffs, NJ: Prentice Hall.

Bratton, S. C. (1994). *Filial therapy with single parents.* Doctoral Dissertation. University of North Texas: Dissertation Abstracts International. ERIC. ED 082890.

Coker, K. H., & Thyer, B. A. (1990). School and family-based treatment of children with attention-deficit hyperactivity disorder: Families in society. *The Journal of Contemporary Human Services,* 276-281.

Cosden, M. (1985). The effects of cooperative and individual goal structure on learning disabled and nondisabled students. *Teaching Exceptional Children, 52,* 103-114.

Denny, R. K., Epstein, M. N., & Rose, E. (1992). Direct observation of adolescent with behavioral disorders and their non-handicapped peers in mainstream. *Vocational Education Classrooms, Behavioral Disorders, 18,* 33-41.

Dorr-Bremme, D. W. (1992). Discourse and society identity in kindergarten-first grade classroom. *Clearinghouse for Teacher Education.* ERIC. ED 352111.

Gemma, A. (1989). Social skills instruction in mainstreamed preschool classroom. *Clearinghouse for Teacher Education.* ERIC. ED 326033.

Gills, W. (1991). Jewish day schools and African-American youth. *Journal of Negro Education, 60,* 566-580.

Goldstein, S., & Goldstein, M. (1990). *Managing attention disorders in children: A guide for practitioners.* New York: Wiley.

Goldstein, A., & McGinnis, E. (1984). *Skillstreaming elementary children.* Chicago, IL: Research Press Company.

Gresham. F. M. (1985). Utility of cognitive-behavioral procedures for social skills training with children: Critical review. *Journal of Abnormal Child Psychology, 13,* 491.

Harris, K. R, & Graham, S. (1996). Constructivism and special needs: Issues in the classroom. *Learning Disabilities Research and Practice, 11* (3), 134-137.

Hedley, C. N. (1987). What's new in software? Computer programs for social skills. *Journal of Reading, Writing, and Learning Disabilities International, 3,* 187-191.

Hines, M. S. (1990). Error monitoring by learning handicapped students engaged in collaborative microcomputer-based writing. *Journal of Special Education, 23,* 407-422.

Istre, S. M. (1993). *Social skills of preadolescent boys with attention deficit hyperactivity disorder.* Doctoral Dissertation. Oklahoma State University, 1992: Dissertation Abstract International, 53.

Johnson, R. T., & Johnson, D. W. (1983). Effects on cooperative, competitive, and individualistic learning experiences on social development. *Exceptional Children, 49,* 323-329.

Johnson, D. W., Johnson, R., & Holubec, E. (1988). *Cooperation in the classroom.* Edina, MN: Interaction Book Company.

Kagan, S. (1990). The structural approach to cooperative learning. *Education Leadership, 47,* 12-15.

Katz, L. G. (1991). The teacher's role in social development of young children. *Clearinghouse on Elementary and Early Childhood Education.* ERIC. ED 331642.

Lane, P. S., & McWhirter. (1992). A peer mediation model: Conflict resolution for elementary and middle school children. *Elementary School Guidance and Counseling, 27,* 15-21.

Lutfiyya, Z. (1991). *Tony Sati and Bakery: The roles of facilitation, accommodation, and interpretation.* Syracuse, NY: Syracuse University, Center on Human Policy.

Odom, S. L., & Strain, P. S. (1984). Classroom-based social skills instruction for severely handicapped preschool children. *Topics in Early Childhood Special Education, 4,* 97-116.

Rizzo, J. V., & Zabel, R. H. (1988). *Educating children and adolescents with behavioral disorders: An integrative approach.* Boston: Allyn and Bacon, Inc.

Salend, S. J., & Whittaker, C. R. (1992). Group evaluation: A collaborative, peer-mediated behavior management system. *Exceptional Children, 59,* 203-209.

Shores, R. E., Gunter, P. L., & Jack, S. L. (1993). Classroom management strategies: Are they settling for coercion? *Behavior Disorders, 18,* 92-102.

Slavin, R. E., & Oickle, E. (1981). Effects of cooperative learning teams on student achievement and race relations: Treatment by race interactions. *Sociology of Education, 54,* 174-180.

Slavin, R. E. (1984). Effects on team assisted individualization on the mathematics achievements of academically handicapped and non-handicapped students. *Journal of Educational Psychology, 76,* 813-819.

Slavin, R. E. (1991). *Using student team learning.* Baltimore, MD: The Center for Social Organization of Schools. Johns Hopkins University.

Storey, K. (1992). A follow-up of social skills instruction for preschoolers with developmental delays. *Education and Treatment of Children, 15,* 125-139.

Taylor, G. (1992). Impact of social learning theory on educating deprived/minority children. *Clearinghouse for Teacher Education, 44,* 349-359.

Thorkildsen, R. (1985). Using an interactive videodisc program to teach social skills to handicapped children. *American Annals of the Deaf, 130,* 383-385.

Chapter 8

BEHAVIORAL MANAGEMENT STRATEGIES

GEORGE R. TAYLOR AND THADDAUS PHILLIPS

INTRODUCTION

BEHAVIOR MODIFICATION TECHNIQUES may be characterized as another form of individualized instruction. These may be adapted to individuals and designed to change unacceptable behaviors in several areas. In this chapter, strategies will be discussed which are necessary to implement a successful behavior modification program.

Behavior modification techniques have been applied with great success in a wide range of problems dealing with exceptional individuals. Successful programs have been developed in the areas of social behavior, academic achievement, motor development, and a variety of other behaviors. Bandura (1969) indicated that behavior includes a complexity of observable and potentially measurable activities, including motor, cognitive, and physiological classes of responses.

Walker, Horner, Suqai, Bullis, Sprague, Bricker, and Kaufman (1996), Reavis, Kukic, Jenson, Morgan, Andrews, and Fisher (1996) have concluded that behavior modification strategy has tremendous potential for working with exceptional individuals. Special educators who employ behavior modification techniques are using an effective strategy; however, they are seldom provided with sufficient guidance as to when the approach should be used, for whom, by whom, and toward what end.

Kazid (1973) wrote that behavior modification programs can be no more successful than the staff who utilizes them. He offered four points which should be considered before implementing a program: (1) staff competencies needed to administer the program, (2) strategies required for developing behaviors in clients which are not controlled by the presence of the staff, (3) techniques for augmenting the performance of intractable clients, and (4) methods for the maintenance of client behaviors after the behavior program has terminated. In essence, certain personnel and facilities should be available before special educators attempt to develop a behavior modification strategy for exceptional individuals, they need to know and explore the limitations and liabilities of the strategy.

On the other hand, current literature abounds with studies reporting on the successful application of behavior modification techniques with the exceptional. The basic principles of behavior modification are neither new nor unique, but the systematic application of its fundamentals to specific problems of human behavior has recently been given increased attention by professionals in the field of education. Principles of direct observation, continuous measurement, and systematic manipulation of the environment were preached early in the nineteenth century; and more recently, behavior modification has received increasing attention, especially within special education during the last decade. This increased attention within special education is, in part, because of the emphasis on task analysis and learning theory (Walker, 1977; Christopollos & Valletutti, 1969; Lovitt, 1970; Breen, 1996; Algozzine, 1991; Kaufman, 1998).

HISTORICAL OVERVIEW

According to Macmillan and Forness (1970), the use of the behavior modification strategy may be traced to 1800 when Itard used reinforcement techniques with the wild boy Victor. The strategy was further refined by Sequin, and during the 1930s and 1940s, psychologists worked to improve the techniques and broaden the application of conditioning principles. During this time span, experiments were mostly confined to the laboratory setting with emphasis on animals and on humans with severe emotional or mental conditions. Skinner's (1950) publications concerning animal behavior gave added impetus to the movement. Efforts were then expanded to apply the principles of reinforcement to a wide range of behavior problems.

The 1960s brought an increase in the frequency of use of behavior modification principles. Macmillan and Forness (1970) reported that researchers launched investigations into several areas of human behavior. Bijou and Baer (1961) focused attention on the interaction between a child and his/her learning environment. Lindsey's (1964) work focused on developing special environments for the retarded, the brain-damaged, and the emotionally disturbed. Ayllon and Haughton (1962) employed behavioral techniques to alter the behavior of patients on a psychiatric ward. Bandura (1969) concluded experiments with modeling techniques.

Around the middle of the present decade, behavior modification was becoming increasingly accepted as a strategy, which had particular values for educating exceptional individuals. More recently, Goodall (1972) remarked that behavior modifiers or controllers have increasingly moved away from laboratory-like settings of mental hospitals, correctional institutions, and special classrooms and have been applied in public schools, halfway houses, private homes, and community health centers.

Modifying behavior has always been one of the principal goals of educational programs for exceptional individuals. According to Christopolos and Valletutti (1969) there is nothing radically new about behavior modification. What does appear to be innovative in the field is the emphasis on evaluation or measurement techniques to determine how effectively behavior is actually modified in the direction identified by the educator. These authors outlined and discussed three aspects related to the behavior modification trend: (1) information about the child, (2) information about the task, and (3) information about the management process. It was concluded that only through the integration of the above aspects of behavior modification could curriculum development truly become a functional tool in the service of educators.

DEFINING BEHAVIOR MODIFICATION

Behavior modification is the application of behavioral analysis to correct an individual's maladaptive behavior. According to Krasner and Ullman (1965) the term denotes a specific theoretical position in regard to changing behavior. The strategy consists essentially of introducing reinforcement contingencies, which encourage the emergence of predetermined response patterns. Both classical and operant conditioning may be employed. The former is achieved by pairing the reinforcer with a stimulus; the latter by making the reinforcer contingent upon a response. Kessler (1966) reflected that in classical conditioning, stimuli are associated with an unconditioned response, whereas in operant conditioning, the response operates on the environment to produce certain results. The organism is not a passive participant in the learning process as in conditioning.

Behavior modification techniques include a variety of approaches such as operant conditioning, contingency management, behavioral modeling, role playing, and other approaches designed to alter maladaptive behavior. In operant conditioning, desired behaviors are reinforced in an attempt to establish new operant behavior. Continuous reinforcement implies reinforcement after each occurrence of the desired response. Intermittent schedules may be one of several types: (1) fixed interval schedule, (2) variable interval schedule, (3) fixed ratio schedule, and (4) variable ratio schedule. Since these schedules are amply discussed in other texts, they will not be elaborated on here. Contingency contracting is that behavior modification strategy wherein the subject knows that a particular reward depends upon the completion of a certain task or tasks. The student is rewarded if he/she successfully completes his/her part of the contract. Modeling refers to copying socially acceptable behaviors. This technique is based upon the premise that most behavior can be imitated by students if they are given a correct model to follow.

Behavior strategy may operate on the following techniques: (1) positive reinforcement contingencies, (2) negative reinforcement contingencies, and (3) a combination of positive and negative reinforcement contingencies. Regardless of the type of reinforcement employed, it is imperative that the reinforcement be scheduled systematically. Initially, the reinforcement should be given immediately after the behavioral act; subsequent reinforcement schedules may be changed depending upon the abilities of the individual. It is of prime importance that the reinforcement scheduled be consistent if the behavior modification strategy is to be successful in changing behavior.

GOAL DETERMINATION IN A
BEHAVIOR MODIFICATION STRATEGY

Goals should come first, not the methods for assessing progress toward the goals. Goals, however, are derived primarily from measures. In the determination of adequate behavioral objectives, one of the steps in a behavior modification strategy requires that a teacher work with both short and long range objectives. Without the association between short and long range objectives, the objectives themselves become fractional bits of behavior with little relationship to the process of educational development.

Goal determination in behavior modification research tends to indicate the following: (1) behavior modification cannot be arbitrarily applied because the strategy does not provide teachers with educational goals or philosophy, (2) behavior modification describes learning as a change in observable behavior, disregarding the entire range of covert and unobserved learning, (3) the use of the strategy limits the target behavior to precise, quantifiable, and measurable behaviors, ignoring less easily defined and difficult to measure behaviors, and (4) the strategy concentrates almost entirely nonobjective measurements, not recognizing the subjective realm of human functioning.

Behavior modification is a recognized approach for the systematic control of certain behaviors. Its effectiveness in the temporary altering of many overt, observable behaviors is not questioned. The approach eliminates long and possibly fruitless searches for underlying psychological causes that may or may not be susceptible to change or therapy. An accurate description of present behaviors is an indication of how subsequent behaviors can be modified or changed. In the case of some exceptional individuals, the crucial task is to affect a reward system, which eliminates undesired behaviors and reinforces those behaviors, which are more socially acceptable. While a review of professional literature supports the value of behavior modification, it nevertheless points out some of the limitations and disadvantages of using the strategy with exceptional individuals.

In the field of special education, behavior modification has developed as an acceptable alternative to the psychodynamic method of resolving behavioral problems. It has helped teachers to focus on specific individual behaviors rather than on a general pattern of behavior such as emotional disturbance or learning disability. Additionally, behavior modification has directed teacher effort away from punitive actions for undesirable behavior to reinforcement and encouragement of desirable behaviors.

Finally, behavior modification has focused attention on the environmental contingencies, which maintain undesirable behaviors. Educators are provided with an approach, which encourages them to analyze and alter classroom environmental situations to bring about desirable changes. No longer are they forced to regard classroom behavior as the result of factors outside the classroom and beyond their control.

Most researchers in the field do not support these views. Opponents of the strategy have attacked the behaviorist position of considering only the overt, observable, and measurable portion of human functioning. They feel that behaviorists are offering a powerful approach to changing human behavior but are neglecting the complex nature of human activity, particularly how individuals learn and how they are motivated. Due to the fact that a behavior modification strategy is based upon specific overt behaviors, it possesses the potential for encouraging teachers to teach those behaviors which fit the system, overlooking affective behaviors.

Behavior modification techniques have proven extremely successful in eliminating maladaptive behavior in children with behavioral disorders (Algozzine, 1991; Breen, 1996). Some of the benefits of applying behavior modification for educational purposes:

- The most significant contribution is that behavior modification helps make education more of a science. It provides a language, including operationally defined terms, which makes precise communication possible. Precise communication helps make possible the replication of studies and the validation of results.
- By utilizing behavior modification techniques, the educator is better prepared to control behavior. Having command of the group or individuals in one way or another guarantee freedom from the discipli-

narian role. Consequently, concern can more appropriately focus on educational programming.

- Any academic subject or problem area can be approached with behavior modification techniques. The contingencies determining the results can be identified whether the task includes reading, writing, arithmetic, or sitting in a seat ready for work. The virtually unlimited potentials for application to a wide range of tasks make it an extremely valuable tool for all educators.

LIMITATIONS OF A BEHAVIOR MODIFICATION STRATEGY

Behavior modification techniques provide systematic procedures which teachers may implement to change or modify deviant behavior and encourage more acceptable behavior. Skeptical, cautious acceptance and application are certainly indicated. Behavioral modification techniques are themselves morally blind. Some of the limitations to the behavioral approach: (1) the behavioral approach treats only the symptoms and not their causes, (2) it stresses remediation and minimized prevention, (3) behavioral problems cannot be nullified by a strategy which fails to penetrate environmental or psychology roots, (4) there is no transferable value because out-of-classroom behavior is not affected, and (5) self-discipline is devalued in favor of extrinsic management.

Teachers are often told to use a positive approach to influence behavior. The danger inherent in this approach is that rewards may impede natural motivation. Better management would help students feel the satisfaction inherent in doing good work for its own sake. Another danger arises when jealousy of the award sets children apart. When this occurs, those who are given an award may be treated as the "teacher's pet," thus, interfering with their social relationships with peers. In cases such as this, receiving an award becomes an unpleasant experience. A third danger is when the reward loses most of its value because it can be attained by only a few and is beyond the reach of most. The use of trinkets, food, and small toys may be ineffective for holding children at a task for any considerable length of time because of situation.

As concern increases with accountability and as the necessity for evaluation increases, another potential source of misuse of a behavior modification strategy is in the area of goal determination. Behaviorally-oriented educators stressed the setting of specific behavioral objectives to determine the direction for effort, and to provide precise means for evaluating that effort (Nelson, 1996, Thompson & Walker, 1999). A dangerous potential is implicit in this desire for accountability and measurability—the situation whereby that which is measurable becomes the goal. The unfortunate situation thus arises in education, i.e., that it may become more rewarding for centers to teach that which is readily measured. Behaviors, which are not easily quantified, particularly those in the effective domain, may thus be excluded from the realm of desirable educational goals.

An approach that does not consider the whole child holds some portents for special education in that it considers the special individual as a collection of indiscrete and unrelated fractions. The basic assumptions underlying the development and utilization of fractional approaches is that human activity may be successfully separated into specific entities, being essentially independent and capable of being individually evaluated and treated. Human behavior is too complex to justify a fractional approach to behavior analysis. A systematic plan is needed. A school-wide approach appears to be an effective strategy to comply.

Discipline has been a major problem facing public schools for several decades. Many exceptional individuals have not responded effectively to traditional measures to learn self-discipline. Behavioral management techniques have been integrated into school-wide discipline plans. These techniques are designed to improve student self-control and responsibility through providing preventive strategies other than punishment (Research Connections in Special Education, 1997).

DESIGNING A SCHOOL-WIDE BEHAVIORAL MANAGEMENT PLAN

A large percentage of behavioral problems may be prevented by a school-wide discipline plan, which is implemented and supported by staff members, administrators, and family members. Consistent school-wide behavioral expectations for various activities and settings need to be established and taught. These expectations should reflect the school community's mission statement and discipline philosophy. The School Wide Discipline Plan includes the following elements:

1. Total staff commitment to the school-wide discipline philosophy toward managing behaviors
2. School-wide rules clearly defined and supported by the staff
3. Common area routines and consequences for breaking rules
4. Plan for teaching rules and procedures and other social skills
5. System for recognizing expected behaviors
6. Description of consistent consequences for infractions

7. Emergency procedures to obtain immediate in-school assistance
8. System for communication
9. Plan for training (Cheney, Barringer, Upham, & Manning 1995; Colvin, Kameenui & Suqai, 1993; Jones, 1993; Suqai, 1993)

Most students will follow the plan and respond with improved behavior if the following are implemented:

1. School and classroom climates are positive and safe and all stakeholders endorse the plan.
2. Staff personal skills should be realistic, be competent and should unify to solve problems.
3. Rules should be systematically taught and correlated with the schools mission. They should be clear, fair, and the consequences of behavior fully understood by the pupils.
4. Behavior, principle of behavioral management should be understood and practiced by all staff members.
5. Parental and student support are essential to any success, parents must be fully apprised of the program, the rules and consequences of non-compliance. They should be totally involved from planning to implementing the behavioral strategy. They are powerful "significant others" for their children.
6. Shared responsibility for all stakeholders should assume discipline. All should support and agree to the plan. In-service training should be provided if needed. A team approach should be evident in solving problems. (Thompson & Walter, 1999)

If implemented, these guidelines will go a long way in promoting support and cooperation from students. As much as possible selected students should be part of the planning and implementation of the plan.

Effective strategic supports are needed for those students who display challenging behaviors resulting from unmet needs. A collaborate team approach is helpful in identifying antecedent strategies such as modification in instructional programs to meet the unique behavioral needs of the pupils. Both physical and human resources will be needed to reduce or minimize many behavioral problems. Changes in schedules and the instructional environment may need to be modified to successfully deal with the behavior problem. Other changes and modifications may include alternative skill training, such as social skills, or adaptive skills and long-term preventive strategies. These strategic support structures are primarily designed for those exceptional pupils who constantly break rules on a regular basis.

The State of Pennsylvania (1995) published guidelines for effective behavioral support. The plan was to balance the rights of all students to a safe learning environment while providing effective programs for students with chronic behavioral problems. To achieve this plan, in-service training was provided to the staff and consisted of conducting functional assessment of the behavioral problem, developing hypotheses relevant to the function of the challenging behavior, designing and implementing the behavioral support plan, evaluating the effectiveness of the plan, and modifying the support plan as needed (Pennsylvania Plan, 1995).

Despite a school-wide discipline plan and positive strategic supports, some exceptional students within a school building will require a personalized student plan to describe an individualized program of intervention. Guidelines will be needed for behaviors in specific settings other than the classroom. Consistent management practices are needed from classroom to classroom as well as the total school. An essential part of the individualized plan must include a problem-solving process. The process should commence with identifying the target behaviors by conducting a functional assessment to assess the behavior. Next, hypotheses statements should be developed relevant to the target behaviors in order to determine to what degree the stated hypotheses were achieved. The intervention strategies should be developed next based upon the functional assessment. Using information cited above, an individual plan should be developed and implemented. Documentation of progress and evaluation of the effectiveness of the plan should be carefully assessed. Based upon the evaluative date, the plan may be modified or terminated. An effective plan should include:

1. Background information on the student.
2. A succinct description of the problem and an assessment of current performance.
3. Clearly defined goal statements should be developed.
4. Well-developed hypotheses statements for the function of the behavior, and intervention strategies related to the function of the behavior.
5. Specific evaluation procedures would be developed before initiating the programs.
6. Appropriate physical and human resources should be identified before implementing the program. (Jones, 1993; Algozzine, Ruhl, Ramsey, 1991; Breen & Fielder, 1996, Colvin, Kameenui, & Suqai, 1993)

STEPS IN CHANGING INAPPROPRIATE BEHAVIORS.

Challenging behaviors are context-related. Behaviors do not occur in a vacuum, individuals select (either consciously or unconsciously) behavior in response to their environment. (Reavis, Kukic, Jenson, Morgan, Andrews, & Fisher, 1996; Suqai, Pruitt, 1993; Walker, Horner, Suqai, Bullis, Sprague, Bricker & Kaufman, 1996).

Challenging behaviors serve a specific function for the student.

Although problem behaviors may be socially inappropriate, they are driven by the belief that they will produce a desired result for the student. Students employ many types of challenging behaviors to achieve their goals. Some commonly used behaviors include, obtaining attention, escaping/avoiding a task or demand, obtaining a desired object or activity, satisfying sensory needs, and gaining control of the situation.

These beliefs can be driven by several factors, including past history, observation of others, and a limited repertoire of alternative behaviors. The ultimate goal of student behavior is to fulfill the need to belong by feeling capable, connected, and contributing. In some instances, goals may need to be modified with acceptable alternatives in order to reduce the inappropriate behavior displayed. (Walker, Horner, Suqai, Bullis, Sprague, Bricker & Kaufman, 1996; Thomas, Grimes, 1995; Mayer, 1995; Colvin, G. (1992); Hudley & Graham, 1995).

Effective interventions are based on a thorough understanding of the problem behavior. In order to produce meaningful long-term behavior change, an intervention must directly address the function and contextual influences of the challenging behavior. Challenging behaviors represent skill deficits, and effective interventions address both the acquisition of appropriate alternatives and the creation of an environment that is conducive to the performance of those alternatives. Effective intervention also aims to prevent the display of challenging behaviors by addressing the role that contextual factors play in the display of problem behaviors.

Changing problem behaviors to socially accepted alternatives require that systematic steps be in place before the behavioral intervention is attempted (Brendtro & Long, 1995). Table 8 reflects recommended steps and process to employ in dealing with problem behaviors. The process begins with identifying the target behavior in question, through evaluating the effectiveness of the program.

In implementing the aforementioned steps, all students should be afforded the same dignity and respect, regardless of their exceptionalities. Intervention strategies should be designed to assist the child to bring his/her behaviors up to social standards. No intervention should stigmatize, dehumanize, or cause emotional or physical distress to individuals in the program (refer to Appendix G).

A variety of recording instruments must be employed to effectively record and analyze behavioral patterns. In some instances, educators must construct their own recording devices. Refer to Appendices H and I for examples of recording instruments.

Data received from these instruments may be analyzed to assist educators in determining the effectiveness of their behavioral program. If evaluative results are negative, the student may need additional practice or expo-

TABLE 8

Steps in Changing Negative Behaviors

Steps	*Strategies*
1.	Identify the behavior you wish to change: to decrease a problem behavior or increase a positive behavior. Pinpoint the behavior by being as specific as possible (i.e., hitting peers during play or at snack times).
2.	Write down the goal you wish to achieve. For example, decrease the number of hitting behaviors towards peers during play or snack times.
3.	List the steps you need to reach the goal (i.e., decreasing the hitting behaviors during snack times, decreasing the behaviors during play times), eliminating hitting behaviors during snack or play times. Reaching a goal via several small steps is usually more successful than attempting to achieve a goal in a single step, especially for young children.
4.	Establish a baseline (how often the behavior occurs now) by counting the frequency of the behavior during snack or play times for a period of 3-4 consecutive days. Record the frequency on a chart that is easily accessible. Golf counters work great for charting the frequency of behaviors.
5.	Decide on the method and type of chart you will use for recording the behavior you are attempting to change. Decide on the consequences (activity, social, and material reinforcers) that will help bring about the desired change.
6.	Evaluate the effectiveness of your behavior management program by recording the child's frequency of targeted behavior over the set period of time to determine if there is a decrease in frequency compared to the frequency of these behaviors recorded on your original baseline. If the behavior is decreasing in frequency, your methods and consequences are appropriate. If not, you will need to go back to Step 5 and make changes.

sure in behavioral management strategies.

The behavior modifier must address three points, if he/she is to successfully implement a behavior modification strategy: (1) define maladaptive behavior, (2) determine the environmental events which support the behavior, and (3) manipulate the environment in order to alter maladaptive behavior. Thompson and Walter (1999) emphasized that a positive atmosphere should be created in implementing a behavior modification strategy. They proposed that the teacher formulate a positive rule, something students can work toward, rather than something to avoid. By this means, the student is directed toward a specific desirable behavior rather than merely castigated without an alternative suggested behavior. The importance of involving students in planning behavior modification strategy was also outlined (refer to Appendix J).

The teacher should establish a working relationship with each individual. The teacher's job is to assign tasks that the student needs to learn, is ready to learn, and could be successful in learning. This approach permits greater teacher-student interaction. The specific behavior modification strategy, the character of its application, and the nature and quality of the teacher-student interaction must arise out of the teacher's assessment of the individual and his/her needs and interests. A behavior modification strategy should be flexible in its application while firmly based in scientific method (Kaufman, 1998; Colvin, 1992; Mayer, 1995).

Due to a wide diversity in mental, physical, and social traits of children with exceptionalities, teachers must develop individual behavioral strategies. These strategies must include the aforementioned traits. We have listed under each area of exceptionality specific behavioral strategies to employ.

THE TEACHER AS A BEHAVIOR MODIFIER

Educators attempt to change the behavior of students in ways which they feel will enhance their desire to learn (refer to Appendix K). Using a behavior modification strategy, educators try to determine those reinforcers which will increase the probability of a desired response or behavior. Several difficulties, however, are inherent in the systematic application of a reinforcer. The first lies in the pupil's perception of his/her current behavior, the target behavior to which he/she is aspiring, and his/her relationship to the reinforcer. By providing an individual with arbitrary reinforcers, a teacher focuses the individual's attention, not on the relationship between his/her behavior and his/her academic or social success, but rather on the relationship between his/her behavior and the reinforcement. He/she sees his/her behavior as related only to the desired consequence and changing his/her behavior has meaning for him/her. The use of natural reinforcers may also be criticized in the same way, although they may more easily be integrated into an individual's frame of reference and thus be more easily related to the desired behavior.

The teacher's attention and praise may function as a negative reinforcer when a teacher utilizes an opportune moment to comment favorably or praise another student in front of the class with the intention of sending a negative message to another student. This type of situation may be called an example of unintended consequences of reinforcement and frequently does not fit the particular life-style of the student. In essence, the method might be harmful to the student unless the teacher has considered his/her individual needs.

Behavior modification is a technique, which may be effectively used in conjunction with educational systems and/or content; it is not a program with content of its own. Generally, teachers of exceptional individuals feel that the utilization of a behavioral modification strategy is too complex and involves too much preliminary training. These concepts can probably be attributed to the fact that special educators are not often familiar with behavioral principles. Teachers who have had adequate training can successfully implement a behavior modification strategy.

Behavior modification techniques can be highly effective in the beneficial changes of social and academic behaviors of exceptional individuals in the classroom or in a school-wide program. Recent research has applied these techniques to preschool children, and to low achieving minority children. The approach that these investigations have taken has been to employ token reinforcers such as colored chips or point cards to improve and maintain improvement of social and/or academic behaviors. Items such as candy, gum, toys, and money have served as back-up reinforcers to these tokens.

SUMMARY

The uniqueness of a behavioral strategy lies in its systematic application of a precise technique to bring about behavioral change. Because of its origin in the scientific laboratory, it requires compliance with and acceptance of the demands of scientific rigor. The development of a behavior modification strategy has established a definite structure whereby a teacher can change a student's behavior. It can be employed to increase the occurrence of desired behavior already within a student's behavioral repertoire or to teach new behavior.

Behavior modification is a valuable tool but should not be used as a total approach to classroom learning. Thomas and Grimes (1995), who stated that alternate developmental theories might be more helpful for determining goals, support this conviction. These developmental theories may suggest to the teacher a specific developmental task that the student must master and what specific skills he/she must acquire in order to achieve subsequent levels of performance.

However, the teacher should be able to recognize the advantages of giving rewards as they relate to a specific goal that is to be obtained. Using this approach, the teacher should be able also to determine when a reward is not working. When the reward becomes the end instead of the means, it becomes a liability. The teacher should become skilled in systematically employing a behavior modification strategy when it will facilitate the acquisition of knowledge and skills designed to make that student a more fully realized individual in his ecological environment.

REFERENCES

Algozzine, B., Ruhl, K., & Ramsey, R. (1991). *Behaviorally disordered. Assessment for identification and instruction.* Reston, VA: The Council for Exceptional Children.

Bandura, A. (1969). *Principles of behavior modification.* New York: Holt, Rinehart, and Winston, Inc.

Breen, M. J., & Fielder, C. R. (1996). *Behavioral approaches to assessment of youth with emotional behavioral disorders.* Austin: Pro Ed.

Brendtro, L. & Long, N. (1995). Breaking the cycle of conflict. *Educational Leadership,* 52-56.

Brigge, M., & Hunt, M. (1968). *Psychological foundation of education* (2nd ed.). New York: Harper and Row.

Cheney, D., Barringer, C., Upham, D., & Manning, B. (1995). Project testing: A model for developing educational support teams through interagency network for youth with emotional or behavioral disorders. *Special Services in the Schools, 10* (2), 57-76.

Christopolos, F., & Valletutti, P. (1969). Defining behavior modification. *Educational Technology, 9,* 28.

Colvin, G. (1992). *Managing acting-out behaviors.* Longmont, CO: Sopris West.

Colvin, G., Kameenui, E. J., & Suqai, G. (1993). Reconceptualizing behavior management and school-wide discipline in general education. *Education and Treatment of Children, 16* (4), 361-381.

Goodall, K. (1972). Who's who and when in behavior shaping. *Psychology Today, 6,* 53-56.

Haberman, M. (1994), Gentle teaching in a violent society. *Educational Horizons,* 131-135.

Hudley, C., & Graham, S. (1995), School-based intervention for aggressive African-American boys. *Applied and Preventive Psychology, 4,* 185-195.

Jones, V. (1993). Assessing your classroom and school-wide student management plan. *Beyond Behavior, 4* (3), 9-12.

Kaufman, J. M. et al. (1998). *Managing classroom behavior: A reflective case-based approach* (2nd ed.). Boston: Allyn and Bacon.

Kazid, A. E. (1973). Issues in behavior modification: With mentally retarded persons. *American Journal of Mental Deficiency, 78,* 134.

Kessler, J. W. C. (1966). *Psychology of childhood.* New Jersey: Prentice Hall.

Krasner, L., & Ullman, L. P. (1965). *Research in behavior modification.* New York: Holt, Rinehart, & Winston.

Lazarus, A. A., Davidson, G. C., & Pollefka, D. A. (1965). Classical and operant factors in the treatment of school phobia. *Journal of Abnormal Psychology, 70,* 225-229.

Lovitt, T. (1970). Behavior modification: The current science. *Exceptional Children, 38,* 58-91.

Macmillan, D., & Forness, S. R. (1970). The origins of behavior modification with exceptional children. *Exceptional Children, 37,* 93-100.

Mayer, G. R. (1995). Preventing anti-social behavior in the schools. *Journal of Applied Behavioral Analysis,* 467-478.

Nelson, J. R. (1996). Designing schools to meet the needs of students who exhibit disruptive behavior. *Journal of Emotional and Behavioral Disorders, 4,* 147-161.

Pennsylvania Department of Education, Bureau of Special Education. (1995). *Guidelines: Effective behavioral support.* Harrisonburg, PA: Author.

Reavis, H. K., Kukic, S. J., Jenson, W. R., Morgan, D. P., Andrews, D. J., & Fisher, S. (1996). *Best practices.* Longmont, CO: Sopris West Publishers.

Research Connections in Special Education. (1997). ERIC/OSEP Special Project. *The Eric Clearinghouse on Disabilities and Gifted Education, 1* (1), 1-8.

Suqai, G., & Pruitt, R. (1993). *Phases, steps, and guidelines for building school-wide behavior management programs: A practitioner's handbook.* Oregon: Behavior Disorders Program.

Thomas, A., & Grimes, J. (1995). *Best practices in school psychology III.* Silver Spring, MD: National Association of School Psychologists.

Thompson, J. C., & Walter, J. K. (1999). School disciplines becoming proactive, productive, participatory, and predictable. *Annual Editions, Education,* 99-100.

Walker, H. M. (1997). *First step: An early intervention program for anti-social kindergartners.* Reston, VA: The Council for Exceptional Children.

Walker, H., Horner, R., Suqai, G., Bullis, M., Sprague, J., Bricker, D., & Kaufman, M. (1996). Integrated approaches to preventing anti-social behavior patterns among school-age children and youth. *Journal of Emotional and Behavioral Disorders, 4,* 193-256.

Chapter 9

PERCEPTUAL REMEDIATION

GEORGE R. TAYLOR

INTRODUCTION

ELSEWHERE IN THE TEXT the discussion was focused upon the many deficits found among exceptional individuals. Causes and methods for remediating the deficits were reviewed. This chapter is designed to focus on an important approach in remediating many of the deficits experienced by some exceptional individuals. The literature is abounded with perceptual strategies to employ in working with children who have learning disabilities. Early researchers perceived perceptual-motor disorders as a major cause of learning disabilities. They proposed learning disabilities were due to disordered motor skills, perceptional integration, balance, and tactile and kinesthetic disorders (Cruickshank, 1961; Frostig, 1972; Kepart, 1974). Many remedial activities were advocated to improve perceptual-motor integration. Lyons (1994) indicated that today the focus has changed to accent techniques for remediating specific deficits such as reading spelling, and mathematical disorders, rather than on activities stressing perceptual-motor integration.

We maintain the view that perceptual-motor integration may constitute problems with any exceptional individual, not only the learning disabled. Therefore, strategies outlined in this chapter can be adapted or modified to assist any exceptional individual who has problems in perceptual-motor integration. As a general principle, the mechanisms of perceptual behavior are dependent on three functions:

1. Awareness of conditions of internal and external environment.
2. Ability to communicate these conditions by the appropriate affecter organs.
3. Ability of affectors to cause the organism to effect overt adjustment to the environment.

Information received from the environment is called sensation. Interpretation of sensory stimulation from the environment is called perceptual (Neisser, 1967; Ornstein, 1972; Abrams, 1994; Irwin, 1996). Physically, the neural aspect of the simple reflect arc is represented by the nervous system which includes the brain.[1] The function of the nervous system is to transmit impulses generated through the sensory structure to the appropriate musculature (Freemen, 1995; Calvin, 1996). This phenomenon, associated with the awareness of the external world through the exterocepter sense, is called perception.

When an individual is thrust into a new environment at birth, he/she suddenly has the responsibility of caring for his/her complex systems. He/she must learn what to do with the radiant energy that enters his/her eyes, with the sound waves that impinge on his/her ears, with the mechanical energy applied to his/her skin, as well as the chemical energy exerted on his/her tongue and nose (Koutulak, 1996).

Gestalt psychologists indicated that perception is innate, but reflected that one must learn what to do with the stimuli that approach his/her senses. The infant must learn to interpret sensory stimuli before he/she can use them to process information in his/her environment. Development of conceptual configuration is governable by manipulative experiences to which the individual is exposed. If he/she is to develop proper concepts, he/she must be motivated by larger perceptual structures commensurate with increase in age. The degree to which each individual's perceptual configuration is organized and its wealth of content depend on one's experiences and native ability to perceive (Ausubel, 1978; Alexander, Kulikowich, & Schulze, 1994; Dole, Duffy, Rochler, & Pearson, 1991; Novak & Musonda, 1991; Rouet, Favart, Britt, & Perfetti, 1997; Schneider, 1993).

Perceptual learning is dependent on the level of material achieved by a child. Full achievement of maturation can be facilitated or inhibited by the occurrence or non-occurrence of specific learning experiences. Neither maturation nor learning can fully unfold independently. To this concept individual differences can be added. Individuals do not perceive situations with equal realism. As humans vary in physical characteristics, so do they vary in endowment and development to exteroceptive capacity. This bears out Gesell's approach to individual differences through the stages of growth and development (Smith, 1994; Reid, 1988).

Hannaford, 1995; Gilbert, 1977, and Ayers, 1991 envisioned perception as involving a complex system of integration between sense fields and between past and present sensory impressions and experiences. Premised upon the aforementioned research, we support the notion that perception is a panoramic screen, storing the past and allowing individuals to utilize long forgotten perceived experiences. Accumulation of old perceptual experi-

---

[1] An excellent source to consult on the structure and function of the human brain is Eric Jensen (1999). *Teaching with the Brain in Mind.* Alexandra, VA: Association for Supervision and Curriculum Development.

ences helps to explain intellectual growth and ability as they combine to make past events meaningful. Changes that take place in perception from early childhood to adult life; that perceptions are not fixed from one year to the next.

AUDITORY PERCEPTION

Begley (1996) contended that auditory and visual perceptions are learned from infancy. The same holds true for the three other basic senses. The child learns to make associative discriminations of similarities, differences, and combinations in each sensory area.

In auditory perception, characteristic sounds have a quality all their own. Sensory data in audition comes through vibrations transmitted from the outer air to fluid in the inner ear. It is from these impulses that one evaluates pitch (frequency) and intensity. From association and learning one can discriminate similarities, differences, and combinations of sound. As in all perceptions, discriminations are stored so that they may be called upon whenever needed for further learning. The ability to recall auditory sounds is called auditory memory (Bender, 1995).

In the very young child, audition supports and reinforces motor activities before the skill and dexterity for writing is developed. In the preschool age child, the use of sounds through language allows him to visualize and report on his visualization sound. Several authors, Curtis and Tallal (1991), Tallal, Miller, and Fitch (1993), and Torgesen (1998) agreed that auditory processing is slower in exceptional children with language problems. It was voiced that these children take longer to process sensory information, respond to questions, and to solve problems. Deficits in auditory perception can have significant impact upon learning. We have provided strategies later in the chapter to remediate auditory perception problems.

VISUAL PERCEPTION

Sensory information to the eye comes in the form of light. When an image from the light falls on the retina, a series of impulses are set off along the optic nerve to the brain. The output of the sensory stimuli is a patterned response based on past and present experiences with environment. Visual perception is perhaps the most important skill required in our culture. Vision reaches the highest achievement when all developmental processes are incorporated in the guidance and training routines presented as learning situations. The use of motor-integrative-perceptual processes enhances every skill in that it prepares the child's entire visual machinery (Bruce & Green, 1990; Swanson, 1987).

Visual perception is the most significant of our perceptual skills in that it is an interpretive skill. It assists us in understanding texture, size, shape, direction, and color. The senses of taste, smell, and touch need more specific contact before they can furnish information on decision and interpretation.

The spiral of development in perceptual skills can progress to where vision alone provides adequate information. For example, one can see an orange and know it is an orange from past perceptual experiences. One does not have to touch, taste, smell it to know it is an orange. As a distance receptor, vision can help us to understand our world more completely than any other sensory mechanism. Perceptual organizations and conceptual orientations in space start with the child's awareness of his/her own position in space. A child must learn to know the meaning of up and down, near and far, right and left, vertical and horizontal. In other words, he/she must learn directionality. This is especially important in learning to read.

The location of objects in space is the result of integration of a series of visual impressions. Kepart (1960) outlined that it is necessary to locate objects laterally, with relation to each other and our own bodies. There are clues one may get which enter into the perception of distance under various circumstances.

1. Kinesthetic sensations produced by the convergent and divergent eye movements that stigmata the distance away from an object.
2. Kinesthetic sensations of the accommodatory movements of the eye to make accurate judgments of distance.

If one has an idea of the relative size of objects in a field of vision, one can learn to estimate relative distances. One can also learn that brightness, clearness, and color saturation decrease as distance increases.

The differences and similarities which an individual observes in space are accomplished, not only on the basis of space but time as well. He/she can learn to change complicated spatial series into a temporal series and back again. The individual can learn to understand that changes in parts of the pattern change the pattern and present a variation. Kepart (1960) further stated that a child must build up the whole, which has its own characteristics and which differs from any of its parts.

Distinguishing figure-ground organization is the final process of structuring precepts. According to Bender (1995), distinction between figure and ground can be learned. The figure is more easily definable by color connected with meanings and feelings. Knowing these differences is important in reading in that one has to distinguish the symbol (figure) from the page on which it is printed (ground).

Smith (1994) concluded that an individual must achieve maturation in the areas of perceptual-motor-conceptual behavior as a reading readiness measure. Movement, like perception, requires patterning. Certain levels of motor skills are indicative of an individual's overall maturity, for one must attain neurological saturation in order to activate specific muscle groups (Brink, 1995; Palmer, 1980).

It is not within the scope of this chapter to discuss detailed relationships between perception and reading, but to review perceptual training techniques that can be successfully implemented by the teacher in remediating reading disabilities found among many exceptional individuals.

READING

Reading is not one skill, but a number of interrelated skills. For the beginning reader, reading is mainly concerned with learning to recognize printed symbols which represent speech and to respond intellectually and emotionally as if the material were spoken rather than printed. The beginning reader learns to develop skills in the mechanics of reading such as developing a sight vocabulary and identifying unfamiliar words. He/she also learns to develop skills in comprehension by learning to grasp meanings, to understand main ideas, and to understand sequences of events as well as recalling details. He/she learns to associate printed words with concrete objects and abstract ideas and use them in arranging sentences (Bender, 1995; Billingsley, & Ferro-Almeida, 1993; Englert & Palinscar, 1988; Hardman, Drew, & Egan, 1996).

Reading involves the following simultaneously:
1. Sensation of light rays on the retina, reaching the brain.
2. Perception of separate words and phrases.
3. Function of eye muscles with exact controls.
4. Immediate memory for what has been read.
5. Organization of the material so that it can be used.

In order to perceive symbols, there must be good visual mobility in the left to right movements across the reading page as well as visual orientation to the symbols on the printed page (Swanson, 1997). Related to the precepts of form are the precepts of space since forms do involve special relationships. Tactile perception gives an indication of size and shape. Visual perception gives one an orientation in space as in left to right, up and down. Visual perception also gives an orientation in space as to size, shape, figure/ground, as well as distance as in near and far. Auditory perception gives one a sense of rhythm, time, and community, as he/she relates to sounds. Space, position, and direction will only have meaning for the child if he/she has sense of his/her own body image.

DEVELOPMENTAL READINESS

Educators have placed much stress on the concept of readiness as a prerequisite for learning. From the field of child development, the emphasis has been drawn on individual differences in maturational patterns, especially as they relate to children in the earliest school years. Differentiated from intelligence and experimental influences, the factor of biological readiness, which appears to be a reflection of specific integration patterns, plays a major role in the acquiring of speech and the learning of reading and arithmetic (Greenberg, 1991). While, for example, aphasia in the adult can generally be traced to known cerebral trauma, in children it is more often maturational in origin and represents a lag in the development of specific language functions. Usually, following the delay, spontaneous compensation occurs, although on later examination a residuum of difficulty may be diagnosed in the form of motor, sensory, conceptual, or mixed aphasia. A similar pattern is followed in older children in relation to reading. Differences in the development of such fundamental techniques as directional orientation and auditory discrimination may be wide in a group of first grade children of comparable intelligence, and the influence of this factor on the learning process is crucial.

A vexing clinical problem for the child psychologist is suggested by these developmental considerations. In some cases, early disability can be expected to be overcome spontaneously through growth, and in other cases specific help is needed. Notwithstanding the validity of the developmental lag concept, too often there is a tendency to wait too long for spontaneous compensation to occur, while the individual is neglected, sometimes beyond remediation.

Bryan (1965) listed five principles which still have relevance today, that should be employed if remediation is to be effective with individuals who have exceptionalities.

1. Remediation should initially focus on the simplest, most basic perceptual associational elements in reading: perception of details within the Gestalt of words and association of sounds with the perceived word elements.
2. Perceptual and associational responses should be overlearned until they are automatic.
3. The remedial teacher should plan the learning experience and modify the presentation of the task and material on the basis of the individual's performance, so that the child is correct in nearly all of his/her responses.
4. When two discriminations or associations are mutually interfering, the following steps should be taken consecutively:
   a. one of the discriminations or associations should be learned on an automatic level;

    b. the second should then be learned on an automatic level;

    c. the first should be briefly reviewed;

    d. the two should be integrated, starting with tasks where the only difference between the two need be perceived; and finally

    e. in graduated steps, both should be made automatic when the task requires demonstrations and associations in addition to the mutually interfering ones.

  5. There should be frequent reviews of basic perceptual associational, and blending of skills, and as rapidly as possible these reviews should involve actual reading.

It appears from the aforementioned principles that successful reading remedial instruction can be influenced by the extent to which the teacher can couple the richness of previous teaching experience with modification in skills and instructional techniques to remediate severe reading problems. Principles advocated by Bryant parallel those advanced by M. Frostig (1972). It was voiced by Frostig that certain perceptual skills need to be practiced until they become fully automated. She further stated that the more automatic the individual's perception and decoding is when he/she reads, the more fluently he/she can direct his/her attention toward the task. Reading readiness should develop precepts of form as they involve the printed letters or symbols a child will need in reading. Vertical, lateral, and oblique lines, plus circles, squares, and angles are the forms singly, or in combination, that make up letter symbols.

PERCEPTUAL REMEDIATION

When discussing perceptual handicaps, reading is one of the most important topics, since nearly all perceptual handicaps affect reading abilities. Reading involves not only language processes, but results upon incredibly rapid perceptual activity derived from sequentially presented brief exposures of complex information (Taylor, 1999). Furthermore, since reading is so dependent upon constructive processes, anything which disrupts the translation of ongoing perception will have disastrous consequences for reading skills.

Perceptual skills are improved when the individual has opportunities to explore and learn the characteristics of distance and spatial relationships. Often exceptional individuals have not mastered sizes and distances because interpretation and reorganization skills have not been perfected. The individual must learn to perfect this reorganization through repeated perceptual-motor activities of matching experiences with an object to the perception of that object at a distance. The process involves matching eye movement with feeling of the body before the size and distance of an object can be judged (Swanson, 1987).

READING RETARDATION

By far the most common area of learning difficulty experienced by children is reading. Estimates of incidence vary widely but probably more than 10 percent of the children who have average intelligence in our schools are reading so inadequately for their grade placement that their total adjustment is impaired. The earliest descriptions traced etiology to a known, specific, focal cerebral lesion. Later, numerous other etiologic correlations were cortical dominance, developmental lag, generalized neurological dysfunctions and emotional problems. In the presence of these and many more etiological possibilities, it is evident that inadequate reading, like other learning deficiencies, is a symptom rather than a discrete clinical entity in itself. Because of this, the term "reading inadequacy" is suggested to describe all cases of reading difficulties.

The term is used in reference to all individuals whose level of reading achievement is two years or more below the mental age obtained in performance tests. It appears valid to use performance rather than verbal tests as the index of mental age, because functioning on the verbal portions of such psychometric tests as the Wechsler or the Binet is significantly affected by the reading inadequacy itself, whereas the performance subtests are much less so influenced. The two-year discrepancy between mental and reading age is arbitrary, but it has the value of limiting the definitive diagnosis to cases showing significant functional reading inadequacy that inevitably affects school adjustment.

While visual, general health, and other causes occasionally operate alone to produce reading retardation, the large majority of cases fall into three major groups:

1. Capacity to learn to read is intact but is utilized insufficiently for the individual to achieve a reading level appropriate to his/her intelligence. The causative factor is exogenous, the individual having a normal reading potential that has been impaired by negativism, anxiety, depression, emotional blocking, psychosis, limited schooling opportunity, or other external influences.

2. Capacity to learn to read is impaired by brain damage manifested by clear-cut neurologic deficits. History usually reveals the cause of the brain injury—common agents being prenatal toxicity, birth trauma or anoxia, encephalitis, and head injury. These cases of brain injury are frequently associated with severe reading retardation.

3. Capacity to learn to read is impaired without definite brain damage suggested in history or on neurological examination. The defect is in the ability to deal with letters and words as symbols, with resultant diminished ability to integrate the meaningfulness of written material.

Based upon the research in reading, it may be concluded that most reading difficulties can be remediated through perceptual training. Premised upon the fact that a detailed assessment has been conducted, isolating is the source of the problem.

PERCEPTUAL TRAINING

The individual may be deficient in any one or more of his/her perceptual abilities; furthermore, the impairment may range in degree from mild to severe. The teacher must ascertain the area and the degree of involvement before initiating therapy. Many of the listed therapies can be integrated and infused with curricula strategies outlined in Chapter 11. The remaining portion of that chapter will be devoted to strategies teachers and educators can employ to conduct perceptual training in the classroom. Some suggested therapies are as follows:

1. Visual Perception
   a. Space
      Develop a left to right sequence (a prereading skill) by the following:
      (1) Arrange story pictures in a left to right sequence (may use flannel board).
      (2) Arrange blocks or squares of colored paper of varying sizes, small to large, in a left to right sequence.
      (3) Use peg and form board placing objects from left to right.
   b. Figure-Ground
      The teacher's goal is to increase the individual's tolerance for distracting backgrounds (gray colors seem to be distracting), thereby, increasing his/her awareness of the foreground. This might be accomplished in two ways: increase the "strength" of the background by first using light lines, dots, and small figures, and then heavier lines; secondly, gradually decrease the "strength" of the foreground by decreasing its size and using lighter shades of color.

PERCEPTUAL MOTOR TRAINING

1. Visual Motor
   a. Eye-Hand
      (1) Show the individual different colored geometric forms, letters, and numbers, and have him/her trace them in a sandbox, on a chalkboard, on paper, or on sandpaper cutouts. Then have him/her copy them, and then draw them without copying.
      (2) Throw rings on a stake and throw beanbags at holes in a board.
   b. Eye-Leg
   Hopping, skipping, jumping, walking a rail.

RESTRICTED PERCEPTUAL MOTOR ABILITIES

A number of individuals with impaired perceptual motor abilities have restricted approaches to activities. They can be helped by exercises designed to foster different solutions to motor problems (e.g., going across a mat in different ways, crawling, walking, hopping).

The importance of gross motor training in the development of curriculum for exceptional individuals has been well documented by research findings. Hannaford, 1995; Ayers, 1991, implied that whereas motor training is important to overall motor development, it is not sufficient in itself. Individuals with exceptionalities need the opportunity to experiment with body movements. Three categories were outlined to assist in the total development of the individual. They were: (1) movement exploration through distance activities, he/she must seek his/her own solution, (2) creative expression were the individual improvises physical movements, and (3) structured physical activities in which the individual is guided to practice certain skills and games. The importance of setting a definite time for activities were discussed as being essential to the success of movement training.

AUDITORY ACUITY

In order to rule out the possibility of deafness, one must get some idea of the individual's auditory acuity. Auditory tests for individuals may be classified as formal or informal. The formal tests include pure tone audiometry, tuning forks, and speech audiometry, all of which require active cooperation on the part of the individual. Another formal but more objective test is Electrodermal Audiometry (E.D.R.), otherwise known as Psycholgalvanometry (P.G.S.R). Informal tests do not require active cooperation and they include sound instruments, sound toys, and free field noise and voice tests.

PROGRAM FOR DEVELOPING AUDITORY DISCRIMINATION

The teacher should begin with the "Awareness Program." In this program, the child will develop an awareness of sounds in his/her environment. These sounds may include sounds in the classroom, at home, at school, in town, at the zoo, and many other places. This is done so that the child can understand what he/she hears. The teacher should develop with him/her a vocabulary for these sounds.

The child should be taught to: (1) discriminate between gross sounds, (2) develop an awareness of likenesses and differences between gross sounds, (3) differentiate between loud and soft sounds, fast and slow frequency, high and low pitch, and the location of gross sounds, (4) imitate gross sounds, and (5) use the vocabulary of sounds.

The child then may proceed to the "Auditory Memory" program. Here the child develops the ability to follow directions in sequential order. The child should be aided in developing auditory recognition, retention and recall through stories and questions (increase length of stories and difficulty of questions). This also can be done through rhymes, poems, finger plays, music, creative dramatics, etc. Creative interpretation can be done without music.

Next, the child learns to discriminate between words and sounds. Before moving to this step, the child must have some of his visual problems corrected. After this has been done, visual clues are developed to discriminate among words using objects as visual clues. Discrimination among words can be made by using pictures and figures. For example:

1. The teacher puts three concrete objects on the table in view of the child. Two are the same (e.g., two boats and one car). In a left to right progression, the teacher points to each object and names it. The teacher asks the pupil to choose which is different or the one that is named only once. The teacher varies the objects in many ways.
2. The teacher puts two different objects in full view. She points to each object naming one of them twice. She asks the child to name the one he/she has heard only once. She varies the order of the objects named.

In using no visual clues, the discrimination is developed in the sounds of words as the phonetic structure change. Other auditory exercises are as follows:

1. A game with silly questions answered by "Yes," or "No," or "Maybe."

2. Another game in which the child looks for a hidden object and is aided by being told he/she is "hot," "cold," or "warm," along with other clues. Verbal directions should be given one at a time. Stories can be told after which the child may be asked to retell parts of the story or answer questions about it.
3. The teacher could have the child to classify objects such as naming objects that belong in a house, etc.
4. Have the child state how objects are alike or different.
5. Ask the child many cause and effect questions like, "What would happen if . . . ?"
6. Have the child complete sentences generated by the teacher.
7. Sentence structure could be developed with the child. The child should be asked to speak in complete sentences.
8. Have the child repeat sentences word for word.
9. Have the child repeat a short story that has been read to him/her.
10. Have the child chant groups of words after you chant them.
11. Have the child say sounds separately before attempting to put them into words.
12. Have the child listen to taped lessons and the record player. Here, you could have the child make use of the "Language Master."
13. The teacher should stand near the child when she speaks so that the child can imitate his/her sounds as well as being able to hear him/her.

VISUAL DYSFUNCTION

The following is suggested for visual dysfunction:
1. Space Perception
   a. Have the child read a simple passage (if capable of reading).
      (1) Does he/she reverse words?
      (2) Does he/she read from the wrong coordinate (right to left?)
      (3) Is he/she a poor reader?
2. Figure-ground Disturbance
   a. Does the child misread words, numbers, letters, or detect incorrect figures when presented on a checkered or on a different colored background?
   b. Is he/she unsuccessful in manipulating simple puzzles? (If so, examiner must first rule out perceptual motor or any eye-hand coordination difficulty before deciding on figure-ground as the factor).
3. Distance Perception

  a. Have the child write a sentence.
    (1) Is his/her writing close enough to the line?
    (2) Are his/her words cramped together?
  b. Have the child color within a circle.
    (1) Does color extend within a circle?
    (2) Does color extend over the line?
  c. Have the child throw an object at another object.
    (1) Does he/she completely overshoot his/her mark?
    (2) Does he/she completely undershoot his/her mark?

The following is suggested for tactile dysfunction: Tests in this area might first include having the child feel certain objects while blindfolded or while his/her eyes are closed. He/she is then instructed to open his/her eyes and identify the object he/she felt from a group of several objects placed in front of him/her.

PROGRAM FOR DEVELOPING VISUAL DISCRIMINATION

The teacher should help the child develop an awareness of shapes before the awareness of the configuration of letters and words. The child should also be helped to develop the ability to use the words for shapes (square, circle, etc.).

The child should learn top to bottom, left to right progression. He/she should be aided in developing the concept of order in the placement of objects, and should develop the use of words such as first, last, second, next.

The child should be taught to develop an awareness of self in relation to his/her environment (body image) and be helped to identify right and left in regard to self. He/she should develop memory for position in space (location of articles in the room, route to school, or the library).

The child should be taught to discriminate among details (shades of colors, concepts of soft and hard, rough and smooth). Also, the child should learn to comprehend shapes through tactile sense. He/she should be aided in developing the ability to identify objects by feeling and in developing a suitable vocabulary of shapes using the tactile sense.

The following are a few exercises that will help the child improve in the visual areas:

  1. Visual Memory
    a. Show the child slides of movies that tell a story; have the child talk about it or retell it after it is over.
    b. Have the child look at a page of pictures and after the pictures have been removed, have him/her try to pick out the pictures like those he/she has seen.

c. Place objects in a certain order, mix them up, and have the child put them back in the original order.

d. An idea for sequencing numbers is to help the child learn his/her telephone number and the telephone number of friends and relatives. If there is a toy telephone, he/she should be allowed to dial the numbers at appropriate times.

e. Provide sequential exercises progressing from the very gross discriminations to the very fine ones.

f. Place three pictures in front of the child. Have the child hide his/her eyes. Remove one picture. Ask: "Which one is missing?" Show the child three letters. Take them all away. Have the child write the letters he/she saw.

2. Visual Reception

   a. Have the child identify objects in picture dictionaries, catalogs, or magazines.

   b. Have the child identify colors, letters, numbers, and geometric forms.

   c. Have the child identify the meaningful content of an action picture.

   d. Have the child tell stories of pictures.

3. Visual Association

   a. Have the child group pictures by class (birds, animals, etc.).

   b. Have the child find the picture that is not like the others in a group, and have him/her tell how the other pictures have something in common (i.e., truck, car, bike, house).

   c. Give the child pictures, each of which tells a part of a story, and have him/her place them in sequential order.

4. Visual Closure

   a. Have the child name shapes of shadows, ink blots, or cloud formations.

   b. Have the child find partially hidden objects in a picture.

   c. Have the child complete a picture by looking at a finished model.

   d. Have the child connect dots or numbers to make some shape or picture and name it before it is finished.

5. Verbal Expression

   a. Have the child describe an object and tell a story about it.

   b. Show the child pictures of home life, children playing in the street, etc., and have him/her talk about it.

   c. Have the child explain how to do some task or play some game.

SUMMARY

Before anyone can professionally treat an individual's needs, he/she must be aware of what the needs are. This can only be accomplished after a correct diagnosis has been obtained. Even then, however, an individual cannot be helped to achieve his/her potential until stumbling blocks which might impede his/her progress are removed. Behavior problems must first be obviated if learning is to take place. The individual cannot retain stimuli if he/she cannot attend to the stimuli for a sufficient length of time. Similarly, the hard-of-hearing individual must be provided with improved channels (and/or new channels should be developed) through which he/she can learn.

No rigid rehabilitation program can be devised for any group of exceptional individuals; rather, each individual must have an individual program that is geared to his/her individual needs, as outlined throughout this text. Not every individual will need all of the perceptual training discussed in this chapter. However, many exceptional individuals exhibit different kinds of minimal problems which often go undiagnosed or untreated. The teacher and the principal should know the individual's abilities and his/her limitations before a program of treatment is started.

The individual needs of several hours each week of specialized remedial instructions in very small groups with teachers who are competent in both diagnosing and presenting alternate instructional techniques. Alternate instructional strategies are covered in Chapters 5, 7, and 8.

REFERENCES

Abrams, R. A. (1994). The forces that move the eyes. *Current Directions in Psychological Services, 3*, 65-67.

Alexander, P. A., Kulikowich, J. M., & Schulze, S. L. (1994). How subject-matter knowledge affects recall and interest. *American Educational Research Journal, 31*, 312-337.

Ausubel, D. P., Novak, J. D., & Hanesian, H. (1978). *Education psychology: A cognitive view* (2nd ed.). New York: Holt, Rinehart, and Winston.

Ayers, J. (1991). *Sensory integration and learning disorders*. Los Angeles: Western Psychological Services.

Begley, S. (1996, February 19). Your child's brain. *Newsweek*, 55-62.

Bender, W. N. (1995). *Learning disabilities: Characteristics, identification, and teaching strategies* (2nd ed.). Boston: Allyn and Bacon.

Billingsley, B. S., & Ferro-Almeida, S. C. (1993). Strategies to facilitate reading comprehension in students with learning disabilities. *Reading and Writing Quarterly Overcoming Learning Difficulties, 9* (3), 263-273.

Brink, S. (1995, May 15). Smart moves. *U.S. News and World Report*.

Bruce, V., & Green, P. (1990). *Visual perception*. East Sussex, UK: Lawrence Erlbaum and Associates.

Bryan, D. (1965). Some principles of remedial instruction for dyslexia. *The Reading Teacher, 18,* 562-572.

Calvin, W. (1996). *How brains think.* New York: Basic Books.

Cruickshank, W., Bentzon, F., Rotsburg, F., & Tannhauser, M. (1961). *A teaching methodology for brain-injured and hyperactive children.* New York: Syracuse University Press.

Curtis, S., & Tallal, P. (1991). On the nature of impairment in language in children. In J. Miller (Ed.), *New directions in research on language disorder.* Boston: College-Hill Press.

Dole, J. A., Duffy, G. G., Rochler, L. R., & Pearson, P. D. (1991). Moving from the old to the new: Research on reading comprehension instruction. *Review of Educational Research, 61,* 239-264.

Englert, C. A., & Palinscar, A. S. (1988). The reading process. In D. K. Reid (Ed.), *Teaching the learning disabled: A cognitive developmental approach.* Boston: Allyn and Bacon.

Freeman, W. (1995). *Societies of brains.* Hillsdale, NJ: Lawrence Erlbaum and Associates.

Frostig, M., & Horne, D. (1964). *The Frostig program for the development of visual perception.* Chicago: Follett.

Frostig, M. (1972). Visual perception integrative functions and academic learning. *Journal of Learning Disabilities, 6.*

Gilbert, A. C. (1997). *Teaching the three R's through movement experiences.* New York: MacMillan Publishing.

Greenberg, D. (1991). Learning without coercion: Sudbury Valley School. *Mothering,* 102-105.

Hall, W. S. (1989). Reading comprehension. *American Psychologist, 44,* 157-161.

Hannaford, C. (1995). *Smart moves.* Arlington, VA: Greet Ocean Publishing Company.

Hardman, M. L., Drew, C. J., & Egan, W. M. (1996). *Human exceptionality: Society, school, and family* (5th ed.). Boston: Allyn and Bacon.

Irwin, D. E. (1996). Integrating information across saccharic eye movements. *Current Directions in Psychological Services, 5,* 94-100.

Kepart, N. (1960). *The slow learners in the classroom.* Ohio: Charles C. Merrill Books, Inc.

Kepart, J., Kepart, C., & Schwartz, G. (1974). A journey into the world of the blind child. *Exceptional Children, 40,* 421-429.

Koutulak, R. (1996). *Inside the brain.* Kansas City, MO: Andrews and McMell.

Lyon, G. (1994). *Frames of reference for the assessment of learning disabilities.* Baltimore: Paul H. Brookes.

Mann, V. A., & Liberman, A. M. (1984). Phonological awareness and verbal short-term memory. *Journal of Learning Disabilities, 17,* 592-599.

Neisser, U. (1967). *Cognitive psychology.* New York: Appleton-Century Crofts.

Novak, J. D., & Musonda, D. (1991). A twelve-year longitudinal study of science concept learning. *American Educational Research Journal, 28,* 117-153.

Ornstein, R. E. (1972). *The psychology of consciousness.* San Francisco: W. H. Freeman.

Palmer, L. (1980). Auditory discrimination through vestibulo-cochler stimulation. *Academic Therapy, 16* (1), 55-70.

Reid, D. K. (1988). Learning disabilities and the cognitive developmental approach. In D. K. Reid (Ed.), *Teaching the learning disabled: A cognitive developmental approach.* Boston: Allyn and Bacon.

Rouet, J. F., Favart, M., Britt, M. A., & Perfetti, C. A. (1997). Studying and using multiple documents in history: Effects of discipline expertise. *Cognition and Instruction, 15,* 85-106.

Schneider, W. (1993). Domain-specific knowledge and memory performance in children. *Educational Psychology Review, 5,* 252-273.

Smith, C. R. (1994). *Learning disabilities: The interaction of learners, task, and setting* (3rd ed.). Boston: Allyn and Bacon.

Swanson, L. (1987). Verbal decoding effects on visual short-term memory of learning disabled and normal readers. *Journal of Educational Psychology, 70,* 539-544.

Tallal, P., Miller, S., & Fitch, R. (1993). Neurological bases of speech: A case for preeminence of temporal processing. *Annals of New York Academy of Success, 682,* 27-47.

Taylor, G. R. (1999). *Curriculum models and strategies for educating individuals with disabilities in inclusive classrooms.* Springfield, IL: Charles C Thomas.

Torgesen, J. (1988). Problems in the study of learning disabilities. In M. Hetherington and J. Hagen (Eds.). *Review of Research in Child Development, 5,* 162-184.

Chapter 10

ASSESSING CHILDREN WITH EXCEPTIONALITIES

GEORGE R. TAYLOR, FRANCES HARRINGTON, AND THADDAUS PHILLIPS

INTRODUCTION

ASSESSMENT IS A PROCESS of collecting relevant information on individuals in order to make valid decisions about them in areas of learning and human functioning. It is a multifaceted process, which involves more than the use of standardized or informal tests. The process included assessing individuals in a variety of mental, physical, and social tasks. (See Appendix L for additional details.) This text is designed to address the use of tests to make sound educational decisions which may be used by individualized education teams to make valid instructional decisions (Taylor, 1997; Salvia & Ysseldyke, 1998; Witt, Elliott, Daley & Kramer, 1998).

Assessing, identifying, and placing children in the least restrictive environment require the use of non-discriminatory and multidisciplinary assessment in developing the IEP (Taylor, 1998; Thurlow, Elliott, Ysseldyke, 1998). Once educational need is established through formal and informal testing, the student is referred to a multidisciplinary team. Based upon the type of data assessed by the team, the student's disability is defined and classified.

MULTIDISCIPLINARY TEAM MEMBERSHIP

The team must include a "teacher or other specialist with knowledge in the areas of suspected disability" (34 CFR 300.533). In practice, diagnosticians and parents are usually members of Multidisciplinary Teams.

Responsibilities of the Multidisciplinary Team

Salvia and Ysseldyke (1998) wrote that the team is responsible for gathering information and making a recommendation about a student's exceptionality. In theory, the decision-making process is straight forward. The MDT assesses the student's performance to see whether it meets the criteria for a specific exceptionality. It must collect information required by the definition of exceptionality. Federal regulations (34 CFR 300.533) also require the team to do the following:

1. Draw on information from a variety of sources, including aptitude and achievement tests, teacher's recommendations, physical conditions, social or cultural background, and adaptive behavior.
2. Ensure that information obtained from all of these sources is documented and carefully considered.

Team members should be competent in the areas, which they assessed. They should be certified or licensed in their respected disciplines. The focus of assessment is to determine the nature and type of exceptionality, type of placement, how well the student is meeting the stated goals and objectives, and related services needed.

MAJOR TYPES OF ASSESSMENT DEVICES AND STRATEGIES

Several types of assessment devices and strategies are used to make decisions relevant to student's abilities and disabilities. They are too numerous to be listed in this chapter. The reader seeking additional information is referred to any basic book on "Assessment." The purpose of this chapter is to overview the educational use of assessment information; for evaluating children with exceptionalities; such as observation, portfolio assessment, self-assessment, and various types of tests employed to assess human behavior (McLoughlin & Lewis, 1991; Browder, 1991).

OBSERVATIONS

Observation is a prime assessment strategy. It should be an essential part of assessment. There should be some predetermined system or structure to guide the observational process of utmost importance, educators must define the behavior to be observed as well as the place, time, and duration of the behavior to be observed. Once the educator has selected the types of behavior to be observed, it will be necessary to develop or use some type of recording instrument to record the observations as projected in Figure 6.

Educators may use check marks to observe the occurrence of the behaviors or simply write *yes* or *no* to each behavior as shown in Figure 6. These observational data may be used to determine strengths and weaknesses in various areas and indicate areas where intervention will be needed. As indicated, students may be observed in different settings. The teacher should choose those settings and times when the behaviors are most likely to occur. Certain types of behaviors may manifest themselves at certain times in the day. Several types of recording systems may be used such as event, duration, and interval recording (Pike & Salend, 1995).

ANECDOTAL RECORDS

Anecdotal records provide a written account of the child's behavior. Data from rating scales and checklists may be used to validate narrative statements in anecdotal records. Educators should exercise caution in recording events in separating facts from their interpretations of behaviors. Another caution is that to validity, data should be kept over a period of time to note trends.

Educators' biases known or unknown tend to influence the information contained in anecdotal records. There is both observer bias and observed bias. Observer bias may be evident from the observer recording invalid behaviors because of some like or dislike of a special characteristic of the observed. Observed bias may result from the fact that the observed may behave differently simply because he/she knows that they are being observed.

There are many valuable use of anecdotal records. To be useful in the instructional program, they should be systematically updated and kept over a period of time and used to strengthen the instructional program by programming the student's strengths and weaknesses into the curriculum (Rhodes & Nathenson-Mejia, 1992). The issue of collecting and organizing information in anecdotal records must be carefully considered by the teacher. Some type of systematic plan should be evident according to Pike, Compain, and Mumper (1994). A three-ring binder that is sectioned off alphabetically by students' last names, a separate notebook on each content area, or a card file system may be employed.

FIGURE 6

DEVELOPMENTAL PROFILE

Student Name: _____
Address: _____

System: _____

Sex: __ M __ F   City   State   Zip Code

Birth Date: __/__/__ Mo. Day Year

Developmental Learning Outcomes

Race/Ethnicity

__ African American   __ White (not Hispanic origin)
__ Hispanic   __ American Indian/Alaskan Native
__ Asian/Pacific Islander   __ Other

Prepared by: _____
School: _____ Local School

Date of Analysis: __/__/__ Mo. Day Year

	Communication Language	Living Skills	Social Emotional	Recreation Physical	Cognitive Vocational
42	talks on phone for purpose	cares for small injuries	follows game rules	gets around immediate neighborhood	knows city, rural, suburb
41	talks with family	cleans up after snack	readies self for school	coord to draw, cut, pants	identifies landmarks
40	talks about real events	concept of saving	aware of others' feelings	coord for riding, jumping	knows facts of simple story
39	dials phone with no help	reads a traffic light	readies self for bed	coord for some kitchen tasks	knows city lives to
38	reads 5 words	does household task	confides in a friend	cuts pictures by self	picks out 10 of 10 objects
37	knows service people	ties shoes by self	plays no supervision	uses opener with no help	gives own street and number
36	tells cause and effect	brushes, combs hair	tells feelings	handles hot and sharp things	knows meaning of 10 words
35	ask meaning abstract	dresses self with no help	plays in small group	plays jump rope	reads 2 words
34	prints name	has bladder control at night	cares for property	rakes, mops, carries broom	sounds out letters
33	takes easy phone messages	prepares simple food by self	prefers same sex friends	plays hopping games	drawn a triangle
32	states birthday	puts things away neatly	comforts playmate	throws ball 8 ft. in direction	draws stick person
31	knows sequence of story	uses a knife	does simple errands	dances rhythm to music	rhymes simple words
30	gives correct address	plays outside by self	gives appropriate apology	skips	counts by 2's
29	has understandable speech	brushes teeth with no help	knows boys and girls	uses a pencil	draws a square
28	names penny, nickel, dime	washes self adequately	displays concern	somersaults without help	attempts pouring
27	counts serially to 10	helps prepare dry cereal	initiates adult roles	catches ball from 5 feet	names 2 persons
26	tells age, knows past/present	keeps nose clean by self	uses cultural courtesy	balances on one foot	drawn person's head
25	likes stories	dresses self completely	asks permission	climbs objects with no help	can draw a+
24	tells use of things	buttons clothes	uses pretend play	jumps off bottom step	ask why
23	repeats rhymes or songs	cleans face and hands	30 min cooperative play	somersaults with help	tells about day and night
22	uses regular plurals	brushes teeth	occupies self on own	opens doors by self	knows when lunch is

FIGURE 6 (CONTINUED)

DEVELOPMENTAL PROFILE

	Communication Language	Living Skills	Social Emotional	Recreation Physical	Cognitive Vocational
21	gives whole name	toilets without help	performs for attention	swings, slides, hike	knows concept of five
20	tells story with pictures	dresses and undress	affection to youngsters	runs for 10 feet	knows times of day
19	listens to story 5 minutes	wipes nose when reminded	enjoys helping around the house	throws objects in direction	can draw a -
18	tells correct sex	uses utensils with no spills	takes turns when reminded	uses alternative feet on steps	points 3 colors
17	holds up fingers for age	undoes button and laces	shares feelings	jumps for 10 feet	gives your 4 of something
16	uses simple sentences	undress except for fasteners	parallel plays	turns one page at a time	makes basic circle picture
15	ask "what's this?"	goes to bathroom by self	initiates play activities	uses chair	says big and little
14	recognizes objects and uses	walks independently of you	greets people with verbal clue	stopped drooling food	draws lined up and down
13	recognizes songs	avoids danger	accepts mother's absence	imitates marks on paper	groups objects by shape, etc.
12	makes two word sentences	knows food and non-food	imitates adult behavior	unwraps candy without help	points to 15 names objects
11	names 5 foods	removes coat without help	jealous of others	walks stairs with help	takes extra step if asked
10	names 2 family members	gets around home by self	interested in others	stoops and pick up things	recognized self in photo
9	uses gestures meaningfully	drinks from glass	interested in other's toys	gets out of chair not falling	points to one body part
8	says own name	begins undressing	wants to help in simple tasks	turns small knobs	marks on surface
7	labels objects	eats with a spoon	responds to adult commands	walk without falling	explores environment
6	meaningful one word use	helps with own dressing	knows own possessions	sit to stand with aid of object	
5	responds to "no"	has stopped drooling	socially some interactions	uses pincer grasp	
4	uses gestures	finger feeds self	initiates some interactions	crawls with arms and legs	
3	responds to name	eats mashed table food	willing to interact	explores objects	
2	responds to sound	holds own bottle	responds to facial expressions	rolls over without aid	
1	vocalizes and babbles	grasps objects for few seconds	wants attention	sucks and swallows liquids	

Source: Maryland Department of Education

SELF-ASSESSMENT

Self-assessment can yield valuable information to assist the teacher in understanding how the child feels towards educational issues. Self-assessment data may come from a variety of sources, such as interviews, journals, log questionnaires checklists, and rating scales. Construction of instruments used in self-assessment must consider the development level of the child in all of the principle areas such as mental, social, and physical. In the case of exceptional children, the type of exceptionality must be carefully considered. In some instances, the teacher will have to assist the child in completing his/her self-assessment (Davison & Pearce, 1992).

PORTFOLIO ASSESSMENT

The values of using portfolios in assessing the strengths and weaknesses of children with exceptionalities have been well documented in the professional literature (Pike & Salender, 1995; Salinger, 1991; Wolf, 1989). Effective portfolio assessment requires a cooperative effort on part of teachers, children, and sometimes parents. The assessment should reflect the learning as well as the products of learning. Scoring rubrics should be developed by teachers with input from students. Students should be instructed on how to use the scoring rubrics. Objective information should be reviewed periodically by teachers, children, and parents to update, delete, document, or expand information items selected for inclusion. Items should be directly related to objectives specified in the student's instructional program. Items should also be related to the IEP strategies developed. Several authors cited above advocated that captions should be developed to: (1) identify the document, (2) show a description of the content, (3) explain why items were included, and (4) summarize and synthesize information.

TYPES OF RECORDINGS

Several types of recordings are necessary to record information from assessment instruments and devices. Event recording involves recording specific behavior which occur. Duration recording is done on a continuous basis, all behavior are recorded. Interval recording is reserved for specific times to record behaviors. Teachers should select the types of recording they deem best for recording behaviors of children. In general, short observations conducted over a period of time are frequently the best method to employ. This approach appears to provide a better sample of the child's behavior. Teachers and educators should rotate the time of observations to reduce getting biased behavior patterns.

MAJOR TYPES OF ASSESSMENT TESTS

Assessment tests and instruments have been developed to assess and evaluate all aspects of human behavior. Some are paper and pencil tests, others are tests administered by specialists, some are norm-referenced, and others are criterion-referenced. Norm and criterion-referenced tests are chiefly used by educators. These tests are based upon norms of a particular age group. Criterion-referenced tests are based on the curriculum or objectives of a school district.

NORM-REFERENCED TESTS

These tests are based upon the average performance of a typical age group using standardized procedures. Items in the tests are designed to provide a sample of curriculum content that students should have had in a certain age group or subject area. An example would be that a fifth grade student should have been taught multiplication; test items are constructed to measure this skill. Students who score at or above the established score are considered to be on grade level; those who score below the established score are considered being below grade level. In essence, NRT's scores show how students' scores compare with each other within school districts and across the country. NRT scores typically do not fall below the established norm or school (Salvia & Ysseldyke, 1998; Epstein, Bursuck, Polloway, Cumbland, & Jayanthi, 1993).

Types of interpretive scores given on norm tables are grade equivalent, intelligence quotients, mental ages, percentile ranks, and stanines. Sometimes raw scores are converted to standard scores or converted weighted scores. Standardized or norm-referenced scores are the most objective instruments available for measuring factual recognition, certain skills, concepts, understanding, problem solving, and sometimes personality traits such as interests and attitudes.

Standardized or norm-referenced tests should reflect the following characteristics:

1. They should be available in at least two equivalent forms. It is best to

use a different form when pre- and posttesting pupils.

2. They should have acceptable face validity, the tests should look valid.

3. They should use symbols and pictures, which are familiar to pupils from various cultures.

4. They should reflect descriptive normative data on pupils selected for the normative groups. Educators can match and compare characteristics of the normative group with their pupils before selecting tests.

5. They should have tables reflecting appropriate standard scores to which the raw scores are transposed. Educators may use these tables to convert raw scores to standard scores.

CRITERION-REFERENCE TESTS

Unlike norm-referenced tests, criterion-referenced tests may be locally normed. They provide information on how well students are performing based upon school districts' goals and objectives in various subject areas. They are designed to compare an individual's performance to some criterion or behavior. Test items are constructed to measure the attainment of the stated objectives. Students not performing up to the criterion will probably have difficulty mastering the next instructional sequence. These test items may be constructed in several basic domains from the curriculum. Strategies employed in constructing criterion-referenced tests are beyond the scope of this chapter.[2]

These tests are commonly used to determine how well students have mastered the domains outlined in the curriculum (Witt, Elliott, Daly, Gresham & Kramer, 1998). Several states have begun to employ criterion-referenced testing. These are designed more for individualized instruction then norm-referenced tests. Specific standards have been set for mastery of the curriculum domains. Students not meeting the standard or criterion are judged as working below grade level. The State of Maryland is one state which has adapted criterion-referenced testing statewide. Criterion tests, as with most assessment devices, have some accommodations that will have to be made when assessing children with exceptionalities due to the nature and extent of their exceptionalities. Some of the commonly used norm and criterion-referenced tests and their usage are reflected in Figure 7.

The tests listed in Figure 7 reflect the basic academic areas covered, the grades in which they should be administered, the time needed to administer them, and the type of response made. Many of these tests will have to be

---

[2] For a comprehensive view of constructing and interpreting criterion-referenced test, refer to Wiersma, William, Jurs, & Stephen. (1990). *Educational Measurement and Testing*. MA: Allyn and Bacon.

FIGURE 7

COMMONLY USED NORM AND CRITERION-REFERENCED TEST

Name of Test	Reading	Mathematics	Spelling	Handwriting	Written Language	Perceptual	PreK-2	3-5	6-8	9-12	Individual	Group	Time	Norm	Criterion	Verbal	Performance	Written	Comments
Analytical Reading Inventory	X						X	X	X	X	X		20-40		X	X			
Ayres Speed Copying Scale				X			X	X	X	X	X			X				X	
Basic School Skills Inventory-Diagnostic	X	X		X			X						20-40	X		X	X	X	
Berry Buktenica Developmental Test of Visual-Motor Integration						X	X	X	X	X		X	10-15	X				X	
Brigance Diagnostic Inventories	X	X	X	X	X	X	X	X	X	X		X	15-90		X	X	X	X	
Cognitive Skills Assessment Battery						X	X				X		20-30		X	X	X	X	
Cognitive Skills Assessment Battery						X					X		20-30		X	X	X	X	
Denver Handwriting Analysis				X				X	X	X	X	X	20-60		X	X		X	
Diagnostic Achievement Battery	X	X	X	X			X	X	X	X	X		30-60	X		X		X	
Diagnostic Reading Scales	X						X	X	X		X		40-50		X	X			
Early Learning Accomplishment Profile						X	X	X			X		Varies	X		X	X		
Ekwall Reading Inventory	X						X	X			X		20-40		X	X			
Kaufman Test of Educational Achievement	X	X	X				X	X	X				30-60	X		X		X	

FIGURE 7 (Continued)

**COMMONLY USED NORM AND
CRITERION-REFERENCED TEST**

Name of Test	Reading	Mathematics	Spelling	Handwriting	Written Language	Perceptua	PreK-2	3-5	6-8	9-12	Individual	Group	Time	Norm	Criterion	Verbal	Performance	Written	Comments
Key Math Diagnostic Arithmetic Test-Revised	x						x	x	x	x	x		30	x		x	x		gross & fine motor cognition self-help, language
Kattmeyer Diagnostic Spelling Test			x					x	x		x	x	10-15		x			x	
Kraner Preschool Math Inventory		x					x				x	x	20-30	x		x	x		
Learning Accomplishment Profile (#LAP-D)						x	x				x		Varies	x		x	x		gross & fine motor, cognition, self-help, language
Mann-Suiter Visual Discrimination & Memory							x	x	x	x	x	x			x	x			
Morrison-McCall Spelling Test			x					x	x	x	x	x							
Motor Free Visual Perception Test						x	x	x	x	x	x		10-15	x		x			
Myklebust Picture Story Language Test					x			x	x	x	x		10-15			x			
Peabody Individual Achievement Test-Revised	x	x	x				x	x	x	x	x		20-30	x		x		x	
Stanford Diagnostice Reading Test	x							x	x	x	x	x	30-40	x					
Sucher-Allred Reading Placement Test	x						x	x	x		x	x	90-150	x	x	x			
													20-45		x	x			

**FIGURE 7 (Continued)
COMMONLY USED NORM AND
CRITERION-REFERENCED TEST**

Name of Test	Academic Area						Administration							Reference		Response Mode			Comments
	Reading	Mathematics	Spelling	Handwriting	Written Language	Perceptual	PreK-2	3-5	6-8	9-12	Individual	Group	Time	Norm	Criterion	Verbal	Performance	Written	
Test of Early Learning Skills	X	X					X			X			30-40	X		X			
Test of Early Math Skills	X	X					X				X		20-30	X		X			
Test of Reading Comprehension	X						X				X		15-20	X					
Test of Written English					X		X			X	X		30-50	X				X	
Test of Written Language					X			X	X	X		X	30-45	X				X	
Test of Written Spelling				X		X	X				X		20-30	X				X	
Wepman Auditory Tests						X	X	X			X		10-20	X		X			discrimination memory
Wide Range Achievement Test	X	X	X				X	X	X	X	X		20-30	X		X	X	X	
Woodcock-Johnson Psychoeducational Battery-Revised	X	X	X		X		X	X	X	X	X		90-120	X		X		X	
Woodcock Reading Mastery Test	X						X	X	X	X			30-45	X		X			

modified and adaptive for use with many children with exceptionalities. Suggestions for modifying and adapting tests are discussed under assessment accommodations later in the chapter.

TEACHER-MADE AND INFORMAL TESTS

Teacher-made and informal tests may be used to supplement or compare results from standardized tests. They also may be employed where standardized tests are not adequate for reasons of content, difficulty, scope, or sensitive cultural materials. Teacher-made tests are based on objectives of the course. One of the first things a teacher should consider in constructing a test is the type of test format to be employed. There are several types of testing formats: (1) True-False, (2) Multiple-Choice, (3) Matching, (4) Completion, and (5) Essay. The type of format chosen will greatly depend upon the disabling conditions of the children being tested. An example, an essay type may not be suited for a child with cerebral palsy. Several adaptations and modifications may need to be made in the testing command and response.

A variety of teacher made and informal assessment devices and techniques are at the espousal of the classroom teacher such as observations, questionnaires, interviews, and inventories. Informal assessment provide information relevant to the students' current level of performance, and assist in pinpointing goals, objectives, and needed adaptation and modification in the instructional program. Student performance is compared to specific learning tests or objectives within the curricula. These techniques permit the direct assessment of student behavior which may be compared with norm-referenced test data. They may be adapted for use with children who have exceptionalities.

QUESTIONNAIRES

Questionnaires may be developed to fit different formats such as surveys, checklists, rating scales, multiple-choice, matching, completion, and true/false items. Questionnaires are designed to collect specific information from students. Little training is needed in constructing questionnaires. The only requirement is knowledge of the content being solicited. They are easily administered and scored.

INTERVIEWS

For many children with exceptionalities, alternate means must be evident for collecting information rather than questionnaires. Their disabilities frequently prohibit them from responding to questionnaires appropriately. Interviews may be substituted to elicit information. The teacher may control the length, time, and provide directions during the interviewing process. Frequently, teachers need detailed information that students can provide. Parents and other professionals must be interviewed to secure the necessary information. The validity of information secured from interviews greatly depends upon the accuracy of the information provided by the interviewer. Teachers must be aware and proceed with caution when interpreting information.

INVENTORIES AND SUBJECT MATTER TESTS

Inventories and subject matter tests may be used to assess a variety of skills in curricula areas for children with exceptionalities. They provide information on children's present levels of functioning with the curriculum. Inventories may be developed by the teacher or purchased commercially for many subject areas. In designing inventories and subject matters tests teachers should be knowledgeable about:
1. The curriculum area being assessed.
2. Developmentally appropriate skills.
3. Breaking tasks or skills into small manageable parts.
4. Preparing test items for each subtest of the curriculum being assessed.
5. Adapting and modifying the number of test items based upon the exceptionalities of the children.
6. Sequences the test items from easiest to degree of difficulty.

OTHER FACTORS TO BE CONSIDERED

WRITING SPECIFICATIONS FOR THE TEST. The purpose of the test must be clearly articulated and specifications for the test developed. Steps include arranging items in order of difficulty, preparing directions for administering the test, setting the time limit, conducting an item analysis, constructing a scoring system, and establishing reliability and validity of the test.

ASSESSMENT ACCOMMODATIONS

New regulations of the Individuals with Disabilities Education Act (IDEA) mandates that students with exceptionalities are to be included in general state and district-wide assessment programs with accommodations if needed. An assessment accommodation is an alteration in the way a test is given. It is designed to permit students with exceptionalities to show what they know without the impediment of the exceptionality (Elliott, Ysseldyke, Thurlow, & Erickson, 1998). In essence, accommodations make the playing field equal for students with exceptionalities. The legal ramifications of testing have been detailed in Chapter 2.

Most NRTs are normed on children without exceptionalities and will not permit modifications or adaptations to accommodate children with exceptionalities. Without accommodations in NRTs, children with exceptionalities most likely will score lower on the test if accommodations are not provided. The new IDEA makes it abundantly clear that school districts must describe in the IEP what accommodations will or will not be used. Thurlow, Elliott, and Ysseldyke (1998) have developed a checklist for teachers, educators, and the IEP team to employ in making decisions to determine what accommodations are valid in altering the testing format in norm-referenced tests. Accommodations may take many forms such as; (1) extending time, (2) reduced stimulus response, and (3) the use of assistive devices. Alternative assessment is another technique that educators can employ in adapting and modifying assessment devices. (See Appendix M for suggested assessment modifications.)

ALTERNATIVE ASSESSMENT

Elliott, Ysseldyke, Thurlow, and Erickson (1998) stated that alternative assessment is a substitute way of gathering meaningful information on students' learning for those who are unable to take, even with accommodations, the regular assessment. Many children with exceptionalities in the cognitive, social, and physical domains are enrolled in different courses of studies, because their exceptionalities will not permit them to complete the regular curriculum. Typically, these students are working on life skill curricula, which are designed to prepare them for supported or competitive employment, sheltered workshops, group homes, or supervised independent living situations.

Alternative assessment may involve using several formats. Portfolio assessment is commonly used in conducting alternative assessment. As indicated earlier in the chapter, portfolio assessments may include summaries and examples of all of the students learning, which is checked by the teacher and updated frequently. Other informal types of assessment instruments such as rating scales, checklists, questionnaires, surveys, interviews, and self-report inventories name but a few strategies to implement alternative assessment strategies (Witt, Elliott, Daly, Gresham & Kramer, 1998).

SUMMARY

There are many uses that educators can make of assessment data; however, the major purpose is to document strengths and weaknesses of children in the basic domains. For the purpose of this text, assessment data supply the necessary information needed to make decisions about children with exceptionalities relevant to: (1) strengths and weaknesses in areas of human fund extending, (2) categorize areas of exceptionalities, (3) identified appropriate instructional and related services needed, (4) formulating the IEP, and (5) making appropriate placement decisions.

Various specialists, depending upon the disabling conditions of exceptional individuals, are needed to assess them. These specialists must also assist in providing education and other strategies to minimize or reduce the affects of the disabling conditions. They should also make recommendations relevant to the type and extent of related services needed. Finally, specialists should be available to interpret and assist the schools by examining technical data in their reports.

Due to the many disabling conditions of children with exceptionalities, accommodations and modifications are frequently needed in the testing format and responses. Without these modifications, many children will not be successful. Federal laws permit this modification. School districts must report in IEPs what, if any, modifications have been made.

REFERENCES

Browder, D. M. (1991). *Assessment of individuals with severe disabilities: An applied behavior approach to life skills assessment* (2nd ed.). Baltimore: Brookes.

Davison, D. M., & Pearce, D. L. (1992). The influence of writing activities on the mathematics learning on Native American students. *The Journal of Educational Issues of Language Minority Students, 10,* 147-157.

Elliott, J., Ysseldyke, J., Thurlow, M., & Erickson, R. (1998). What about assessment and accountability? Practical implications for educators. *Teaching Exceptional Children, 31* (1), 20-27.

Epstein, M. H., Bursuck, W. D., Polloway, E. A., Cumbland, C., & Jayanthi, M. (1993). Homework, grading, and testing. National Surveys of School District Policies. *OSERS News (in print), 5, 4,* 15-21.

McLoughlin, J., & Lewis, R. (1991). *Assessing special students: Strategies and procedures* (3rd ed.). Columbus, OH: Charles E. Merrill.

Pike, K., & Salend, S. (1995). An authentic assessment strategy. *Teaching Exceptional Children, 28* (1), 15-19.

Rhodes, L. K., & Nathenson-Mejia, S. (1992). Anecdotal records: A powerful tool for on-going literacy assessment. *The Reading Teacher, 45* (7), 502-509.

Salinger, T. (1991). *Getting started with alternative assessment methods.* Workshop presented at the New York State Reading Association Conference, Lake Kiamesha, New York.

Salvia, J., & Ysseldyke, J. E. (1998). *Assessment.* Boston: Houghton-Mifflin.

Taylor, G. R. (1997). *Curriculum strategies: Social skills intervention for your African-American males.* Westport, CN: Praeger Press.

Taylor, G. R. (1998). *Curriculum strategies for teaching social skills to the disabled.* Springfield, IL: Charles C Thomas.

Thurlow, M. L., Elliott, J. L., & Ysseldyke, J. E. (1998). *Testing students with disabilities: Practical strategies for complying with district and state requirements.* Thousand Oaks, CA: Corwin Press.

Wiersma, W., & Jurs, S. (1990). *Educational measurement and testing.* Boston: Allyn and Bacon.

Witt, J. C., Elliott, S. N., Daly III, E. J., Gresham, F. M., & Kramer, J. J. (1998). *Assessment of at-risk and special needs children.* Boston: McGraw-Hill.

Wolf, D. P. (1989). Portfolio assessment: Sampling student work. *Educational Leadership, 46* (7), 35-39.

Chapter 11

CURRICULUM DEVELOPMENT: STRATEGIES AND IMPLEMENTATION

GEORGE R. TAYLOR AND LORETTA MACKENNEY

INTRODUCTION

A CURRICULUM SHOULD REFLECT all of the experiences afforded a child; its contents must be broad enough in scope to prepare a student to meet their present as well as future needs. In order to achieve these goals, Dever and Knapczyk (1997) advocate the following eight principles of curriculum development:

1. A curriculum should have social validity; refers to how well the curriculum addresses the social skills needed by learners to function successfully in society.
2. A curriculum should focus on integration; refers to how well all of the major components in a curriculum addresses the various developmental stages of the learners.
3. A curriculum should contain all required skills, as reflected in the goals and objectives as well as those skills required to function successfully in the school and the community.
4. A curriculum should reflect the demands of both current and future environments, indicates that curricula should address skills needed for learners to react successfully in a variety of settings at different developmental stages.
5. A curriculum should have objectives and pathways broad enough to respond to the needs of all learners in the program; curriculum experiences should be based on realistic goals and objectives. These goals and objectives should be formulated on the basis of the needs, capacities, and interests of disabled learners as they interact with their environment. Diverse learning styles and other characteristics should be taken into consideration and curriculum experiences modified and adapted to the unique needs of each exceptional learner.
6. A curriculum should serve as a referent for monitoring instructional assessment data which enables educators to order and sequence tasks as

189

well as changing tasks when objectives are not being met.

7. A curriculum should be seen as a local responsibility and define the purpose of the instructional program, curricula must be a local responsibility since local school districts are in the best place to assess the needs of children with exceptionalities in their school districts. Additionally, local school districts can readily identify and coordinate the instructional program.

8. A curriculum should promote coordination, collaboration, and continuity across instructional programs; due to the complex problems faced by exceptional learners in most areas of human functioning, services must be well coordinated.

CHARACTERISTICS OF CURRICULA

Curricula are written to assist exceptional learners to achieve broad goals as deemed important by society. Depending upon the type of exceptionality, these broad curricula are written for groups of exceptional learners who have common needs and traits or characteristics. Individualization of instruction is an attempt to adapt the broadly defined curricula to the unique needs and learning styles of the exceptional in inclusive classrooms and other community settings. Characteristics of curricula differ based upon the abilities and disabilities, subject content, location of the facility, and the educational environment where the instruction of the exceptional will be conducted.

According to Bigge (1988) and Shujaa (1995), the curriculum consist of all experiences offered the child in his/her logical environment and is based upon the development of the child and the culture of the society in which he/she lives. Cultural values significantly influence the nature and type of curriculum experiences reflected. In the case of many individuals with exceptionalities, curriculum experiences and development must reflect the immediate and long range goals for the child correlated with his/her developmental sequence and functional levels. Thus, scope, objective, and sequence are essential factors in planning curriculum (Tanner & Tanner, 1995).

Curriculum development is designed to reflect the course of study in schools. It is intended to present information to students in an organized manner through various methods and instructional strategies. Educators much be cognizant of creative and innovative ways to individualize and maximize learning for pupils by providing practical learning activities.

The curriculum should be designed to:

1. develop the exceptional child's mental capabilities.
2. strengthen the exceptional child's emotional stability.

3. fulfill the exceptional child's health and social needs.

4. promote the exceptional child's occupational adjustment.

PRINCIPLES OF CURRICULUM DEVELOPMENT

It is not within the scope of this chapter to develop a complete curriculum guide, rather to present concepts and strategies needed to develop one.[3] It is readily recognized that curriculum development requires participation from many segments of our society, including local education agencies and specialists from various disciplines.

Coordination of services must be established between all agencies in the public and private sectors that provide services to disabled learners. Planning curriculum experiences, if they are to be successful, must include collaboration with community agencies serving children with exceptionalities (Wilson & Cervero, 1996). Consultant services may be needed in various disciplines to assist in curriculum development. All integrated approach is needed which may require the assistance and services of several specialists and coordinated with the school (George, 1996). Joint participation of school and allied disciplines enables research and current findings to be applied to develop a general and broad framework which may be adapted for developing curricula.

Designing curriculum involves two major methodologies. The first methodology is experimental instruction. Experimental instruction is designed to intrinsically motivate students' interest inside and outside of the classroom. The second approach is systematic instruction. Teacher-student interaction underline this methodology. The major purpose of systematic instruction is to develop a skill on concept and develop materials and activities which will enable students to achieve selected objectives.

Curriculum development in most school districts are concerned with developing academics in order to equip pupils to master complex tasks in our society. This point of view is endorsed for most pupils including individuals with exceptionalities.

CURRICULUM GOALS AND OBJECTIVES

Curriculum goals drive the instructional program and indicate in concise terms what the learner is expected to achieve and strategies for achieving the

---

[3] Refer to George R. Taylor (1999). Curriculum Models and Strategies for Educating Individuals with Disabilities in Inclusive Classrooms: Charles C Thomas.

stated goals. Goals also assist in the selection of objectives, assessments, instructional program with sequenced activities, identification of resources, both physical and human. They also indicate what to include as well as what not to include in a curriculum pattern. Basic skills needed to attain and to achieve the tasks are clearly delineated (Taylor, 1999).

Through a systematic approach some evidence should be noted in the changes in performance of the learner, psychologically speaking, if no changes occur as a result of the instructional process, no learning has taken place. Consequently, objectives and goals must be concisely stated if expected behaviors are to be adequately assessed. Teachers who state goals or objectives in terms of student behavior are showing a more systematic approach to learning, and are in a unique position to judge the efficiency of the teacher-learner process.

It should appear that some hierarchy of needs should be evident for individuals with exceptionalities in order to guide them in reaching their optimum growth. A first step for administrators and teachers of exceptional individuals would be to identify goals or objectives. Secondly, to divide them into manageable parts so that the children can succeed. Before sequencing tasks, detailed information should be gathered on each child. Observations appear to be one useful technique for this source. Careful observations will promulgate the status of each child's growth and development. Since all behavior is purposeful, each behavior that the child displays is an effort to meet some need. A good instructional technique is to directly and consciously modify that behavior which is present. Observations will also show the types of environment and conditions in which certain types of behavior are likely or unlikely to occur. Capitalizing on this aspect of child development, goals and objectives will be realistic and relevant.

Another point of interest is that goals should emphasize skills and activities that are within the scope of the children's daily lives. It is both psychologically and educationally sound to begin with known experiences and gradually expand these experiences based upon the abilities of the child. The degree to which goals and objectives are reflected, in academic, social, and personal skills will depend upon the level of disability and other deficits that the child might have.

PRETESTING

Before administrators and teachers can successfully determine if goals and objectives have been accomplished, some prior student input concerning acquired knowledge and skills must be known. The success of any instructional program cannot be fully realized until some initial assessment is made before children begin the instructional process. It is almost impossible to determine whether goals or objectives have been met unless some precriterion test has been administered.

Pretesting is deemed important for several reasons: (1) to determine if stated objectives are realistic, (2) to guide school personnel in redefining or stating objectives, (3) to give a cross section of abilities and interests in a class, (4) to assist in determining the nature and extent of the program content, including equipment and materials for conducting the program, and (5) to pinpoint the teacher's strengths and weaknesses in the subject.

INSTRUCTIONAL PROCEDURES

As postulated, pretesting will allow administrators and teachers to gauge the instructional process, and to sequence learning tasks in a more objective manner. The evaluation of an instructional program should include evidence that the program has or has not reached its objectives, and should also provide the basis for conclusions and recommendations for improving the program. All relevant data should be matched and developed to meet the program's objectives. Data and information not germane to the objectives should not be included in the instructional process.

Recognition by the school of the exceptional individual as a whole, from the time of his/her identification to the time of his/her discharge, would seem to warrant methods of instruction that would take into account all of his/her general and specific behaviors. The behaviors would include the development of desirable general personality characteristics and the acquisition of specific knowledge and skills that should emanate from the instructional program. In essence, the instructional program should be directly associated with the goals and objectives set forth. Needs, interests, abilities, and prior background are also important. These components should be reflected in the objectives and expanded into the instructional program.

The curriculum for individuals with exceptionalities would then be based upon realistic goals and objectives of the individual. School experiences can then be adopted to the reasoning power, the ability to perceive abstract relationships, and other mental, physical, and social limitations that characterize and handicap the behavior of these pupils.

Individual differences and program scope must be recognized when planning an instructional program. Program scope includes the totality of experiences and activities to which an individual is exposed during a specific period of time. Therefore, teachers must be skilled in informal assessment procedures so that both the general and specific characteristics of the children can be described and reacted to in the instructional program. A further criterion of scope is the predicted level of performance each child will be able to attain as an adult. Thus, once the child has been assessed and some prediction made concerning his/her future capabilities, an instructional program should be tailored to meet his/her needs. Awareness of the need for sequencing experiences and activities within and between classrooms at each level is another important consideration if the educational objectives for these children are to be met (Ediger, 1996).

By defining goals on a continuum of levels of difficulty, a twofold purpose is accomplished. First, the teacher is assisted in establishing objectives for each class in such a way that they are sequential in an ascending order of difficulty and are also achievable in a foreseeable future. Second, because individual capabilities and competencies vary among children with comparable measurable abilities, such as sequencing, permits some to move further and faster than others in a single class.

The key position of the teacher in improving the educational program for individuals with exceptionalities requires that the teacher have a basic understanding of the characteristics and needs of these exceptional children and the modification and adaptations required in the total school program. To accomplish this goal, they must insist that instructional procedures match the program objectives and that tasks are sequenced, based upon the abilities of the children.

SEQUENCE IN CURRICULUM DEVELOPMENT

The initial step in developing a curriculum is to identify the scope. The scope refers to the breadth and width of those general behaviors that are critical to successful functioning. These general behaviors should be written as general objectives. These general objectives provide the framework for constructing other components of the curriculum (Ediger, 1996).

The second stage is sequence-specific objectives as they relate to the general objectives. All specific objectives should be designed to achieve the general objectives. Specific objectives should be stated in behavioral and measurable terms (Taylor, 1997).

The third step is to identify activities and resources that will achieve the objectives. The activities should be functional and reflect real-life experiences that disabled individuals are exposed to. The use of computer technology should be infused with activities. Refer to Chapter 4 for additional details.

The fourth step is to include cultural, ethnic, and racial diversity into the curriculum. This approach affords the exceptional individual the opportunity to appreciate and understand his/her sense of importance and identifying with minorities who have made significant contributions in all fields (Banks, 1995). As much as possible, parents should be involved in reinforcing the skills taught. They may be used as resource individuals, and offering suggestions relative to material and activities.

A curriculum that does not highlight the contributions of minorities gives an inaccurate and distorted view of the many significant contributions made by them. Multicultural activities and strategies enriches the curriculum by showing differences in cultural styles, patterns, and interests of diverse groups (Wood & Lazzari, 1997). Strategies for incorporating diversity and cultural activities are highlighted in Chapter 8.

The fifth step involves structuring each activity to follow a set sequence: (1) The teacher models the behavior, (2) The student attempts to repeat the demonstrated behavior, (3) Other students critique the behavior, and (4) The student practices the skill independent of the group. These steps assist disabled individuals in internalizing their behaviors and assessing how their behaviors impact upon others (Taylor, 1997).

A structured learning program should follow the listed format for each behavior taught:

1. Behaviors should be written in behavioral terms.
2. The application of task analysis should be followed until each skill is mastered before moving to the next skill.
3. Some classroom arrangements will be necessary to accomplish some of the skills.
4. No specific time of the day should be devoted to skill training, rather the training should be devoted to skill training, rather the training should be infused into the regular curriculum whenever possible. (Taylor, 1997)

Effective teaching mandates that the special educator be skilled in the art of posing questions, sensitive to the individual needs of individuals with exceptionalities competent in sequential aspects of curriculum development, and knowledgeable about modifying and adapting instructional strategies based upon the unique needs of these individuals. Frequently, there is no updated curriculum, teachers must be prepared to develop their own curricula or units of instruction or modifying existing.

A FUNCTIONAL APPROACH

A functional approach to teaching individuals with exceptionalities can easily be infused throughout the curriculum. A functional approach involves exposing the learner with real-life situations and activities which he/she will experience in life. Each curricula area we have discussed emphasizes a practical and functional approach (Taylor, 1998).

Several group activities under each of the curriculum domains reflect a functional and holistic viewpoint within the content of real-life experiences. In essence, individuals with exceptionalities should be taught to model, imitate, and demonstrate appropriate skills in the reality in which they exist. A functional approach for developing curricula may be demonstrated by using certain segments from them to develop instructional units.

The degree of variability among exceptional learners becomes greater as they become older, thus, school experiences should be provided at an early age and programmed in sequential steps throughout their school experiences. One of the major means of achieving the aforementioned is through developing curricula based upon achievable objectives. The curriculum should encompass all the planned experiences provided by the school to assist exceptional learners in attaining learning outcomes. It bridges the past, the present, and indicates future changes needed to prepare them to become functional and contributing members of our society.

Curriculum planners for programs must anticipate the shifts and changes in society in order to make curriculum relevant to those changes. Curriculum experiences should be designed to meet the short as well as the long range needs of exceptional individuals. In order to achieve this goal, functional approaches and activities for developing curricula may be demonstrated by using certain segments from them to develop instructional units.

A SUGGESTED FORMAT FOR DEVELOPING INSTRUCTIONAL UNITS FROM CURRICULA

There are several formats that educators may employ in developing curricula, depending upon the standards adapted by a school district. Any format developed should be logically sequenced from stating observable and measurable objectives to assessment and evaluation of progress. We have abstracted from several areas of the curriculum, instructional units commonly used to instruct individuals with exceptionalities. Additionally, a recommended format for educators to use has been provided. In the researchers' opinion, employing the use of common format enables educators to become more competent and better able to carry out an effective instructional program. The format in Table 9 is recommended.

In each of the curricula areas addressed in this chapter, this common format is recommended. Each instructional objective is achieved through using realistic and functional instructional strategies. Under instructional objectives, all objectives are sequenced, teaching model activities, students model activities until mastery has been achieved. Students practice the skills independently. Under resources, both human and physical types should be list-

TABLE 9

Format for Developing Curricula

Description of the Lesson:

Major Objective:

Instructional Objectives	Instructional Strategies	Resources		Assessment and Evaluation
		Human	Physical	

ed. The use of cultural diversity and learning styles under the human category, and computer technology under the physical category should be stressed. Strategies for assessing and evaluating each curricula area should be summarized.

This chapter is designed to assist teachers of individuals with exceptionalities with strategies and methods for developing functional curricula and units of instruction as systematical functional approach should be stressed in developing curricula. Curriculum development is a time-consuming and complex process, involving making major decisions relevant to the instructional program. Various approaches may be taken in developing curricula; however, it is commonly agreed by several authorities that curriculum should provide measurable and observable objectives, functional instructional activities, outcomes, and evaluation.

EVALUATION OF SOCIAL, ACADEMIC, AND PSYCHOMOTOR SKILLS

If evaluation results are to be effectively used to gauge to what extent the stated objectives have been achieved, then the evaluation process must be properly planned prior to employing procedures for assessing basic skills of exceptional individuals. A decision must be made on what to evaluate. This approach will facilitate the selection of appropriate methods and techniques, such as:

1. evaluating the competence of a particular skill;
2. determine the baseline behavior for a particular skill;
3. using results to revise the unit;
4. providing information to gauge the progress of individuals with exceptionalities;
5. appraising the effectiveness of selected skill activities;
6. making sure that individuals with exceptionalities have the necessary prerequisites for performing the skills;
7. having the necessary physical and human resources to conduct the unit;
8. eliciting the cooperation of parents;
9. providing training for parents to follow-up skills at home; and
10. determining the reactions of disabled individuals toward selected activities. (Taylor, 1992)

SPECIFIC EVALUATION TECHNIQUES

Specific evaluation techniques for evaluating skill development of exceptional individuals are many. There are both formal and informal techniques which may be applied. This section will address information procedures to employ. These techniques appear to be readily accessible or can be easily developed by the classroom teacher. Some recommended strategies outlined are:

1. Develop a brief checklist to assess skills in a variety of situations.
2. Simulate social, academic, and psychomotor activities requiring individuals with exceptionalities to portray different roles that can be used to assess the understanding of appropriate behaviors in various settings. Group and individual appraisal of the activity may be conducted by the class.
3. Group assignments can be used to evaluate the ability of exceptional individuals to work cooperatively. Record specific incidents, appropriate, and inappropriate incidents.
4. Model and provide illustrations of appropriate and inappropriate behaviors.
5. Structure activities and situations which call for specific kinds of behaviors and observe the performance of exceptional individuals. A rating scale may be used.
6. Assess the frequency of inappropriate behaviors, assist exceptional individuals in monitoring their own behaviors.
7. Use a variety of audio-visual aids, such as films and filmstrips depicting appropriate and inappropriate social skills, have exceptional individuals to critique what is taking place and give alternative responses.

Additionally, experiences and activities should be sequenced so that stated goals and objectives may be effectively achieved (Choate, Enright, Miller, Poteet, & Rakes, 1995).

EVALUATING THE PUPIL'S ACHIEVEMENT

Evaluation of pupil's progress should be an ongoing process based upon measurable and observable objectives of the instructional program. As indicated, it is of prime importance to assess prior skills before instruction is attempted. After the instructional process, pretest, and posttest data should be compared and analyzed to pinpoint changes in the pupil's behavior as a result of instruction. Evaluation will also show possible needed changes in the instructional program. Lack of changes in behavior can be attributed to many factors such as: (1) program content not being relevant to children, (2) lack of materials to implement the program, (3) objectives not being stated in behavioral terms, (4) insufficient time allowed, (5) types of instruments used, (6) tasks not properly sequenced, based upon interest needs and abilities of the children, and (7) poor planning and administration to effect change.

A well-planned program will have identified many ways of measuring desired changes and will lend itself to effective evaluation of exceptional children. The following points appear noteworthy of mentioning if educators are going to assess their achievements in a scientific manner:

1. The objectives must be specified in realistic and relevant terms, which will denote the behavior to be changed.
2. The characteristics, needs, interests, and abilities of the children must be identified.
3. The types of measurement to determine whether the objectives of the program were met should be clearly evident.
4. Content of the precriterion must match the postcriterion if discrepancies are to be minimized.
5. Some systematic approach should be evident for recording data.

Through the scientific approach, the end product of evaluation should reflect in behavioral changes shown by the students, that is what the student does after the instructional program compared with what he/she did before he/she initially entered. Results from this type of evaluation will enable administrators and teachers to objectively evaluate the achievement of individuals with exceptionalities, as well as reflect needed changes or modifications in the program.

A SYSTEM FOR EVALUATION INSTRUCTION

System evaluation (task analysis) has traditionally been associated with trades and vocational types of programs. Recently, educators have realized the importance of extending this concept of education. Their rationale was predicated upon the principle that identifying tasks and sequencing are two of the chief components of learning. The model below is a simple explanation of how system evaluation can be extended to instruction in the schools. It pinpoints the importance of goals and summarizes how activities may be sequenced. Curriculum activities may be monitored, changed, and individualized by using the model. Additionally, realistic evaluation of learners achievement can be objectively stated. Evaluative data will clearly indicate strength and weakness in the instructional program. Data will indicate whether or not skills are above or below the achievement levels of the learner and indicate the next instructional sequence or task to pursue. Table 10 shows the various steps employed in evaluating instruction.

TABLE 10

A Systematic Model for Evaluating Achievement of Disabled Children

(1 Observe, Collect, and Record Data on pupils. (Needs, Interests, Abilities, Behavior, etc.) Specific activity, conditions, and standards.	(2 Write, Sequence, and Integrate Terminal and Specific Objectives (To characterize pre-test)
(4 Administer and Evaluate Pre-test (Record Date)	(3 Pre-test (To assess prior knowledge and skills)
(5 Based on Results from pre-testing, Adjust Proposed Instructional Program and the Sequencing of Terminal and Specific Objectives	(6 Develop Instructional Program, Identify Materials, Activities and Timing
(8 Post-tests to ascertain if Terminal Objective has been met, or any changes in pupil's behavior as a result of instruction. (Compare pre and post data)	(7 Conduct Instructional Program. (Observe, Collect, and Record Data on pupil's progress, Validate program)
(9 Feedback results of Post-testing. (Repeat or refine system based on results)	(10 *Recycling can be made at any point in the system where a breakdown in learning occurred.

Description of a System for Evaluation

The system is an attempt to visually portray some component parts that should be reflected in sequencing skills and tasks for evaluating achievement of individuals with disabilities. Instruction begins with identifying and recording the pupil's needs, interests, etc., stating the activity and conditions under which the program will operate, as well as denoting the minimum standard that will be accepted toward the achievement of the objective. From this point, objectives, testing, and instruction may all be sequenced or broken into tasks. Refining and recycling at any point in the program might be necessary, if expected behavior was not obtained, in light of evaluative data. Negative results might be attributed to tasks not properly sequenced, need for revision in stating objectives, and lack of materials or activities. At any rate, the negative alternatives should be identified before revision in the system is proposed.

Long-and short-term evaluation requires a definite statement of objectives. Evaluation concerns the extent to which goals have been reached, and can only pose sensible questions when the long-and short-term goals are clearly stated. To be effective, evaluation must be a continuous process and an answer to two basic questions: (1) is there evidence of pupil's growth, and (2) are the experiences received worthwhile for the children?

SUMMARY

The degree of variability among individuals with exceptionalities become greater as they become older. Thus, the school should provide formal education experiences for them at an early age and program their learning in sequential steps throughout their school experiences. One of the basic means of achieving this end is through developing a functional curriculum based upon measurable and achievable objectives. The instructional process should encompass all the planned experiences provided by the school to assist pupils in attaining designated outcomes to the best of their abilities. It bridges the past, the present, and indicates future changes and needs mandatory by society in preparing an adequate way of life for the exceptional in our society. Programs should be designed to develop and promote the child's mental, emotional, social, physical, and occupational needs and adjustment for the present as well as for the future. The changes in social forces, appraisal of instruction, and contribution of research should be combined for relevancy in educating the exceptional. Program modification includes the understanding of exceptional children, as individuals, and understanding of his/her home and community in order to sequence educational tasks toward objectives.

Curriculum planners for programs dealing with exceptional individuals should anticipate the shifts and changes in society and make curriculum relevant to those changes as indicated in Chapter 4. Instruction should be based on the nature of the children and of the society in which they live. Many exceptional individuals do not have access to many learning experiences that are common for their normal peers, consequently, more than ordinary care must be taken to see that their experiences are feasible and realistic. Experiences offered individuals with exceptionalities should be strongly based on the possible roles that they will assume in society (Grossen & Carnine, 1996). Activities should be sequenced and integrated so that realistic goals and objectives can be achieved. They should be feasible for these individuals and relate to the roles that they may play in society. Modifications should be made in the instructional program as new societal trends and information dictate. School personnel should not be restricted from experimenting with a variety of activities in search for a program adapted to the needs, interests, and abilities of individuals with exceptionalities (Green, 1991).

The attainment of goals for individuals with exceptionalities basically is not different from other children, as long as realistic behavioral objectives are developed, based upon needs, characteristics, interests, and ability of the exceptional individual in question. Equally important will be the assessment of areas where they can achieve some level of success, and to methodically sequence his/her educational experiences towards stated objectives, as reflected in Chapters 11 and 12. Program content must be individualized and modified to meet the unique needs of each child. No one instructional procedure can serve the needs of any group of exceptional children. Moreover, the type of curriculum or instructional procedure used will greatly depend upon the observation of each child.

During the course of a school year, school personnel may need to request the consultative services of specialists in various disciplines. The integrated approach to learning, which is so necessary for the exceptional, requires that the services of specialists be coordinated and integrated with the work of the school. Joint participation of school and allied disciplines enables research and current finding to become a part of daily classroom teaching.

If the schools are going to be committed to providing universal education for individuals with exceptionalities, special services must be provided in order that they might have equal educational opportunities. Many of them deviate so greatly in physical, mental, emotional, and cultural needs until special services and modification in the instructional program must be made if they are to attend school or to profit from its instruction. The schools have not been very effective in serving many of the needs of individuals with exceptionalities. Curricula interventions and strategies outlined in this chapter, if implemented, will assist the schools in providing quality education to all individuals with exceptionalities under their supervision.

REFERENCES

Banks, J. A. (1995). Multicultural education and curriculum transformation. *Journal of Negro Education, 64,* 390-400.

Bigge, J. (1988). *Curriculum-based instruction for special education students.* Mountain View, CA: Mayfield.

Choate, J., Enright, B., Miller, L., Poteet, J., & Rakes, R. (1995). *Curriculum-based assessment and programming* (3rd ed.). Boston: Allyn and Bacon.

Dever, R. B., & Knapczyk, D. R. (1997). *Teaching persons with mental retardation: A model for curriculum development and teaching.* Madison, WI: Brown and Benchmark Publishers.

Ediger, M. (1996). *Sequence and Scope in the Curriculum, 117,* 58-60.

George, P. S. (1996). Arguing integrated curriculum. *Education Digest, 62* (96), 16-21.

Green, G. et al. (1991). Instructional strategies for students with special needs in integrated vocational education settings: Enhancing education opportunities. *Journal of Vocational Special Needs Education, 13* (2), 13-17.

Grossen, B., & Carnine, D. (1996). Considerate instruction helps students with disabilities achieve world class standards. *Teaching Exceptional Children, 28,* 77-80.

Kaufman, J. (1993). *Characteristics of emotional and behavioral disorders of children and youth.* New York: Merrill.

Kazdin, A. (1980). *Behavior modification in applied settings.* Homewood, IL: Dorsey.

Shujaa, M. J. (1995). Cultural self meets cultural others in the African-American experience: Teachers responses to curriculum content reform. *Theory and Practice, 34,* 194-201.

Tanner, D., & Tanner. L. (1995). *Curriculum development: Theory and practice.* New York: Macmillan.

Taylor, G. R. (1997). *Curriculum strategies in social skills intervention for young African-American males.* Westport, CN: Praeger Publishing Company,

Taylor, G. R. (1998). *Curriculum strategies for teaching social skills to the disabled.* Springfield, IL: Charles C Thomas.

Taylor, G. R. (1999). *Curriculum models and strategies for educating individuals with disabilities in inclusive classrooms.* Springfield, IL: Charles C Thomas.

Wilson, L., & Cervero, R. M. (1996). Who sits at the planning table: Ethics and planning practice. *Adult Learning,* 20-22.

Wood, J. W., & Lazzari, A. M. (1997). *Exceeding the boundaries: Understanding exceptional lives.* New York: Harcourt Brace Publishers.

Chapter 12

INDIVIDUAL EDUCATION PROGRAM REQUIREMENTS

FRANCES HARRINGTON AND GEORGE R. TAYLOR

INTRODUCTION

INDIVIDUAL EDUCATION PROGRAM (IEP), as defined by SECTION 614 (d) of IDEA, means a written statement for each child with an exceptionality that is developed, reviewed, as revised in accordance with the above section. The regulations further stated than the IEP should also designate responsibilities, tasks, and time lines for implementation (refer to Appendixes N &O). The regulations in PL 94-142, PL 101-476, and PL 105-17 are specific in describing what the IEP must include and the manner in which it must be developed although some flexibility is permitted in developing, formalizing, and monitoring the IEP. Some basic legal requirements to consider in writing IEP's:

1. All of a student's unique needs must be addressed, not only academic needs.
2. The availability of services may not be considered in writing the IEP. If a service is needed it must be written on the IEP and if the district does not have the service available, it must be provided by another agency.
3. The IEP is a firm, legally binding "commitment of resources." The district must provide the services listed or the IEP must be amended.
4. IEP's must be individualized. The same goals, same content areas, same discipline or the same amounts of therapy on many IEP's do not reflect individualization. The Office of Special Education programs (OSEP) and federal legislation have directed school districts to implement the above procedures.

Statements regarding the student's present levels of educational performance, special educational performance, annual goals, special education and related services to be provided, projected dates for the beginning and end of services, and transition services for youth are all mandated by law to be included in IEP development. The chief modification made to these familiar components has been to place more emphasis within the law upon involving students with exceptionalities in the general curriculum and into the general education classroom, with supplementary aids and services as appropriate. With these new IEP requirements, there is a clear intent to strengthen the connection between special education and the general curriculum. The new emphasis on participation in the general curriculum . . . is intended to produce attention to the accommodations and adjustments necessary for children with exceptionalities to access the general education curriculum and the special services which may be necessary for appropriate participation in particular areas of the curriculum . . . (Committee on Labor and Human Resources, 1997).

The IEP concept is a major improvement over most instructional planning centered on placement decisions. The improvement comes largely from requiring a written plan with all of the major components of IEP developments. Components of the IEP will undergo significant changes effective July 1, 1008. Premised upon this fact will we address only those changes, which will be in operation after July 1, 1998.

INDIVIDUAL EDUCATION PROGRAM REQUIREMENTS

For specific strategies and examples of IEP development, refer to George R. Taylor (in press) *Individualized Education Programs Perspective and Strategies* published by Mellon Press. Each student's Individualized Education Program, or IEP, is a vital document, for it spells out the special education and related services that he or she will receive. The IEP is developed by a team that includes both parents and school professionals and, when appropriate, the student. The new IDEA maintains the IEP as a document of central importance and, in the hope of improving compliance, moves all provisions related to the IEP to the one place in the law-section 614(d). Under the prior law, IEP provisions were found in several different places.

At the same time, several key changes have been made to what information the IEP must contain and the way in which the IEP is developed. The exception is provisions related to children with exceptionalities who have been convicted as adults and incarcerated in adult prisons. These provisions take effect immediately (National Information Center of Children & Youth with Disabilities, 1997).

THE INFORMATION THE IEP MUST INCLUDE. The IEP retains many familiar components from previous legislation, such as statements regarding the student's present levels of educational performance, annual goals, special education and related services to be provided, projected dates for the beginning and end of services, and transition services for youth. However, some modifications have been made to these familiar components to place more emphasis within the law upon involving students with disabilities in the general curriculum and in the general education classroom, with supplementary aids and services as appropriate.

For example, "present levels of educational performance" must now include a statement of how the child's disability affects his or her involvement and progress in the general curriculum. Similarly, the IEP must contain a statement of supplementary aids and services, that the child or youth needs in order to be involved and progress in the general curriculum and to participate in extracurricular and other non-academic activities; and . . . to be educated and participate with other children with exceptionalities and non-exceptional children.

With these new IEP requirements there is a clear intent to strengthen the connection between special education and the general education curriculum (the Committee on Labor and Human Resources, 1997).

The new emphasis on participation in the general education curriculum is intended to produce attention to the accommodations and adjustments necessary for children with exceptionalities to access the general education curriculum and the special services, which may be necessary for appropriate participation in particular areas of the curriculum (Sack, 1997).

Along the same line is the requirement that the IEP include an explanation of the extent to which the student will not be participating with non-exceptional children in the general education class and in extracurricular and non-academic activities. This explanation of the extent, to which the child will be educated separately in a new component of the IEP, is clearly in keeping with the changes noted above.

Other aspects of the IEP are entirely new as well. For example each student's IEP must now include a statement of how the administration of state and district-wide assessments will be modified for the student so that he or she can participate. If the IEP team determines that the student cannot participate in such assessments, then the IEP must include a statement of (a) why the assessment is not appropriate for the child, and (b) how the child will be assessed. These changes work in tandem with changes elsewhere in the IDEA requiring that students with disabilities be included in state and district-wide assessments of student achievement.

Other new IEP requirements are statements regarding: (a) informing the student about the transfer of rights as he or she approaches the age of majority; (b) how parents will be regularly informed of their child's progress toward meeting the annual goals in the IEP; (c) where services will be delivered to the student; and (d) transition service needs of the student beginning at age 14.

DEVELOPING THE IEP. The new IDEA maintains essentially the same process for developing the IEP namely; a multidisciplinary team, including the parents, develops the document. However, the new legislation increases the role of the general educator on the IEP team, to include, when appropriate, helping to determine positive behavioral interventions and appropriate supplementary aids and services for the student.

Also added to the IEP process are "special factors" that the IEP team must consider. These factors include:

1. Behavior strategies and supports, if the child's behavior impedes his or her learning or that of the others;
2. The child's language needs (as they relate to the IEP) if the child has limited English proficiency.

PROVIDING FOR INSTRUCTION

In Braille and the use of Braille (unless not appropriate), if a child is blind or visually impaired; and the communications needs of the child, with a list of specific factors such as:

1. Deaf
2. Hard-of-hearing
3. Whether the child requires assistive devices and services

REVIEWING AND REVISING THE IEP

The language in the new IDEA emphasizes periodic review of the IEP (at least annually, as previously required) and revision as needed. A new, and separate requirement exists; schools must report to parents on the progress of non-disabled children, which seems likely to affect the revision process for IEP's. If it becomes evident that a child is not making "expected progress toward the annual goals and in the general curriculum," the IEP team must meet and revise the IEP.

IDEA 97 specifically lists a variety of other circumstances under which the IEP team would also need to review and revise the IEP, including the child's anticipated needs, the results of any reevaluation conducted, or information provided by the parents.

PARENT PARTICIPATION IN ELIGIBILITY
AND PLACEMENT DECISIONS

Under the old IDEA, parent participation was not required for making decisions regarding a student's eligibility for special education and related services. As was mentioned above, under the new legislation parents are specifically included as members of the group making the eligibility decision.

Parent participation in placement decisions is similarly required. Under the old legislation, parent involvement in deciding the placement of their child was not required. The new IDEA clarifies the parents' right to be involved in such decisions.

REEVALUATIONS

Under the previous law, each exceptional student receiving special education and related services was reevaluated every three years in all areas related to his or her disability. The purposes of this evaluation were to determine if the child continued to be a child with a disability, (as defined within IDEA) and what his or her present levels of educational performance and educational needs were.

Under IDEA 97, an LEA must ensure that a reevaluation of each child with a disability is conducted if "conditions warrant a reevaluation of the child's parent or teacher requests a reevaluation, but at least once every 3 years" [Section 614(a)(2)(a)]. The new law, however, has streamlined the reevaluation process. Many of the aspects described above under initial evaluation apply as well to reevaluation. Now, at least every three years, the IEP Team and other qualified professions, as appropriate, must review existing evaluation data on the child and, based upon that review and upon input from the parents, must identify what additional information (if any) is needed to determine:

1. If the child continues to have a particular category of disability (as described within IDEA) and continues to need special education and related services;
2. What the child's present levels of performance and educational needs are;
3. Whether any additions or modifications to the special education and related services are needed to enable the child to meet the goals set out in the IEP and to participate, as appropriate, in the general curriculum.

As members of the IEP Team, parents participate in the review of existing data.

If IEP Team members (and other qualified professionals, as appropriate) feel that they do not have enough information to answer the above questions, then the LEA must administer such tests and other evaluation procedures as may be needed to produce the information identified by the team. Parents must give informed consent before their child may be reevaluated. Chapter 13 provides specific details. The need for informed parental consent for reevaluation is new to the law; previously such consent was only needed for initial evaluations. If parents fail to respond to the LEA's request for consent to reevaluate the child, the LEA may proceed without it, if the LEA can demonstrate that it took reasonable measures to obtain the consent and the parents failed to respond.

On the other hand, qualified professions (as appropriate) may determine whether or not sufficient data are available to determine whether the child continues to be a "child with a Disability." In this case, the LEA is not required to conduct additional assessments. Parents must be notified of those determinations and the reasons for it, as well as their rights to request that their child be assessed to determine whether the child continues to be a "child with a disability," as defined with IDEA. If parents request such an assessment, the LEA must conduct it. As with initial evaluation, a copy of the evaluation report and the documentation of determination of eligibility must be given to the parent.

The Report provides an explanation regarding the changes IDEA 97 brings to the entire evaluation process—both initial evaluation and reevaluation.

TRANSITION SERVICES

The requirements for providing transition services for youth with exceptionalities have been modified in IDEA 97. Refer to Chapter 4 for additional details. While the definition of transition services remains the same, two notable changes have been made to IEP requirements:

1. Beginning when a student is one, and annually thereafter, the student's IEP must contain a statement of his or her transition service needs under the various components of that IEP that focus upon the student's courses of study (e.g., vocational education or advanced placement);

2. Beginning at least one year before the student reaches the age of majority under state law, the IEP must contain a statement that the student has been informed of the rights under the law that will transfer to him or her upon reaching the age of majority. (National Inter-Communication Center for Children and Youth with Disabilities, 1997).

MEDIATION

IDEA 97 establishes mediation as a primary process to be used in resolving conflicts between schools and the parents of a child with a disability. While prior legislation permitted mediation, the new legislation explicitly outlines the states' obligations for creating a mediation system in which parents and schools may voluntarily participate. Among a state's obligations are:

1. ensuring that the mediation process is voluntary on the part of the parties, is not used to deny a parent's right to due process, and is conducted by a qualified and impartial mediator trained in effective mediation techniques;
2. maintaining a list of qualified mediators; and
3. bearing the cost of the mediation process.

Some parents may choose not to use mediation, and states may establish procedures requiring parents to meet with an impartial party who would explain the benefits of mediation and encourage them to make use of the process.

DISCIPLINE OF CHILDREN WITH DISABILITIES

Some of the most sweeping—and complicated—changes in the new IDEA are in the area of disciplining children with disabilities. To assist schools in understanding and complying with these new requirements, the Office of Special Education Programs (OSEP), U.S. Department of Education, released an initial guidance on September 19, 1997. (You can obtain this guidance from NICHCY or on the Internet at: *www.ed.gov/offices/ OSERS/IDEA/memo.htm*) An essential means of developing an accurate understanding of IDEA 97's disciplinary requirements is to read the law itself. As requested by OSEP, the discussion of discipline in this News Digest is kept to providing verbatim quotations from PL 105-17.

The requirements of law are found in Section 615(k), "Placement in Alternative Educational Setting." This section is divided into 10 subparagraphs (e.g., authority of school personnel, authority of setting, manifestation determination review, and so on).

There is no substitute for reading exactly what the law says. If you are interested in or concerned about the disciplining of children with exceptionalities, read Section 615(k) of IDEA 97 in its entirety.

THE NEXT STEPS

Laws passed by Congress provide a general framework of policy related to a particular issue. Once a law is passed, Congress delegates the task of developing regulations to guide the law's implementation to an administrative agency within the Executive Branch. These Federal regulations are published in the Code of Federal Regulation (CFR). The CFR interprets and further explains the law.

Regulations exist for the old IDEA, in CFR Title 34 Parts 300 to 338. Proposed regulations for IDEA 97 were published in the Federal Register on October 22, 1997. A 90-day period of public comment followed the publication of these proposed regulations, where individuals and groups provided feedback and identified concerns regarding what was proposed. Comments are being reviewed and, if appropriate, revisions will be made, and then final regulations will be published.

Until final regulations are available, states are required to implement IDEA 97 with the guidance available from old regulations (where the IDEA statute) and from the language of the new statute (where new regulations do not exist to reflect and interpret changes that have occurred). Final regulations were to be implemented by the spring of 1998.

In our opinion the New IEP regulations will create additional paperwork for school districts. We are proposing forms to assist. The forms are recommendations only, as indicated districts will have the flexibility to develop their own forms. It is recommended that these forms be computerized in order to reduce the amount of manual labor involved in their completion. These forms will need to be modified based upon the various states' classifications system.

Placement decisions are made by the IEP Committee based upon the assessment and evaluative data submitted. Table 11 shows the various types of public school placements for exceptional individuals. Both categorical and non-categorical are used for the various levels. The State of Maryland employs non-categorical (generic) classification, which apply to all mild to moderate disabled individuals, and categorical classifications to severe to profound disabled individuals.

SUMMARY

A major part of PL 94-142 and PL 105-17 mandates that an individual education program be developed for every disabled individual through a meeting, which includes teachers, resource personnel, parents, and in some

TABLE 11

Placement Criteria For Each Level of Service

Level of Service	Service	Elementary Staff	Secondary Staff	Students Served
Level I (Non-Categorical)	• Consultation to regular class teachers • Diagnostic services (academic, behavioral, psychological, psychiatric) • Case conferences	• Social Worker • Psychologist	• Counselor or Social Worker • Psychologist	• Student mainstreamed from more intense level of service (monitoring) • Students re-entering from hospitalization or out-of-city placement who require monitoring
Level II (Non-Categorical)	• Resource room/average of 5 hours per week • Behavior Management Strategies • Contracting • Remedial Instruction and/or Tutoring • Counseling/Individual or Group • Case conferences for regular and resource teachers • Family Services	• Resource Teacher • Social Worker or Counselor • Psychologist	• Resource Teacher • Social Worker or Counselor • Psychologist	• Student mainstreamed from more intense level of service • Students requiring direct service to improve and/or maintain performance in regular education • Students requiring individual or group counseling to succeed in school • Students requiring specific behavior management plans in regular classes

TABLE 11

Placement Criteria For Each Level of Service

Level of Service	Service	Elementary Staff	Secondary Staff	Students Served
Level III (Non-Categorical)	• Resource Room/up to 15 hours per week • Behavior management strategies • Contracting • Class meetings • Remedial instruction • Counseling/group or individual • Case conference • Family services	• Resource Teacher • Social Worker or Counselor • Psychologist	• Resource Teacher • Social Worker or Counselor • Psychologist	• Student mainstreamed from more intense level of service • Students requiring direct service to improve and/or maintain performance in regular education • Student requiring individual group counseling to succeed in school • Students requiring specific behavior management plans in regular classes • Student requiring direct family involvement in counseling to succeed in school and the community.
Level IV (Categorical)	• Self-contained class/up to 10 students • Potential for full-day programming in special class • Regular curriculum with remedial instruction	• Self-contained Teacher • Paraprofessional • Social Worker or Counselor • Psychologist	• Self-contained Teacher • Paraprofessional • Social Worker or Counselor • Psychologist	• Students who are able to interact appropriate in lunchroom, halls, or auditorium, but require a full-time special education program to succeed in school. • Students requiring intense academic instruction.

TABLE 11

Placement Criteria For Each Level of Service

Level of Service	Service	Elementary Staff	Secondary Staff	Students Served
Level IV (Categorical) (Continued	• Behavior management system			• Students requiring a structured consistent behavior management system throughout their school day.
	• Behavior management strategies			
	• Class meeting			
	• Crisis intervention and support			
	• Counseling/group and individual			
	• Home/school contact/communication system			
	• Family counseling services			
	• Case conferences on a weekly basis			
	• Psychological services as needed			
	• Psychiatric consultation services			

TABLE 11

Placement Criteria For Each Level of Service

Level of Service	Service	Elementary Staff	Secondary Staff	Students Served
Level V (Categorical)	• Self-contained class in separate facility or separate wing of a comprehensive building/ 6-9 students	• On-site Administrator	• On-site Administrator	• Students who are unable to interact appropriately in the halls, cafeteria, or auditorium and require intense supervision even when not in the classroom.
	• Regular or modified curriculum based on student needs	• Self-contained Teacher	• Self-contained Teacher	• Students requiring ration to control behavior.
		• Paraprofessional	• Paraprofessional	• Students requiring intense academic instruction.
	• Behavior management system	• Social Worker or Counselor	• Social Worker or Counselor	• Students requiring a highly structured, consistent behavior management system throughout their school day.
	• Behavior management strategies	• Psychologist	• Psychologist	• Students requiring crisis intervention and counseling available at all times.
	• Class meetings	• Music Therapist	• Physical Education Teacher	• Students requiring individual counseling.
	• Crisis intervention and support	• Art Therapist	• Auxiliary Paraprofessional	• Students requiring direct family involvement in counseling to succeed in school.
	• Counseling/group and individual	• Auxiliary Paraprofessional	• Vocational Education Opportunity (Senior High)	• Students requiring direct and frequent home/school contact to succeed in school.
	• Home/school contact/ communication system	• Physical Education Teacher	• Industrial Arts/Home Economics Home Economics (Junior High)	
	• Family counseling services	• Psychiatrist (consulting)	• Psychiatrist (Consulting)	
	• Case conferences on a weekly basis	• Reading/Math Specialist	• Reading/Math Specialist	

Source: Baltimore City Public Schools

instances the children themselves. The IEP should also designate responsibilities, tasks and timelines for implementation. The regulations of PL 94-142 and PL 105-17 are specific in describing what the IEP must include and the manner in which it must be developed. State and local educational agencies have the flexibility in developing procedures for implementation, formulating and monitoring IEP designs. Formats differ from state to state and frequently within different school districts or the same state, chiefly due to broad governmental regulation concerning the structure of IEP development. The following steps are usually addressed by the states:

Step 1. Identification of problems is the initial step in determining whether or not students' problems are brought to the attention of appropriate personnel.

Step 2. Referrals by appropriate school personnel.

Step 3. Evaluation includes an extensive review of the available service and alternatives required to meet the student's needs.

Step 4. The IEP Conference is where previously collected data and program needs are presented. A written plan is prepared.

Step 5. Implementation of the plan must be disseminated to all persons who will participate in the student's program. Each participant is required to monitor the student's performance and to make any necessary modification to the plan.

Step 6. Evaluation is repeated as a final step. The intent is to determine student progress and the IEP's general effectiveness. Based upon evaluative results, the IEP committee may request additional information or request modifications during the instructional phase.

The IDEA 97 maintains essentially the same process for developing the IEP—namely, the document is developed by the team, including the parents and when appropriate, the child. (Refer to George R. Taylor [in press] *Individual Education Programs: Perspectives and Strategies,* Mellon Press.)

The term "individualized education program team" or "IEP Team" means a group of individuals composed of:

1. The parents of a child with a disability.

2. At least one regular education teacher of such child (if the child is, or may be, participating in the regular education environment).

3. At least one special education teacher, or where appropriate, at least one special education provider of such child; and when appropriate, the child with a disability.

4. A representative of the local educational agency who is qualified to provide, or supervise the provisions of, specially designed instruction to meet the unique needs of children with disabilities; is knowledgeable about the general curriculum; and is knowledgeable about the availability of resource of the local educational agency;

5. An individual who can interpret the instructional implications of evaluation results, who may be a member of the team described in clauses (ii) through (vi); at the discretion of the parent or the agency, other individuals who have knowledge or special expertise regarding the child, including related services personnel as appropriate.

6. Whenever appropriate, the child with a disability. The new legislation increases the role of the general educator on the IEP Team to include, when appropriate, helping to determine (a) positive behavioral strategies and interventions and (b) supplementary aids and support for school personnel are to be provided so that the child can advance appropriately toward attaining the annual goals, be involved in and progress in the general curriculum and other activities, and be educated and participate with other activities, and be educated and participate with other children with disabilities and non-disabled children. (Bateman, 1997)

At the same time, several key changes have been made to what information the IEP must contain and the way in which the IEP is developed. These changes took effect on July 1, 1998. (The exception is provisions related to children with disabilities who have been convicted as adults and incarcerated in adult prisons. These provisions take effect immediately) (National Information Center for Children and Youth with Disabilities, 1997). IEP Content Effective July 1, 1998.

Major changes in the IEP that will take place July 1, 1998 include:

1. A statement of the child's present levels of educational performance including "how the child's disability affects the child's involvement and progress in the general curriculum . . . "(H.R. 5, p. 12-127)

2. A statement of measurable annual goals, including benchmarks or short-term objectives, related to meeting the child's needs that result from the child's disability to enable the child to be involved in and progress in the general curriculum. (H.R. 5, p. 127)

3. A statement of the special education and related services and supplementary aids and services to be provided and a statement of the program modifications or supports for school personnel that will be provided for the child to advance appropriately toward attaining the annual goals and to be involved and progress in the general curriculum. (H.R. 5, p. 127-128)

4. A statement of any individual modifications in the administration of state or district wide assessments of the student achievement that are needed in order for the children to participate in such assessment (H. R. 5, p. 127-128). If the IEP team determines that the child will not participate in a particular state or district-wide assessment of student achievement (or part of such an assessment), a statement of why that assessment is not appropriate for the child and how the child will be assessed. (H.R. 5, p. 128-129)

Beginning at age 14, and updated annually, a statement of the transition service needs of the child under the applicable components of the child's IEP that focuses on the child's courses of study (such as participation in advanced-placement courses or a vocational education program). Beginning at age 16 (or younger, if determined appropriate by the IEP Team), a statement of needed transition services for the child, including, when appropriate, a statement of interagency responsibilities or any needed linkages (H.R. 5, p. 129).

Beginning at least one year before the child reaches the age of majority under the state law, a statement that the child has been informed of his or her rights (H.R. 5, p. 130).

1. The IEP Team shall consider strengths of the child and concerns of the parents for enhancing the education of the child and the results of the initial evaluation or most recent evaluation of the child. (H.R. 5, p. 133)
2. In the case of a child whose behavior impedes his or her learning or that of other, the IEP Team shall consider, when appropriate, strategies, including positive behavioral interventions, strategies, and support to address that behavior.
3. In the case of a child with limited English proficiency, consider the language needs of the child as such needs related to the IEP. (H.R. 5, p. 134)
4. In the case of a child who is blind or visually impaired, provide for instruction in Braille and the use of Braille unless the IEP determines otherwise (designated criteria for that determination are provided). (H.R. 5, p. 134)
5. The IEP Team shall consider the communication needs of the child. (H.R. 5, p. 135)
6. The IEP Team shall consider whether the child required assistive technology devices and services. (H.R. 5, p. 135)
7. The regular education teacher of the child, as a member of the IEP Team, shall, to the extent appropriate, participate in the development of the IEP of the child, including the determination of appropriate positive behavioral interventions and strategies and the determination of supplementary aids and services, program modifications, and support for school personnel. (H.R. 5, p. 135)
8. Each local educational agency or state educational agency shall ensure that the parents of each child with a disability are members of any group that makes decisions on the educational placement of their child. (H.R. 5, p. 138)

The regulations also clearly state that the IEP, once developed and approved by the parents, is a set of goals and objectives to guide the program, not a legally binding contract. That is, a goal, such as the attainment of a specific reading level, does not become a legal requirement. The school district does, however, have a legal responsibility to provide the services stipulated in the IEP for example, specific assistance from a speech or language pathologist or from an occupational therapist. If it does not provide those services, the parents have legal recourse.

Note that we have now reached the third major step in the series of events that lead to special education programming, in which the law specifies that parents must be intimately involved. The first was the initial request for parental approval for assessment and evaluation.

After the assessment is made, federal regulations require that a meeting often called staffing—be held to review and interpret its results. At this meeting, parents and personnel representing the various disciplines involved must determine whether an impairment or disability exists and the way the student may be most effectively served by the school. If the student does not meet the requirements for special education services, the assessment results and reasons why the student was not eligible should be summarized. Recommendations for program modifications and adaptations should be included and forwarded to the teachers. (Gearheart, Mullen, & Gearheart, 1993)

Guidance governing the IEP process must be expressed in written forms to express the IEP guidelines may be developed individually by the various states. The major focuses of an IEP are on instruction. Instruction is designed to minimize, reduce, or correct the assessed deficits displayed by the individuals. Both long and short-term objectives "will as a statement on related services and special educational services" must be provided with strategies and resources for achieving them. Parental involvement is a key component of IEP development. The due process procedures provide parents and their children productive safeguards.

REFERENCES

Committee on Labor and Human Resources. (1997). Washington, D.C.: Government Printing Office.

Gearheart, B., Mullen, R., & Gearheart, C. (1993). *Exceptional individuals: An introduction.* California: Brooks/Coles Publishing Company.

Taylor, G.R. (In press). *Individual education program: Perspective and strategies.* Mellon Press.

Sack, J. L. (1997). Educational officials cite concerns about implementing IDEA rules. *Education Week,* 1-4.

National Information Center for Children & Youth with Disabilities (NICHCY), *New Digest.* (1997), Volume 26.

Chapter 13

PARENTAL INVOLVEMENT IN WRITING INDIVIDUAL EDUCATION PLANS

GEORGE R. TAYLOR

INTRODUCTION

FEDERAL REGULATIONS REQUIRE that the parents of children with disabilities be involved in the design, evaluation, and where appropriate, implementation of school-based improvement plans. I.E.P. (Individual Education Plan), which is part of PL 94-142, mandates parental involvement from initial identification to placement. Other legislative acts require that children with disabilities also have a planned IEP developed. We have given detailed description to parental involvement in IEP construction in Chapter 12.

According to Hardman, Drew, and Egan (19996), IDEA mandated the following rights for parents:

1. To consent in writing before the child is initially evaluated.
2. To consent in writing before the child is initially placed in a special education program.
3. To request an independent education evaluation if the parent feels the school's evaluation is inappropriate.
4. To request an evaluation at public expense, if a due process hearing finds that the public agency's evaluation was inappropriate.
5. To participate on the committee that considers the evaluation, placement, and programming of the child.
6. To inspect and review educational records and challenge information believed to be inaccurate, misleading, or in violation of the privacy or other rights of the child.
7. To request a copy of information from the child's educational record.
8. To request a hearing concerning the school's proposal or refusal to initiate or change the identification, evaluation, or placement of the child or the provision of a free, appropriate public education.

Morsink, Thomas, and Correa (1991) wrote that parents have not been meaningfully involved in the education decision-making involved in developing IEP's. The schools have not done an effective job in meeting federal mandates. Educators must think of an experiment with innovative ways of involving parents in the schools. Over the last several decades the school has had a difficult time in establishing effective partnerships with parents. Much of the fragmentation has occurred because of non-involvement, hostility, or parental indifference towards the school. Many schools serving parents of children with exceptionalities consider them a nuisance, non-productive, uneducated, lacking social issues. The relationship is further strained when parents internalize the negative behavior displayed by the school and view the school as an unaccepted place which have no interest in them as individuals. There must be a total shift in the paradigm. The school must accept these parents and provide training and assistance in desired areas.

It is incumbent upon the school to understand and appreciate the importance of parental and families involvement in order to improve family/school cooperation. Individuals with exceptionalities cannot successfully reach their optimum level of functioning unless their parents become actively involved in their education (Taylor, 1998). The school should assure that parents are involved in: (1) The assessment process, (2) Instructional planning, (3) Decision making (4) Evaluation, (5) Identifying related service needs, (6) Selecting parenting skills, (7) Planning for support learning at home, (8) Strategies for parental education, and (9) Ways for becoming better advocates for educational reforms.

Parental involvement in the school can be expedited through scheduling periodical conferences. This will provide opportunities for the teachers to assess the parents' skills, and completeness for working in the classroom. As the parents become familiar with the academic programs at the school, they may reinforce the skills taught to their children at home. Under supervision, the parents may develop or establish an academic program at home to argument the schools program.

They may also provide the school with valuable information concerning developmental issues, safety concerns, community resources, and demonstrations. Additionally, they may serve as resource individuals and accommodate the class on field trips (Gough, 1991).

A recent *Reader's Digest* Poll revealed that strong families give children an edge in school. Children who socially participate with family functions scored higher on tests than those who did not. The survey also revealed that strong family ties improved self-image and confidence in children. The family is the cornerstone for success in later life. Parent education appears to play a role in how well the student performs in school.

The quality of family life appears to be a significant factor in all of the groups. Children with exceptionalities from intact families performed better than those who lived only with their mothers. Strong family ties appear to reduce some of the anxiety faced by exceptional individuals. Individuals with exceptionalities from families who attend church also scored higher on tests.

INCREASING PARENTAL INVOLVEMENT

Creative and innovated ways relevant to family involvement must be experimented with to improve parental involvement, especially for parents of children with exceptionalities (Mansbuch, 1993). Factors such as: (1) diverse school experiences, (2) diverse economic and time constraints, and (3) diverse linguistic and cultural practices all combine to inhibit parental involvement. Diversity should be recognized as strength rather than a weakness. Parents need to feel that their cultural styles and language are valued knowledge, and that this knowledge is needed and welcomed in the school. The school can assist those parents by providing training programs to assist them in understanding their roles in planning for their children. Any training program, to be successful, must incorporate the language and culture of the parents in order to prepare them to participate and contribute to the educational planning of their children.

COMMUNICATING DIAGNOSTIC
INFORMATION TO PARENTS

Individuals with exceptionalities as well as all childrens' progress may be assessed through using developmental milestones to denote developmental problems. This sequence permits parents to work with their children where there are developmental problems and to pattern the learning of skills in a more predictable manner. It is commonly agreed that parents should be provided with as much information as possible concerning their exceptional children. Heddel (1998) recommended the following guidelines relevant to communicating diagnostic information to parents:

- A doctor should tell parents as soon as possible, preferably. This information should be communicated in an appropriate place, such as an interview room or office.
- There should be no casual observers–this is a private matter.
- Both parents should be told at the same time. It should not be left to one parent to inform the other.
- Parents should be given time and opportunity to ask questions, even though they may be confused and at a loss for words.

- Another interview should be scheduled, not more than a day or two later. Patients should be encouraged to bring questions that will inevitably come up in the interim, and should be told that another person having experienced the specific type of exceptionality will be at the next meeting to help answer questions and suggest sources of help.

Information is also needed on strategies that parents can employ in working with their exceptional children at home. Parents can provide information to augment assessment and diagnosis. Data from the home environment as well as other environments are needed in order to arrive at an appropriate diagnostic evaluation of exceptional children.

PARENTAL CONSENT

Parental consent must be obtained in order for a school district to conduct an initial evaluation or assessment, holding an IEP meeting, developing and implementing an IEP, changes on the IEP, and a written report must be reported to parents. Figure 8 outlines specific procedures to determine if the child qualifies as a child with exceptionality as defined in federal legislation. Parental consents for evaluation shall not be construed as consent for placement for receipt of special education and related services.
SES. 614. Evaluation, Eligibility Determinations, Individualized Education programs and education placements.

SAFEGUARD PROCEDURES FOR PARENTS

Procedural safeguards for parents guarantee a timely administrative resolution of complaints. Any parent aggrieved by the findings and decisions regarding an administrative complaint shall have the right to bring a civil action with respect to the complaint. In addition, parents have the right of confidentiality of evaluation and assessment data relevant to their children. Written consent for the exchange of assessment data must be approved by parents. Parents also have the rights to examine records relating to assessment, screening, eligibility determinations, and the development and implementation of IEP and IFSP Plans, which must be written in their native language.
A review of the professional literature and federal legislation indicate that parents must be apprised of the following due processes concerning assessing, IEP development, and placement. Due process rights of parents are summarized in Figure 9.

FIGURE 8

Timeline–from the Initial Screening to Implementation of the IEP for Exceptional Children

Process	Process Timeline	Cumulative Timeline Total Calendar Days	
Parent Request Screening School Request Screening	0	0	
Screening Completed • Written parental permission must be secured before assessment.	30 Calendar Days	30	
Assessment Completed • Parents/guardians are informed in writing of the assessment results and of the possibility of the need for special education services.	45 Calendar Days	75	
IEP Meeting Held • Parents are invited to attend.	30 Calendar Days	105	
IEP Written and Approved by Committee • Parents are required to be invited to participate in the development of the IEP. • Written parental approval of the IEP is required.	30 Calendar Days	135	
IEP Implemented • Written parental permission is obtained for placement and reporting of placement to the Department of Education.	30 School Days	177	Total Time: 26 weeks, 3 days
IEP Reviewed for Appropriateness • Written consent of the parents must be secured for any change from the original IEP as a result of the 60-day review.	60 School Days	261	Total Time: 40 weeks, 3 days
Written Report To Parents • A review of the IEP must occur annually thereafter, and a written summary must be reported to parents.	10 School Days	275	

FIGURE 9

Due Process and Rights of Parents*

Written permission must be secured before your child is assessed.	Examine school records concerning your child (The right may be exercised at any time by appointment.
You are to be afforded the opportunity to be informed of the results of assessment.	Obtain a free independent evaluation with the prior approval of the school district.
You must be informed of an invited by written notice to participate in Admission, Review, and Dismissal Committee Meetings, which address your child's special educational needs.	An interpreter or translator as needed. Determine whether the hearing will be closed or open to the public.
You must be notified when an Individual Education Program (IEP) will be written for your child and you may participate.	Advice of counsel and representation by counsel at the hearing.
You must sign the IEP before the program can be initiated.	Bring the child to the hearing.
You must give your consent before your child may be placed in an exceptional children's program.	Keep the child in his/her current educational placement until all due process hearing appeals have been completed.
You must give your consent before information regarding your child's special and educational needs are submitted to the State Department of Education.	Written notification about the hearing in your primary language or mode of communication. Present evidence and testimony.
Your child's IEP is subject to annual review and you must be informed in writing of the results of any review.	Prohibit the introduction of any evidence, which has not been disclosed to you at least five (5) days prior to the hearing.
You have the right to request a hearing whenever the IEP Committee proposes to or refuses to change the identification, evaluation, or educational placement/program of your child.	Cross-examine and challenge all testimony presented during the hearing.
Receive a verbatim transcript of the hearing at reasonable cost.	
Appeals the decision of the hearing officer or hearing panel.	

*Source: Baltimore City Public Schools, Division of Exceptional Children

PARENTAL TRAINING

School districts are mandated to provide training and information that meet the training and information needs of the parents of children with exceptionalities particularly underserved parents. They must also assist parents in:

1. Understanding the availability of how to effectively use procedural safeguards, including encouraging the use, and explaining the benefits of alternative methods of dispute resolution, such as the mediation process;

2. Receiving training and information of their rights and protection under the law, in order to develop the skills necessary to effectively participate in planning and decision making relating to intervention, assessment, education and transitional services;

3. Receive coordinated and accessible technical assistance and information to assist such persons, through systemic-change activities and other efforts, to improve early intervention, educational, and transitional services and results for children with exceptionalities and their families;

4. Making available to parents' appropriate technology and media used in the improvement and implementation of early intervention, educational, and transitional services.

5. Assisting parents to better understand the nature of their children's exceptionalities and their educational and development needs;

6. Communicating effectively with personnel responsible for providing special education, early intervention, and related services;

7. Participating in decision-making processes and the development of individualized education programs and individualized family service plans.

8. Obtaining appropriate information about the range of options, programs, services, and resources available to assist their children with exceptionalities.

The federal government supports parental training through grants made to states, local communities, and information centers. Each training center must provide services to meet the training needs of parents with children with exceptionalities as outlined in federal regulations. These service centers network with appropriate clearing houses, including organizations conducting national dissemination activities, and with other national, state, and local organizations and agencies that service parents and families of children with exceptionalities.

REPORTING TO PARENTS

The Committee on Labor and Human Resources (1997) believes that informing parents of children with exceptionalities as often as other parents, will in fact, reduce the costs of informing parents of children with disabilities. This procedure will facilitate more useful feedback on their child's performance. One method recommended by the committee would be providing an IEP report card with the general education report card, if the latter were appropriate and provided for the child. An IEP report card could also be made more useful by including checkboxes or equivalent options that enable the parents and the special educator to review and judge the performance of the child.

An example would be to state a goal or benchmark on the IEP report card and rank it on a multipoint continuum. The goal might be, "Ted will demonstrate effective literal comprehension." The ranking system would then state the following, as indicated by a checkbox: no progress; some progress; good progress; almost complete; completed. Of course, the school and the IEP team when appropriate would use these concepts. This example is not intended to indicate the committee's preference for a single means of compliance with this requirement.

SUMMARY

There has been strong support from the federal government to include the family in the early educational process of their children. Parental involvement permits children to successfully manipulate their environments. The federal government created guidelines for the educational community in developing and implementing a comprehensive, coordinate, multidisciplinary, interagency program of early intervention services for infants, toddlers and their families (Gallagher, 1989). Legislations and federal mandates require the parents be actively involved in constructing the IEP as well as being involved in the total process.

The role of parental participation in educating their exceptional children, according to much of the research in the field, has shown limited participation between them and the school. This view has been interpreted to imply by many that parents simply had no interest in the education of their children (Lynch & Steirn, 1987; Taylor 1998). Several factors may contribute to lack of parental participation and involvement. Many parents do not feel welcome in the schools. They believe that they have little to offer in the education of their children. Cassidy (1988) reported that problems with scheduling, transportation and knowledge of the instructional programs; (IEP) procedures are partly responsible for poor parental participation. Parents must be actively involved in all aspects of planning including assessments, instructional planning and program evaluation and monitoring of programs. Special efforts are needed to develop better working relations of parents from diverse groups (Bauwens & Kornek, 1993).

The role of parents of exceptional individuals in the school must supersede the mandates of PL 94-142. Parents must feel that they are welcome in the school, and be given responsibilities concerned with planning, collaborating with teachers, and being involved in policy making. Parents should have an active role in planning and instructing their children and function as advocates for them if children are to profit significantly from their school experiences. Schools should experiment with various ways of improving parental participation, since they are the foremost educators of their children. Effective parental involvement programs acknowledge the fact that parents are a child's earliest and most influential teachers. Attempting to educate the child without parental support is akin to trying to rake leaves in a high wind.

Chapter 14

TRANSITION AND RELATED SERVICES

Frances Harrington and George R. Taylor

INTRODUCTION

Transition services may be defined as a coordinated set of activities for children with disabilities. It is designed within an outcome-oriented process, which promotes movement from school to postschool activities including postsecondary education, vocational training, integrated employment (including supported employment), continuing and adult education, adult services, independent living, or community experiences, and the development of employment and other postschool adult living objectives, and, when appropriate, acquisition of daily living skills and functional vocational evaluation (Individual with Disabilities Education Act Amendments of 1997).

The transition component should not be a separate entity, rather a part of the regular IEP. The plan should follow the basic plan used with the IEP. Children with disabilities are entitled by law to have a transition plan developed to enable them to profit sufficiently from their special education experiences. These experiences should be transferable to the world of work and a statement relevant to interagency duties and responsibilities for linkage must be already established and articulated before the student graduates.

If children with disabilities are to make adequate adjustment in society as adults, appropriate transitional services must be undertaken to assist them. Recognizing this act, the schools, parents, and the federal government are coordinating services to address some of the issues facing disabled individuals as they prepare to leave school. Public Laws 94-142, PL 101-476, PL 98-524, and PL 105-17 all address in some detail this important issue of transitional services for disabled individuals. All of the federal mandates relevant to the above laws have been summarized in Chapter 2. Hopefully, PL 105-17 passed in 1997 with its strong language relevant to including transitional services in the IEP will increase equality of employment and education for disabled individuals.

LEGAL REQUIREMENTS FOR TRANSITION
SERVICES IN THE IEP

The requirement for providing transition services for youth with disabilities have been modified in IDEA 97. While the definition of transition services remain the same, two notable changes have been made to IEP requirements:

• Beginning when a student is 14, and annually thereafter, the student's IEP must contain a statement of his or her transition service needs under the various components of that IEP that focus upon the student's courses of study (e.g., vocational education or advanced placement); and

• Beginning at least one year before the student reaches the age of majority under state law, the IEP must contain a statement that the student has been informed of the rights under the law that will transfer to him or her upon reaching the age of majority.

NEW REQUIREMENTS

The new law maintains 16 as the age when student's IEP's must contain statements of needed transition services. These two requirements—one for students aged 14 and older and one for students aged 16 and older—seem confusingly similar. However, the purpose of including certain statements for students beginning at age 14, according to the Committee on Labor and Human Resource's Report (1997), "is to focus attention on how the child's educational program can be planned . . . [and] the provision is designed to augment, and not replace, the separate transition services requirement, under which children with disabilities [who are 16 or older] receive transition services."

Preventing school dropout is a major component of transition service. They are a coordinated set of activities designed to keep children with disabilities in school. The IEP Committee must determine the nature, type, services; experiences needed to perform the task. The team considers the students' needs and interests as well as input from his/her parents. Parental input may be in the forms of conferences, interview, surveys or questionnaires. Research by Zigmond (1990) listed areas of program need. First, many of these students need, and too few receive, intensive basic skill instruction. Too many programs slight basic skills altogether, believing it is too late while others require students to "do" basic skills activities, but provide next to no real instruction in survival skills. The third need is for successful completion of courses required for graduation. As schools budgets are reduced, some basic courses disappear, leaving IEP teams to struggle with issues of granting graduation credit for extensively modified regular courses. One legally correct solution is for the district to establish what the essential, minimum requirements are for credit toward graduation. Those may be rigorously adhered to, as long as reasonable modifications are allowed in how the requirement is met. The IEP should lay out these understandings clearly and explicitly.

According to Bateman (1996) transition needs are the last area Zigmond addresses. She points out that about 12 to 30 percent of graduating LD students go on to college and they, of course, have transition needs related to selecting and applying to a school. She also notes that vocational education programs in high school are not necessarily a better ticket to job success than are more academic programs. One of the most important additional skills needed by many students who have learning disabilities is self-advocacy. The students' presentation of his/her needs at the IEP meeting may itself provide one opportunity to assess and discuss self-advocacy skills.

The IEP team should consider input from the family and in some instances the student his/herself when disability does not prevent involvement. All of the areas of needs and social and basic skill instruction needed for successful adaptation in the world of work should be addressed in the transition plan. The transition plan should incorporate the following components:

- Instruction—the major instruction component should be identified, based upon being identified as assessed needs.
- The nature and extent of related services needed should be clearly articulated. Responsibilities, community linkages, and various types of intervention strategies should be evident, such as dramatic play, cooperative groups and role-playing.
- Develop appropriate goals and objectives based upon assessed needs. Specific timelines should be developed to determine to what extent the objectives have been achieved.

The Secretary of Education has acknowledged that not all the IEP content requirements, especially goals and objectives, are appropriate for all transition services (FR 44847, discussion of 34 CFR 300.346). No IEP team should use time or energy trying to fit transition needs and services into a format including annual goals and objectives unless it truly makes sense to do so.

According to Tomey (1996) transition services are a coordinated set of activities for a student designed with an outcome-oriented process, which promotes movement from school to postschool activities, including:

- Postsecondary education,

- Vocational training,
- Integrated employment (including supported employment),
- Continuing and adult education,
- Adult services,
- Independent living, and
- Community participation.

The coordinates-set activities shall be based on the individual student's needs, taking into account the student's performances and interests, and shall include:

- Development of employment and other postschool adult living objectives,
- Instruction,
- Community experiences, and, when appropriate, acquisition of daily living skills and functional vocational evaluation.

NOTE: All IEP's of students age 16 and older must address needed transition services in:

- The development of employment objectives
- The development of adult living objectives
- Specialized instruction in transition areas
- Community experiences to meet transition goals

For each of these areas, if no transition services are needed at the time of the annual IEP, then the IEP committee must document why services are not needed. Some students will require transition services in the areas of acquiring daily living skills and functional vocational evaluation. The inclusion of these areas on the IEP is left to the discretion of the IEP committee.

DEVELOPING THE TRANSITION COMPONENT OF THE IEP

The transition component of the IEP should be a part of the student's regular IEP. It is not a parallel document, a separate or a "transition IEP." All of the IEP development requirements and procedures discussed earlier also apply to the transition component. The legal significance of transition, being but one aspect of the IEP process, is substantial. A student is entitled to those transition services, which for that student are special education or related services necessary to enable the student to benefit from special education. The period of "benefit" to be considered has arguably been lengthened beyond school and into adult life, but the substantive entitlement is still to special education and related services, not to those plus transition services. One logical beginning point for the transition component is with the team reaching agreement about the individual student's needs with regard to the three mandated areas of: (a) instruction; (b) community; (c) vocational training.

In spite of federal laws, parental input and efforts instituted by the schools, many disabled individuals leaving school are not prepared for employment or to enroll in postsecondary education (Bursuck & Rose, 1992; Florian & West, 1991; Nisbet, 1992).

It is generally agreed by most professionals involved with transitional services, that it is a complex and ongoing process that should begin as early as possible. Our view is that the process should begin at the end of the elementary grades, reinforced in middle schools, and refined at the end of secondary school. In our opinion, this strategy would better equip disabled individuals to prepare for the adult world.

PL 98-524 is the vocational act which provides services through rehabilitation counseling in several areas related to employment and training for the world of work in high skill, high salaried careers and postsecondary education with PL 105-17, greater coordination between education and vocational rehabilitation is mandated. We are optimistic that the future outlook for disabled individuals in the area of improved transitional services will significantly improve when the full impact of PL 105-17 is achieved.

As indicated, preparation for the world of work should begin in the elementary grades for disabled individuals. In secondary school, the roles of counselors and educators should be to assess the skills, abilities, job requirements, functional levels, and employment outlook. Resulting data from assessment should be used to develop a transitional plan. The plan should involve disabled individuals to the extent of their abilities; of equal importance will be the coordination of the transitional plan with parents and community agencies. The plan should be revised as needed, depending upon developmental physical, social, and academic changes which may occur in disabled individuals as they progress through school.

SUMMARY

Adaptive skills in the basic areas of social and interpersonal skills must be an integral part of any model of training for disabled individuals. Research has constantly documented that many disabled individuals fail because of personal appearance, poor personal hygiene, and lack of appropriate decision skills (Taylor, 1997; Taylor, 1998). The school must provide appropriate social skills activities to improve interpersonal skills of disabled individuals; through activities designed to develop positive interpersonal skills of disabled individuals and; through activities designed to develop positive interpersonal relationship to teach disabled children how to internalize feelings and behaviors. Bateman (1996) elegantly summed up that related services implied provided transportation, and such developmental, corrective and other supportive services (including: (1) speech pathology and audiology, (2) psychological services, (3) physical and occupational therapy, (4) recreation, including therapeutic recreation, (5) social work services, (6) counseling services, including rehabilitation counseling, and (7) medical services, except that such medical services shall be for diagnostic and evaluation purposes only, as may be required to assist a child with a disability to benefit from special education.

FIGURE 10

Evaluating Related Services

Date: _____

Student: _____   Pupil Number (PIF): _____

Summary of Special Education and Related Services

Special Education	Direct Hours	Indirect Hours	Frequency*	Initiation Date (M/D/Y)	Ending Date (M/D/Y)	Extended School Day/Year (Hours/Day)
Special Education	/	/	/	/ /	/ /	/
Physical Education	/	/	/	/ /	/ /	/
Speech/Language Therapy	/	/	/	/ /	/ /	/
Assistive Technology	/	/	/	/ /	/ /	/
Audiological Services	/	/	/	/ /	/ /	/
Counseling Services	/	/	/	/ /	/ /	/
Early Identification and Assessment of Disabilities	/	/	/	/ /	/ /	/
Medical Services	/	/	/	/ /	/ /	/
Mobility Training Services	/	/	/	/ /	/ /	/
Occupational Therapy	/	/	/	/ /	/ /	/
Parent Counseling and Training Services	/	/	/	/ /	/ /	/
Physical Therapy	/	/	/	/ /	/ /	/
Psychological Services	/	/	/	/ /	/ /	/
Recreation	/	/	/	/ /	/ /	/
Rehabilitation Counseling/Services	/	/	/	/ /	/ /	/
Social Health Services	/	/	/	/ /	/ /	/
Social Work Services	/	/	/	/ /	/ /	/
Transition Services	/	/	/	/ /	/ /	/
Transportation	/	/	/	/ /	/ /	/
Vision Services	/	/	/	/ /	/ /	/
Other	/	/	/	/ /	/ /	/
Total Hours* Intensity	/	/	/	/ /	/ /	/

*Specify Time Per Week (W), Month (M), Year (Y), after mark

Appendix A

INTERNET SITES WITH INFORMATION ON THE IDEA AMENDMENTS OF 1997

The Internet sites listed below offer information related to the IDEA Amendments of 1997 (P.L. 105-17). This list is not comprehensive.

- **US Dept. of Education, Office of Special Education and Rehabilitation Services**
  http:///www.ed.gov/offices/OSERS/IDEA/the_law.html
  This is the origin of federal information on IDEA. It links to the text of the law (P.L. 105-17); speeches about IDEA; general information; articles; letters and memos; IDEA '97 updates; Federal Register notices; and information on training and technical assistance.

- **Council for Exceptional Children (CEC)**
  http://www.cec.sped.org/pp/ideahome.htm
  General and legislative information and publications

- **Federal Resource Center**
  http://www.dssc.org/frc/texton/idea.htm
  Includes links to P.L. 105-17; Notice of Proposed Rule Making (NPRM) for P.L. 105-17 (proposed regulations); Senate Report Language; side-by-side comparisons of IDEA '97; memos from OSEP on IEP Requirements, State Improvement Grants, Initial Disciplinary Guidance, changes in Part B of IDEA; monthly OSEP IDEA updates; questions and answers from OSEP on IDEA, and data sources.

- **Great Lakes Regional Resource Center (GLARRC)**
  http://www.csnp.ohio.-state.edu/GLARRC/idea.htm
  Information on State Improvement Grants/State Improvement Resources (SIG/SIP), professional development, paraprofessionals, funding, alternate assessment, systems change, certification, and data sources.

- **National Early Childhood Technical Assistance Center (NECTAS)**
  http://www.nectas.unc.edu/idea/idea.html
  Information on IDEA '97 in relation to early childhood educational settings.

- **National Information Center for Children and Youth With Disabilities (NICHCY)**
  http://www.nichcy.org/textonly/ideatxt.htm
  General legislative information, publications, training material.

  http://www.nichcy.org/Trainingpkg/order.htm
  OSEP's training package on IDEA '97 and/or Spanish overheads.

- **Western Regional Resource Center (WRRC)**
  offers several documents addressing specific provisions of IDEA '97.

  http://interact.uoregon.edu/wrrc/IDEEA Tech.html
  Assistive technology devices and services.

  http://interact.uoregon.edu/wrrc/IDEAStateadvpan.html
  Establishment, membership, and responsibilities of BIA Advisory Board and State Advocacy Panels.

  http://interact.uoregon.edu/wrrc.IDEADiscipline.html
  Discipline of students with disabilities.

  http://interact.uoregon.edu/wrrc.CRSMemo.html
  Memorandum from the Congressional Research Service (CRS) to Rep. Robert Scott (VA) on discipline issues under IDEA '97. Scott requested this memo to answer questions from the Virginia School Boards Association.

  http://interact.uoregon.edu/wrrc/IDEACorrections.html
  Children with discipline in adult correctional facilities.

  http://interact.uoregon.educ.wrrc/IEP/iephome.htm
  Includes material initially collected for the IEP Institute Series: Training for Trainers; Individualized Education (IEP); Tool for Success in Education and Beyond.

This publication was prepared with funding from the Office of Educational Research and Improvement, U.S. Department of Education, under contract no. RR93002995. Any opinions expressed in this report do not necessarily reflect the positions or policies of OERI or the Department of Education. ERIC DIGESTS are in the public domain and may be freely reproduced and disseminated.

Appendix B

WHAT INCLUSION MEANS
AND WHAT IT DOESN'T

"Is inclusion a good idea?" is a silly question. As one of our colleagues, Bob Bogdan, suggests, it's a bit like asking whether Tuesday is a good idea. We've all had good Tuesdays and bad Tuesdays. It all depends on what we make of Tuesday or any other day of the week. So it is with inclusion.

Many of the criticisms of least restrictive environment, or inclusion, miss the real meaning of the concept. The principle simply means that when a school district educates a child with a disability, it should do so in a way that least limits the child's opportunity to be near and interact with other children. It does not mean, "Do away with special services." It does not say, "Include students, but do not give the necessary support services to the teachers to make it work."

Most parents have seen or at least heard about bad examples of inclusion. Just as no one would seriously propose doing away with Tuesdays when a bad one occurs, no one should question the value of inclusion because of one bad example. Let's look at what inclusion means and what it doesn't.

Note: Taken from *Preparing for life: A manual for parents on the least restrictive environment,* prepared for the Technical Assistance Parent Program (TAPP) Project by the Center on Human Policy at Syracuse University, 1985, pp. 19-21.

Appendix C

FEATURES OF INCLUSIVE EDUCATION

- Full membership for ALL students.

- A strong sense of "community" in the classroom, throughout the school, and with parents/caregivers.

- The study and celebration of diversity.

- Curriculum and methods which are adapted for individual needs.

- Active partnership with parents.

- Sufficient supports to students and staff.

- Collaboration which yields increased student achievement.

Appendix D

INCLUSION MEANS . . . .

- Educating all children with disabilities in regular schools.

- Providing special services within the regular school.

- Supporting regular teachers and administrators.

- Having students with disabilities follow the same schedules as other children.

- Involving children with disabilities in as many academic classes and extracurricular activities as possible, including art, music, physical education, field trips, assemblies, and graduation exercises.

- Arranging for children with disabilities to use the school cafeteria, library, playground, and other facilities at the same time as other students.

- Encouraging helper and buddy relationships between typical children and those with disabilities.

- Teaching all children to understand and accept human differences.

- Placing children with disabilities in the same schools they would attend if they were not disabled.

- Providing an appropriate, individualized educational program.

Note: Taken from *Preparing for life: A manual for parents on the least restrictive environment,* prepared for the Technical Assistance Parent Program (TAPP) Project by the Center on Human Policy at Syracuse University, 1985, pp. 19-21.

Appendix E

INCLUSION DOES NOT MEAN...

- Dumping children with disabilities into regular programs without preparation or supports.

- Locating special education classes in separate wings at a regular school.

- Ignoring children's individual needs.

- Exposing children to unnecessary hazards or risks.

- Placing unreasonable demands on teachers and administrators.

- Ignoring the concerns of parents.

- Isolating students with disabilities in regular schools.

- Placing older students with disabilities at schools for younger children.

- Maintaining separate schedules for special education and regular students.

Taken from *Preparing for life: A manual for parents on the least restrictive environment,* prepared for the Technical Assistance Parent Program (TAPP) Project by the Center on Human Policy at Syracuse University, 1985, pp. 19-21.

Appendix F

SOME COOPERATIVE LEARNING STRATEGIES

Circle Activities

Circle activities have been specifically designed to include many different groupings:

Full: The full circle implies that all students would participate in the circle topic and sit together in one circle.

Team: The approach is based on Slavin and Johnson's concepts of cooperative learning (Slavin, 1991; Johnson et al., 1988). Teams consist of five to six students representing different characteristics and abilities. Permanent team assignments are recommended in order to save time assigning teams for each activity.

Recommended strategies for forming cooperative teams include:

Select a name: Team members select a name, take a vote, and then introduce the name to a larger group.

Construct a logo: Members approve of the logo, which will be used to identify the team. The art teacher may be used as a resource if needed.

Develop a group profile: Provide each team with paper and supplies for designing a group profile on the paper showing each separate individual's interests/strengths/desires onto a team profile chart.

Partner: Provide activities for two students to work together. Students may choose their own partner. After a while, ask students to choose another student whom they do not know as well.

243

Cooperative Learning Tools

Many of the materials used in circle activities are already accessible in the classroom. Teachers are encouraged to be as creative and innovative as possible.

Puppets: Any puppet that is friendly-looking is sufficient. The puppet introduces the circle activities and facilitate the discussion. Students may choose a puppet name or use the name of one of their story characters.

Timer: This can greatly facilitate circle discussions because it lets students know when the circle time is up. Set the timer for the designated time and inform students that when the timer buzzes, the circle is over.

Suggestion box: A small box with a removable top will suffice. Cut a slit one half inch by five inches along the top of the box. Have the children decorate the box and write "Suggestions" on the side in big bold letters. Students should be instructed to place their suggestions inside the box. Their suggestions may provide additional circle topics to discuss.

Name cards: Make a set of name cards on three inch by five inch strips of paper. Color code the cards using two colors. Divide the class in half; give the boys alternate colors. Colors may be changed as special events and holidays occur.

Writing book: Make a writing book ditto. Provide space for each student's name in the group. Make several copies of the sheet and staple them between construction paper covers. Use the book during circle time to record students' comments. On selected circles, name the topic at the top of the form and then quickly jot down the main idea of each student's contribution. This is also an incentive for listening.

Recommendations for increasing participation within groups and circles include:

1. **Accent strengths and uniqueness throughout the day.** Students won't be able to verbalize their strengths unless they are made aware of them.

2. **Have students keep individual records of their positive self-statements.**

3. **Model positive self-statements.** If students hear the teacher saying positive comments periodically about themselves, they'll begin to feel it's safe to do so too.

4. **Praise and support students for their use of positive self-statements.** Attempt to create an environment that's secure for such growth.

5. **Be supportive of any student who cannot quickly verbalize a positive self-statement in the circle.** Use whatever statement is generated and make a positive remark about it; seek approval and endorsement from the student.

6. **Discuss real-life experiences of students in the beginning circles.** Students are often more comfortable about sharing things that they have experienced. Invite students to bring something from home of which they are proud or have an interest in.

7. **Invite students to draw a picture of what they will be saying for the circle.** This is particularly helpful for shy students. The picture will provide support for the student during discussions.

Appendix G

SUGGESTIONS FOR EFFECTIVE
CLASSROOM MANAGEMENT

A classroom that is managed effectively is necessary if desirable pupil learning is to occur. Prevention of difficulties rather than punishment for misbehavior is desirable. The use of the following suggestions will be valuable in establishing and maintaining effective management in the classroom.

Have a Good Program

Busy pupils are not troublemakers. Provide a program that interests, challenges, and satisfies pupils. Include activities that enable pupils to "let off steam" in acceptable ways.

Help Pupils Set Standards

Work cooperatively with the pupils to set up reasonable standards of behavior. State the standard positively. Post the standards.

Be Consistent

The good teacher is not mercurial. Children like to know what to expect.

Let Them All Help

Don't leave any child out when the room chores and responsibilities are assigned. A sense of belonging reduces discipline problems.

Divert Mischief-Makers

Invite disturbers of the peace to give some service to the class or to the school. Commend them for the service. Aggressive behavior may be an expression of hunger for attention.

Avoid Creating Discipline Problems

A classroom ruled by fear, threats, or unreasonable punishment creates more problems than it solves.

Make Learning an Adventure

Boredom is a potent cause of discipline trouble. If your teaching is interesting and exciting to you, it will be to your pupils too. Interest, like enthusiasm and the measles, is contagious. Without interest, the pupil learns little.

Don't Talk Too Much

Use posture, facial expressions, and silence to cut down on the need for talking. Talking isn't necessarily teaching. The good teacher induces his/her pupils to talk and guides their discussion.

Don't Try to Talk Above Confusion

If what you say is worth saying, it's worth hearing. Keep your voice down and refuse to talk about confusion.

All children are entitled to the kind of discipline that results in self-control, in emotional stability, and in the moral and spiritual values that contribute to the self concept.

Appendix H

CHARTING FREQUENCY OF BEHAVIORS

Example 1: Record the frequency of behaviors for obtaining baseline data (the number of times a behavior occurs before an intervention is initiated) and the effectiveness of the interventions.

Behavior Frequency Chart

Child's Name: _____ Date: _____

Behavior: _____

Date	Activity	Time Interval	Number of Behavior

Use one color for baseline data and a different color to record the frequency of behaviors once you have started the intervention. It is best to use one chart for each activity. However, if you wish to record more than one activity on a chart, use a different color for each activity.

Example 2: Record the frequency of behaviors for obtaining baseline data (the number of times a behavior occurs before an intervention is initiated) and the effectiveness of the interventions.

Behavior Frequency Chart

Child's Name: _____ Date: _____

Behavior: _____

	Baseline Frequency			Frequency of Behaviors with Intervention								
FREQUENCY 30x 25x 20x 15x 10x 5x												
1	2	3	4	1	2	3	4	5	6	7	8	etc.
					Day							

Appendix I

TRANSITION CONDUCT SHEET

(Teacher: Please indicate class and initial/sign your name.)	Class	Class	Class	Class	Class	Class	Class	Earning Level 60
Name: Date:	Teacher's Initials	Teacher's Initials	Teacher's Initials	Teacher's Initials	Teacher's Initials	Teacher's Initials	Teacher's Initials	
Expresses feelings, thoughts, and needs calmly and politely.								
Follow directions when given and remains on task until assignment is completed.								
Treats self, others, and property with respect and kindness.								
Remains in class unless excused and/or escorted by an adult.								
Personal Goal:								
POINTS AWARDED								
SUBTOTAL								

Points earned:

2 points = Excels Displaying Expected Behavior
1 point = Displays Expected Behavior
0 points = Does Not Display Behavior
TO   = Time Out

SCORE _____ X _____ = _____   EARNINGS _____

Comments: _____

250

Appendix J

TEACHING ROUTINES

Most effective managers spend considerable time in the beginning of the year teaching routines. However, they do not teach these routines all at once. They begin by first teaching the routines that are absolutely necessary to run a classroom; then, using a piece-by-piece approach, new routines are added after the students are regularly mastering those expectations that have been established first.

Establishing management routines requires slow, regular, and consistent implementation, as indicated in the following guidelines:

1. Mentally walk through each routine to be sure that it is both efficient and possible for the ages of your students.

2. Instruction:

   a. Relate the new behaviors to previous ones and set expectations for new behavior (anticipatory set).
   b. Teach new behaviors directly through structured activities.

3. Model:

   a. Walk the students through the routines during the first few weeks.
   b. Demonstrate the set of desired behaviors.

4. Checking for understanding/guided practice:

   a. Be sure that the children understand the directions by asking them to restate them in their own terms.
   b. Give directions for each step as students practice.
   c. Provide for practice by...
      • giving less frequent directions
      • giving cues to start the routine
      • having students orally repeat the "cue" directions, and
      • having students repeat the directions.

5. Independent practice:

   a. Give students an opportunity to practice on their own.
   b. Constantly monitor the use of the routine through observation.
   c. Provide for reinforcement by evaluating the use of the routine with the students (provide both positive and negative feedback).

Appendix K

SUGGESTIONS FOR HANDLING
UNACCEPTABLE CLASSROOM BEHAVIOR

Prevention is better than cure; therefore, look for signs, as children enter the classroom, that will alert you to possible outbreaks later on.

Below are listed some possible infractions of the regularly accepted rules and regulations that permit a well-managed classroom. To the right are listed possible ways of handling the infractions.

Means of Handling Incidents

Unacceptable Behavior	Immediate	Deferred
Yelling Out	1. Ignore 2. Teach Courtesy 3. Encourage pupils to follow routine set up earlier	1. Explain reasons for not allowing this. 2. Set up a system of giving rewards for remembering to follow rules.
Hitting Another Child	1. Separate the two (physically or/and geographically). 2. Send a letter to parents if this is a reoccurring infarction. 3. Send pupils involved to the office with a pass and a note.	1. Allow each child to explain what he/she thinks caused the behavior. 2. With inductive questioning, help children decide how this behavior could have been avoided.
Making Loud Noises with Pens, Pencils, Books, Desks, Lips, etc.	1. Remove object that is being used from child without a word. 2. Put your fingers to your lips to remind child he/she is disturbing others. 3. Move desk several inches away from other furniture.	1. Encourage children to practice self-control. 2. Encourage child to try to qualify for the "Good Citizenship Award."

Unacceptable Behavior	*Immediate*	*Deferred*
Defacing Property	1. Remove object that is being used from the child. 2. Remind child what he/she is doing; he/she may be daydreaming; therefore, not consciously aware of his/her actions. 3. Provide change of pace activities at regular intervals during the school day.	1. Discuss with child the difficulties involved and the expenses incurred in having school property repaired. 2. Initiate a clean-up campaign emphasizing "Pride in Our School." 3. Encourage child to qualify for the "Good Citizenship Award."
Calling Bad Names	1. Have pupil tell what the other child's name really is. 2. Have pupil participate in game telling as many words as possible that begin with the same sound.	1. Discuss self-respect and respect for others. 2. Discuss reasons for remembering not to say unkind things.
Teasing	1. Separate pupils geographically in the classroom. 2. Redirect the accused to a specific individual activity. 3. Redirect the accuser to a specific individualized activity.	1. Discuss with pupils the necessity for ignoring teasing acts sometimes. 2. Discuss the consideration each human should have for the feelings of others.
Illness	1. Whisper to find out why child does not feel well today. 2. Send child to nurse if necessary. 3. Send note to parents about your concern.	1. Discuss the social problems child may be having; help him/her to solve his/her problem and change his/her attitude. 2. Try to impress upon parents the necessity of a good breakfast and sufficient sleep.
Getting Out of Seat	1. Teachers should be observant at all times so that this incident can be stopped before it is carried through. 2. Be sure that all children are listening and following specific directions. 3. Ask child if the teacher can help, as you walk toward him/her, showing your interest in whatever concerns him/her. 4. Have impromptu "change of pace" activities when children appear restless.	1. Redirect child's path toward the book case to get a specific book; to the cupboard to bring you something needed to pick up trash and put it in the trash container; etc. 2. Send letter to parents asking for assistance in training child to develop self-control.

Unacceptable Behavior	*Immediate*	*Deferred*
Throwing Things Across the Room or Shooting Paper Balls with Rubber Bands	1. Caution child that such behavior cannot be accepted in the classroom. 2. Cite possible dangers and confusion caused by such behavior. 3. Find out why child is not gainfully employed with his class work. 4. Redirect the child's energies to some profitable (to him/her) activity.	1. Discuss with child his reasons for such behavior (in private). 2. Send letter to parent if this is a recurring act. 3. Direct a discussion concerning the profitable results discerned from forming good amiable relationships with peers.
Playing with Toys	1. Have child to talk for 30 seconds or one minute during a show and tell period. 2. Take toy and place on exhibit table for child to share with other pupils during free time. 3. Encourage children to bring article for display pertaining to topics being studied.	1. Be sure children are aware of what materials are necessary and important to bring to school each day. 2. Be sure children know when it is permissible to bring specific articles. 3. Send a letter to parents explaining one and two above. 4. Ask in written communication that parents visit school to retrieve dangerous objects.
Holding Private Conversations with Nearby Pupils	1. Ask child to share his interesting statements with the entire class. 2. Ask child to relate his/her story to his/her peers during free time.	1. Have child indicatively give reasons for not carrying on private conversations during class time. 2. Send letter to parents asking for assistance in helping child remember his/her responsibilities in the classroom to himself/herself and to his/her classmates.
Quiet, Retiring Behavior or Apparent Daydreaming	1. Make some remark that will gain child's attention such as; "Listen carefully, Mary," you might want to answer our next question, or "John, do you see something outside the window that will help us?" etc. 2. Make child realize that his/her contribution is needed (i,e., "Jane, will you explain our directions to your group?" or "Michael, do you agree with Anthony? Tell us what you are thinking.")	1. Help pupils realize that without oral expressions it is difficult to know if they really understand or whether or not more teaching is needed. 2. Encourage parents to do some small but rather exciting activity with this child that he/she may share with his/her classmates. (Child may help prepare a meal; may be given a birthday party; may receive a new frock; may receive a new toy, book, or game, etc.)

Appendix L

BALTIMORE CITY PUBLIC SCHOOLS
EDUCATIONAL ASSESSMENT REPORT

Date of Assessment:_____

Parent/Guardian/Parent Surrogate   Student   Date of Birth (Month/Date/Year)

Address (Street, Apartment Number)   Pupil Number (PIF)   Social Security Number

City, State, Zip Code   School (Name and Number)   Grade

Primary/Native Language_____

Assessment Techniques (Check as appropriate)

☐ Record Review   Testing: ☐ Formal   ☐ Informal   ☐ Observation   ☐ Interview

Type of Assessment

☐ Initial   ☐ Reevaluation

Background Information

_____

_____

_____

Description of Classroom and/or Test Behavior

_____

_____

_____

_____

Assessment Data Summary

Test Administered	Date (s)	Age/Grade Equivalents	Standard Scores

Purpose   To document the results of student assessment., more than one procedure may be addressed in a single report, however, each examiner should prepare his/her own report. Each report must be completed prior to sharing information with the parent and/or prior to any team meeting to discuss the results. (34CFR 300.532 and 300.534; COMAR 13A.05.01.05C(3)-(5) and 13A.05.01.05E.

Distribution   A copy of the report must be provided to the parent at the meeting at which the assessment is initially reviewed. If the parent does not attend the meeting, a copy of the report must be mailed to the parent within five (5) school days of the meeting.

Directions for Completion

Date   Enter the date of assessment.

Identifying
Information   Each name of parent, guardian, or parent surrogate.
Enter address of parent, guardian, or parent surrogate (Street, Apartment No).
Enter City, State, Zip Code for above address.
Enter student's name (First, Middle, Last).
Enter student's date of birth (Month/Day/Year).
Enter PIF# for enrolled student.
Enter social security number of student.

> **Note: If the parent does not have the social security number available, please ask them to forward it to you as quickly as possible. Retrieval of the social security number must not delay any aspect of the ARD process.**

Assessment Techniques   Check all appropriate assessment techniques used to gather information for the report.

Type of Assessment   Check the type of assessment.

Background Information   Include developmental history, health information, school history (retention, attendance patterns), classroom behaviors, functional levels, support services provided, etc., as appropriate.

Description of
Classroom and/or
Test Behavior   Discuss the student's behavior during the testing situation or in the classroom, if possible.

Assessment Data
Summary   List the tests administered or the informal techniques used and the scores (age equivalents, grade equivalents, standard scores, as appropriate).

Data Interpretation

_____

Specific recommendations for instruction

_____

Performance that deviates from developmental milestones or general education objectives

_____
_____
_____
_____
_____
_____
_____

Educational Assessment Report
Page 2 of 3
Rev. August 27, 1996
1120-25-313

Data Interpretation   Interpret test results or discuss the student's progress in the Data Interpretation section. Include the student's strengths, weaknesses, and learning patterns.

Performance Deviation   Describe how the student's performance deviates from average developmental milestones and/or general education objectives.

Recommendations
For Instruction   Make specific recommendations on how to teach the student.

Areas that may require special education/support services
    __Mathematics   __Written Language
    __Physical Education   __Other_____
    __Reading   __Other_____
    __Self-Help Skills   __Other_____

Rationale

_____
_____
_____

Recommendation for instructional and testing modifications

_____
_____
_____
_____

Test Validity (address each area)

Based on this report the examiner believes:

    __the assessment procedures are valid for the purposes intended.   __Yes   __No

    __the results are a valid report of the student's current achievements.   __Yes   __No

    __the assessment procedures measure what the test purports to measure   __Yes   __No
    rather than the student's impaired sensory, manual, or speaking skills
    or cultural/linguistic characteristics.

Comments/Explanations

_____
_____
_____

_____   _____   _____
Signature   Title of Examiner   Date Report Completed

1120-25-314

Appendix M

SUGGESTED ASSESSMENT MODIFICATIONS FOR COMPETENCY TESTING OF DISABLED STUDENTS' TAKING THE MARYLAND FUNCTIONAL READING, MATHEMATICS, OR WRITING TESTS, OR THE TEST OF CITIZENSHIP SKILLS

(see page 260)

Modification	MR	VI	DEAF	HI	SLD	SI	ED	OI	OHI
A. Scheduling Modifications: Tests may be administered									
1. At time of day most beneficial to student.	X	X	X	X	X	X	X	X	X
2. Over a number of sessions, to be determined by the ARD Committee.	X	X			X	X	X	X	X
3. Until, in test administrator's judgment, student can no longer sustain the activity due to physical disability or limited attention span. Additional session(s) may then be scheduled.	X				X	X	X	X	X
B. Setting Modifications: Tests may be administered									
1. Individually.	X	X	X	X	X	X	X	X	X
2. In a small group.	X	X	X	X	X	X	X	X	X
3. In a carrel.	X				X		X		
4. In the special education classroom.	X				X	X	X	X	X
5. At student's home.									
6. With student seated in front of classroom.			X	X					
7. With teacher facing student.			X	X					
8. By student's special education teacher.	X	X			X	X	X	X	X
9. Using an Interpreter during the time oral instruction is given to the student(s)			X	X					
C. Format and/or Equipment Modification: Tests may be administered									
1. In large print.		X							
2. In Braille.		X							
3. With student using magnifying equipment.		X							
4. With student wearing noise buffers.							X		
5. Using templates and/or graph paper.		X			X				
6. By teacher or proctor reading the test to student**.	O	O			O			O	O
D. Recording Modifications									
1. Student may mark answers in test booklets.	X	X			X			X	X
2. Student's answer choices may be recorded or recopied by proctor or assistant.	X	X			X			X	X
3. Student may mark answers by machine.	X	X						X	X
4. Student may dictate response to proctor or special education teacher***.					O			O	
5. Student may sign response to a total communication interpreter for the hearing impaired.****			O						

*The definitions for each: MR - (Mentally Retarded); VI - (Visually Impaired); HI - (Hearing Impaired); SLD - (Specific Learning Disability); SI - (Speech and Language Impaired); ED - (Emotionally Disturbed); OI - (Orthopedically Impaired); OHI - (Other Health Impaired).

**Note for use with the MFRT. Items from all other tests may be read to student, except items on the MFMT which say "choose the word name,"

***For the MFWT only. Please read the attached "Special Procedures for a Dictated Response."

****For the MFWT only.

Modifications for multi-handicapped students should be selected from all of the listed modifications, depending upon the student's handicap.

Note: The modifications recommended above for a particular handicapping condition are simply recommendations or suggestions. Any modifications listed may be used with any disabling conditions listed, at the discretion of the ARD Committee and sometimes the test maker.

Source: Maryland State Department of Education.

Appendix N

ARD PROCESS

Admission, Review, and Dismissal Team (ARD Team)
The Admission, Review, and Dismissal processes are implemented by an interdisciplinary committee whose purpose is to evaluate the program for the education of disabled children.

The local school ARD team is composed of the following personnel:
(a) Administrator (Principal or designee)
(b) Chairman, if other than administrator
(c) Classroom Teacher (s), including the regular educator
(d) Others, as needed who would be helpful in contributing information regarding a particular student, diagnostic personnel, individuals expected to become deliverers of direct services to the student, and/or a specialist trained in the area (s) of the student's disability should be present.
(e) Student's parent (s) if they choose to attend.
(f) A representative of the local educational agency.

In order to effectively meet the individual needs of the potentially disabled student, the participants should only be those individuals who can make significant contributions to the disposition of a student's care.

Responsibilities of the ARD Team

- Secure the appropriate local assessments necessary to determine the disabling condition (s).
- Determine the designees for writing an Individualized Education Program (IEP) with the parents as full participants in this writing.
- Conduct a review within 60 calendar days of the student's placement to determine the appropriateness of the placement. The parents will be notified in writing of the team review date at least ten days prior to this review.
- Conduct a periodic review of the student's program. The law requires a minimum of an annual review.
- Determine when the student is to be dismissed from special education program (s).
- See that each member signs the written IEP.
- Notify parents at appropriate steps (see Timeline).

Team Personnel, Role Expectations, and Contributions

Every team member has certain obligations to the team process. Each participant should:

- Understand the team approach process and dynamics, and function within this framework.
- Assist in the selection of appropriate cases for the team conference.
- Prepare fully, well in advance of the meeting, for the team conference by reviewing and/or updating available pertinent data and, where applicable, observe the student and report these observations.
- Present pertinent information about cases referred to the team in a concise and understandable manner.

261

- Assume responsibilities based upon team decisions and follow-up on assigned courses of action.
- Communicate follow-up information, as appropriate, among team members, including classroom teacher.

An ARD team may include the following professionals. The contributions and tasks of these individuals are described below.

Contributions of Team Members

Person	Perspective	Tasks in Team
Administrator	Child in relation to total school population and in other schools; program options available throughout country; policies and procedures affecting options; staff abilities in relation to pupil's needs.	Final responsibility for team functioning and all aspects of school's response to child's needs.
Guidance Counselor	Child's individual social and emotional needs; group dynamics of child in class setting; interaction of child and staff; family dynamics and parental concerns.	Present information about child's social/emotional functioning; may present educational information; may report observations of child and contacts with parents.
General Educator	Child in relation to others in class; expectations of children at same chronological age and grade level; subject matter of specific grades; range of average abilities and characteristics below and above.	Report on child's performance and behavior specific to child and in relation to class group, discuss strategies used and effectiveness of each.
Special Educator	Child in relations to disabling condition; implications of handicapping conditions; learning (educational performance); specialized techniques and materials relevant to child's needs/strengths.	Same as above; child's special needs and special strategies required; child's readiness for mainstreaming.
Medical Staff (Nurse, Pediatric Consultant, Other Consultants)	Child's health status and history; implications of surgical procedures, and medical conditions; symptoms of health and medical problems to be aware of in the classroom.	Present summary of health status; report and interpret medical reports; discuss child's health status in relation to school activities.
Speech-Language Pathologist	Child's speech and language functioning in relation to others of same age and ability; impact of speech and language problems on learning and behavior.	Provide summary of speech/ language evaluations and/or therapeutic intervention; discuss implications of child's speech/ language in the classroom.

Person	*Perspective*	*Tasks in Team*
Reading Specialist	Child's reading ability (word attack, comprehension) in relation to others of same age; specific reading problems and their effect on learning and behavior.	Provide summary or reading evaluations and/or special intervention; discuss implications of reading problems in the classroom.
Psychologist	Child's cognitive and/or affective development in relation to others of the same age; characteristics of abnormal/normal psychosocial development; impact of abnormal development on learning and behavior.	Provide summary of cognitive projective and/or achievement testing; discuss test results in terms of implication for school program.
Pupil Personnel Worker	Child's family background and present family dynamics; the effects of this on child's learning and behavior; community resources available and dynamics of community; procedures and policy related to truancy, expulsion/ suspension, boundary changes, and other pupil personnel issues.	Provide summary of social history and/or other contacts with family; provide information about community resources.

Others, as needed for specialized programs/services, can provide information on testing in special areas, services available, other perspectives of child-physical therapist, occupational therapist, vocational education personnel, teachers of the gifted and talented...

Person	*Perspective*	*Tasks in Team*
Team Chairman	Child's special needs in relation to school team's ability to provide services individual team member strengths; policies and procedures related to Pupil Services or ARD Team functioning.	Provide group leadership, organize tasks, assign responsibilities, monitor completion of tasks within legal time limits.

Appendix O

LEGAL TIME LIMITS P.L. 94-142

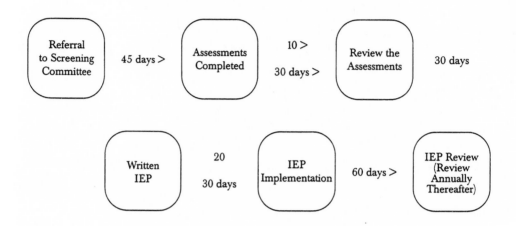

NOTES:

Inform parents 10 days before the screening meeting and 20 days before placement. Parents may sign a waiver of the 20 day notice to permit rapid placement.

All required actions can be completed very quickly in inclusive placements. Additional meetings may require more time for special education placement; however, close adherence to the timeline is recommended.

GLOSSARY

Acquired immune deficiency syndrome (AIDS): A breakdown of the body's immune system, allowing the body to become vulnerable to a host of fatal infections that it normally is able to ward off.

Adaptive behavior: The effectiveness or degree with which individuals meet the standards of personal independence and social responsibility expected for their age and cultural group.

Alexia: Inability to read written or printed language, although there is no organic visual pathology.

Amblyopia: Weakness of vision without any apparent change in the structure of the eye itself.

American Sign Language (ASL): A manual language used by many people with hearing impairments that meets the universal linguistic standards of spoken English.

Amniocentesis: A procedure for analyzing factors in the amniotic fluid in which the embryo is suspended, that may indicate the presence of problems for the offspring.

Anoxia: Lack of oxygen or the disturbance of bodily functions resulting from lack of oxygen.

Aphonia: Loss or disturbance of the capability of producing appropriate sounds.

Aphasia: The loss of the ability to speak as a result of brain injury or trauma.

Applied behavioral analysis (ABA): A learning approach that is based on individual analyses of a student's functioning and relies on the learning of behaviors to remediate learning problems.

Aptitude-achievement discrepancy: A discrepancy between a student's ability (measured on intelligence tests) and academic achievement; a factor in the diagnosis of learning disabilities.

Arthritis: Inflammation of the joints that causes them to swell or stiffen.

Articulation: The movement of the mouth and tongue that shapes sound into speech.

Assessment: A process for identifying a child's strengths and weaknesses; it involves five steps: screening, diagnosis, classification, placement, and monitoring or discharge.

Assistive technology: Tools that enhance the functioning of persons with disabilities.

Asthma: A condition affecting a person's breathing.

At-risk-infant: An infant who has a greater chance of displaying developmental delays or cognitive or motor deficits due to a variety of factors.

Athetosis: A form of cerebral palsy marked by involuntary, wormlike movements.

Atoxia: A form of cerebral palsy marked by an impairment of muscular coordination which makes it difficult to walk or maintain balance.

Audiometry: The evaluation of hearing ability, usually made by the use of standardized testing and devices.

Attention deficit disorder (ARD): A conduct disorder that leaves children unable to pay attention or work at a task; impulsiveness is another characteristic of the disorder. Often found in combination with hyperactivity (attention deficit hyperactivity disorder [ADHD]).

Attention-deficit hyperactivity disorder (ADHD): A disorder that causes children to have difficulty settling down to do a particular task, especially desk work.

Audiogram: A graphic record of hearing acuity at selected intensities throughout the normal range of audibility, recorded from a pure-tone audiometer, which creates sounds of present frequency or intensity.

265

Audiometer: An instrument for testing hearing acuity.

Audition: Thought transformed into words and received by a listener through hearing.

Auditory method: A method of teaching deaf students that involves auditory training and makes extensive use of sound amplifications to develop listening and speech skills. Also called acoupedic method, acoustic method, auditory global method, aural method, and unisensory method.

Augmented communication: Methods of communicating that are based on symbols or gestures rather than speech.

Authentic assessment: Measuring a child's ability by means of an in-class assignment.

Autism: A neurological disorder that leads to deficits in functioning, particularly in communication and social skills.

Behavioral modification: The practice of applying behavior principles to educational, therapeutic, and social problems; a technology built upon principles of operant and respondent conditioning designed to change inappropriate behavior.

Blindness: A state of severe visual impairment in which there is no measurable or useful vision.

Brain-injured: Characterizing one who before, during, or after birth has received an infection of the brain, which prevents or impedes normal brain functioning and which may be related to disturbances in sensing, responding, and learning.

Cataract: A condition of the eye in which the lens of the eye is clouded, resulting in dimming of vision.

Cerebral palsy: Any one of a group of disorders affecting control of the motor system and due to brain damage, before, during, and after birth.

Chromosomes: Very small bodies in the nucleus of a cell which carry the genes or hereditary factors.

Cleft palate: A congenital failure in development of the roof of the mouth, often associated with cleft lip.

Compulsion: A rigidly enacted behavior often resembling the "fixed," ritualistic behaviors of animals.

Congenital: Present at birth.

Crippled: Characterizing orthopedic impairment that interferes with the normal functions of the bones, joints, or muscles.

Cystic fibrosis: A hereditary disorder producing a generalized malfunction of the pancreas leading to numerous organic and functional deficiencies.

Deafness: A condition in which one has sustained severe impairment of the hearing; nonfunctional for normal purposes.

Decibel: A relative measure of the intensity of sound; hearing loss is measured in decibels.

Developmental period: That time period during which major, relatively stable characteristics of the individual are established; frequently designated as that interval between conception and 18 years of age.

Deviation: From a social view, any departure from the norm sufficient to produce differential social consequences.

Diabetes mellitus: Disorder of pancreatic insulin production resulting in excessive amounts of glucose in the blood and in the urine.

Diplegia: Paralysis affecting similar parts of both sides of the body.

Disability: A deviation of body or functioning that results in functional inadequacy in view of environmental demands.

Discriminative stimuli: Mark the time or place when an operant behavior will have reinforcing consequence and, thus, sets the occasion for a behavior.

Dysarthria: Disorder of articulation due to a loss of control and coordination of the muscular movements of tongue, lips, jaw, and palate required for speech.

Dyslalia: Any of the disorders in the articulation of speech not due to damage of the central nervous system.

Dyslexia: Inadequate reading skill, lack of understanding the relationship between sounds and letters.

Dysphemia: Any speech disorder due to a psychoneurotic condition having no known organic base.

Echolalia: Repetition of words or phrases spoken by others.

Ectomorphic: A term for body types characteristically tall and thin, fragile and lightly muscled.

Electroencephalogram: An instrument used to measure changes in the electric potential of different areas of the brain; the record of such measurements.

Encephalitis: Viral infection of the brain.

Epilepsy: A group of nervous diseases in which the person has seizures; related to disorders in the brain's electrical activity; may be present at birth or developed after illness or injury.

Etiology: The study of the causes of a disorder.

Exceptional child: A child who differs from the norm in mental characteristics, sensory abilities, communication abilities, social behavior, or physical characteristics to the extent that special education services are required for the child to develop to maximum capacity.

Exceptional individual: Any person whose physical attributes or functioning deviate from the norm sufficiently to evoke or require differential interpersonal or environmental response or arrangements.

Exogenous: Externally or environmentally caused.

Formative assessment: Frequent evaluation designed to provide feedback to permit adjustments in educational or therapeutic programming (e.g., progress checks).

Frustration: Emotional tension resulting from the blocking of a desire or need of a subjective state experienced under conditions of ratio strain (i.e., absent reward for continued effort).

Functional assessment: A step-by-step assessment of the student's behavior to better understand the intent of the behavior.

Genetic counseling: Information provided to parents and potential parents on the probabilities of hereditary assets and liabilities, based on a detailed medical pedigree, pregnancy histories, and certain laboratory tests.

Gifted: A term used to describe persons with intellectual gifts.

Grand mal seizure: Epileptic seizure consisting of several phrases in which the person loses consciousness, thrashes about, stiffens, and goes into a deep related state.

Hydrocephalus: Presence of excess cerebrospinal fluid within the brain resulting in damage to brain tissue; frequently results from spinal injury.

Hypernasality: Speech sounds which should be emitted through the mouth being emitted instead through the nasal cavity. This often occurs in partial or complete paralysis of the soft palate.

Immaturity: A pattern of deviant behavior in which children are inattentive, sluggish, uninterested in school, lazy, preoccupied, and reticent.

Incidence: The number of new cases occurring in a population during a specific interval of time.

Inclusion: The process of bringing children with exceptionalities into the regular classroom.

Individual education program (IEP): A program written for every study receiving special education; it describes the child's current performance and goals for the school year, the particular special education services to be delivered, and the procedures by which outcomes are to be evaluated.

Individualized family services (IFSP): An intervention program for young children and their families that identifies their needs and sets forth a program to meet those needs.

Instructional technology: The computer and tools that support the use of computers.

Language disorder: The impairment or deviant development of comprehension or use (or both) of a spoken, written, or other symbol system.

Learning disability: A disorder that manifests itself in a discrepancy between ability and academic achievement.

Least restrictive environment: The educational setting in which a child with special needs can be taught successfully in the regular classroom.

Mental retardation: A combination of subnormal intelligence and deficits in adaptive behavior; manifested during the developmental period.

Modalities: Ways of sensing and responding; thus, visual, auditory, tactile, verbal, motor, etc., capabilities.

Multidisciplinary team: A group of professionals who work with children with disabilities to assist them achieving their optimum level of growth.

Muscular dystrophy: A condition characterized by weakness of the skeletal muscles with increasing deformity as the disease progresses.

Neurologist: Medical specialist in the diagnosis and treatment of disorders of the nervous system.

Normalization: The concept that the educational and therapeutic goal for exceptional individuals must be normal functioning and status, and that procedures employed in attaining the goal must be as close to normal as is feasible.

Operant conditioning: A learning process in which the behavior of the subject is modified as a consequence of his own behavior. Behaviors which "operate" on and thus change the environment are themselves changed by the new environment.

Ophthalmologist: Medical specialist in the diagnosis and treatment of diseases of the eye.

Orthopedic: The area of medicine concerned with bones, joints, and muscles. Also, the area of surgery dealing with the correction of deformities and the treatment of chronic diseases of the joints and spine.

Otolaryngologist: Medical specialist in the diagnosis and treatment of disease of the ear, nose, and throat.

Otologist: Medical specialist in the diagnosis and treatment of disease of the ear.

Perceptual-motor disabilities: Difficulty in understanding or responding to the meaning of pictures or numbers.

Performance assessment: A measure of the application of knowledge.

Perinatal: Occurring at or pertaining to the time of birth.

Petit mal seizure: Mild and quite brief epileptic seizure in which there may be only a slight loss of consciousness.

Phenylketonuria (PKU): A hereditary metabolic disease transferred through genetic action; resulting in a lack of the necessary enzyme for oxidizing phenylalanine, which in turn promotes accumulation of phenylpyuric acid with resulting mental retardation.

Physical disability: A condition that interferes with the individual's ability to use his or her body.

Positive reinforcement: The application of a positive stimulus immediately following a response.

Prenatal care: Monitoring of a pregnancy by the mother and her physician.

Prognosis: Prediction of the course and end of a disorder.

Prosthesis: An artificial replacement of an absent part of the body; adaptation of the environment to minimize sensory and response difficulties.

Psychomotor seizure: A form of epileptic seizure consisting of purposeful but inappropriate acts. A difficult form to diagnose and control.

Quadriplegia: Paralysis affecting all four body limbs.

Reinforcement: A procedure for strengthening a response involving the immediate presentation of a consequence that acts to build the response frequency, duration, or intensity, or all three.

Reliability: Degree to which a test or other instrument of evaluation measures consistently whatever it purports to measure; consistency across persons, tests, or time.

Resource-room specialist: A special educator employed to provide special assistance to exceptional children and others in regular and special classes through the use of specialized materials and methods.

Retardation: Slowness or delay in the acquisition of physical or behavioral characteristics relative to norms for these characteristics.

Rheumatic fever: A chronic infection of the connective tissues of the body, affecting the joints, heart, and blood vessels.

Rh incompatibility: Parental difference in a certain blood group factor (first discovered in Rhesus monkeys) that can result, for example, in an Rh-positive factor present in the fetus; resulting in agglutination of blood with serious consequences for the baby and the mother.

Rubella: German measles, especially hazardous to the fetus during the first three months of pregnancy.

Shaping: The practice of reinforcing only those behaviors that progressively move in the direction of the desired final performance and extinguishing (not reinforcing) all other responses.

Sickle-cell anemia: An inherited abnormality of the red blood cells (with cells shaped like "sickles," rather than spheres) resulting in severe anemia, predominantly, but not exclusively found in persons of African ancestry. Parents who are "carriers" of the disorder may discover this through a sample test and receive counseling relative to treatment and the desirability of reproduction.

Social maladjustment: A syndrome in which one's social behavior is sufficiently deviant that he cannot participate in "normal" activities with others; usually involves violation of social norms and codes of conduct.

Sociogram: A technique which evaluates the social movement and distance of a person within a given group.

Spasticity: Excessive tension of the muscles making control of the muscles difficult.

Special education: The profession concerned with the arrangement of education variables leading to the prevention, reduction, or elimination of those conditions that produces significant defects in the academic, communicative, locomotor, or adjustive functioning of children.

Speech pathologist: One who is engaged in the study of the disorders of speech and language usually responsible for diagnosing a speech problem and supervising the therapy.

Spina bifida (Occulta): A defect of closure in the posterior bony wall of the spinal canal that is not accompanied by associated spinal cord or meninges pathology.

Stuttering: A speech impediment in which the normally smooth flow of words is disrupted by rapid repetition of words, hesitations, or breathing spasms or all three.

Summative assessment: Single, end-of-sequence evaluation (e.g., year-end achievement tests and final exams).

Syphilis: Contagious venereal disease

Target behaviors: Specific, explicitly stated behaviors selected for modification.

Task analysis: A method that breaks down complex tasks into simple component parts, teaches each of the components separately, then teaches them together; a procedure under which a child receives positive reinforcement for each step or part of the total task as it is completed.

Time-out: The physical removal of a child from a reinforcing situation for a period of time, usually immediately following an unwanted response.

Validity: The extent to which a test or other measuring instrument fulfills the purpose for which it is used.

Vicarious learning: Learning that occurs to someone who observes how other's behaviors are reinforced while the learner himself/herself is not an active participant of the event.

Visual acuity: The ability to see details clearly or identify forms at a specified distance.

Visual-auditory-kinesthetic (VAK) method: A phonic system for the remediation of reading disabilities.

Voice: The production of sound in the larynx and the selective transmission and modification of that sound through resonance and loudness.

Voice disorder: A variation from accepted norms in voice quality, pitch, or loudness.

Zero reject principle: The principle that all children with disabilities must be provided a free and appropriate public education and that local school systems cannot decide not to provide needed services.

NAME INDEX

SUBJECT INDEX

E DUE